I REMEMBER THE LAST WAR

(ORIGINAL VERSION, RESTORED)

By

BOB HOFFMAN

Former Lieutenant, United States Army

Original Publisher: Strength & Health Publishing Co., York, Pennsylvania, 1940

PUBLISHED BY O'Faolain Patriot LLC, Copyright 2011

info@PhysicalCultureBooks.com

ISBN-13: 978-1467930239

ISBN-10: 1467930237

Published in the United States of America

To Order More Copies Visit: Physical Culture Books.com

RECENT PHOTO OF THE AUTHOR

TABLE OF CONTENTS

Preface	4
I. BATTLES IN THE WOODS	8
II. ACTION ON THE ATLANTIC	21
III. WE LAND IN FRANCE	28
IV. AT THE BRITISH SCHOOL	35
V. A LONG HIKE	46
VI. THE BATTLE OF PARIS	52
VII. THE ROAD TO ETERNITY	64
VIII. OVER THE TOP	74
IX. IN THE HEAT OF BATTLE	83
X. GERMAN PRISONERS	98
XI. BACK TO THE HOSPOTAL	105
XII. TALES OF THE WOUNDED	111
XIII. I REJOIN MY REGIMENT	121
XIV. MOVING TOWARD THE FRONT	133
XV. FOLLOWING THE BATTLE	141
XVI. DEATH FROM THE SKY	150
XVII. THE VESLE RIVER – FISMES AND FISMETTE	158
XVIII. A COUNTER ATTACK IN FISMES	165
XIX. OVER THE TOP AGAIN	174
XX. BACK ACROSS THE VESLE	181
XXI. BATTLE WITH THE SNIPERS	196
XXII. FIRST NIGHT IN FISMETTE	202
XXIII. IN FRONT OF THE FRONT	214
XXIV. A WOUNDED GERMAN	226
XXV. A NIGHT ATTACK	233
XXVI. THE DAYLIGHT PATROL	240
XXVII. OUR LAST BATTLE OF FISMETTE	251

PREFACE

FEW people have been able to learn much about what actually took place in the front line fighting of the World War. They have often asked about the war, and have found few veterans who would talk about it. One of the chief reasons for this is that they had nothing or very little to tell about the war. Approximately four million men were in service during the war. Half of these went to France and of these, half a million were near the front. Ten men are required behind the front to keep one man in action, service of supply, truck drivers, hospital workers, ambulance drivers, guards in the base ports, the replacement and casual camps, many thousands of M P's (military police), artillery, engineers, signalmen, aviators, mechanics, and endless more. And of the infantry organizations alone, only a part were actually at the front. In our own company, Company A, mth Infantry, 28th Division, there were over a thousand men during the war in a normal 250 men company. These were added to replace the men who became casualties— killed, wounded or gassed. We had one man, Oscar Hess, who was the last of the original company to become a casualty and he was wounded on November 10th. All the remainder were killed, wounded, gassed, or hospitalized for some reason.

Our division lost more men than any other former national guard division, more men than any other organization except the First and Second regular divisions. Our regiment lost more men than any other regiment of our division, our battalion more men than any of the three battalions in our regiment and our company more men than any other company in the battalion. Yet we had men who never saw a German who was not a prisoner. Some of our men were cooks, top sergeants, company clerks, supply sergeants, buglers, signalmen, kitchen police, the men who carried up the ammunition, the rations, cared for the wounded at the advanced stations, buried the dead, many were liaison men, carrying messages from company to battalion.

They fired and were fired at as we fought in towns, woods, and hills, but seldom saw the targets at which they fired; bombs and shells were dropped on them, they suffered from gas, and most of the horrors of war, they were killed, but they weren't actually at the front. Men who were trained as I was, scouting, patrolling, observation, sniping, who led patrols, reconnaissance or combat, advance guards, captured prisoners, put a gun out of action, held advanced posts, served as suicide squads when we were being attacked, were the men who actually saw the war, and most of them are dead. While 125,000 American dead in France are not so many when divided among the million men who were at or near the front, it is a tremendous percentage when it is considered how few of these men were doing the fighting. More than 250 men in our company alone were killed, more than the original strength of the company lost their lives in France. They can't tell you the story.

I was phenomenally lucky, so I will tell our story, will try to tell you something of what happened over there. There have been war books written by other men who were better writers than I—more fitted to place what they saw upon the printed page. But I don't believe a book about America's participation in the war has been written by a man who spent days, weeks and months in intensive fighting at or in front of the front, as my comrades and I did.

There is nothing beautiful or particularly glorious about this story. I have told it as well as I could, but have been able to give you only a faint idea of the conditions we encountered during the five worst days any unit of the American army experienced in France—the five days of our battle of Fismette. You could fully appreciate its horrors only if you were there. Never was a group of men harder pressed by superior forces of the enemy, or more ill equipped to fight off those attacks than were we. No artillery support during most of the fighting, no trench mortars, no hand or rifle grenades, just a moderate amount of pistol, rifle and machine gun ammunition. No food, proper medical attention, or the opportunity to bury the dead. Our men in that battle, the handful who held the front of the front lines, covered themselves with undying glory.

The telling of this story will give a better idea of what we did in France than have other war books I have seen. It tells the unvarnished truth about how we lived, slept, hiked, fought and died over there. There is another generation of men since those distant days of 1918. If this book does its part in showing them the folly, the uselessness, the tragedy of war, I'll feel well repaid for the time I spent in writing it.

This story covers the attack on Hill 204, between Chateau Thierry and Vaux, the drive up through the country between the Marne and the Vesle rivers in France. Although I sent the complete details of this fighting home in letters written during and immediately after the ending of hostilities in France, I haven't made use of those notes. I remember enough of the war to write several books. After the episodes described in this volume, there was more fighting in the last half of August, early September, the drive into the Argonne September 25th, weeks and weeks of fighting through the wooded hills and rivers of France, the drive on Metz until the war ended. If you find this book interesting, and would like to hear more of the war, drop me a line care of Strength & Health Publishing Co., York, Pa. I may write another book.

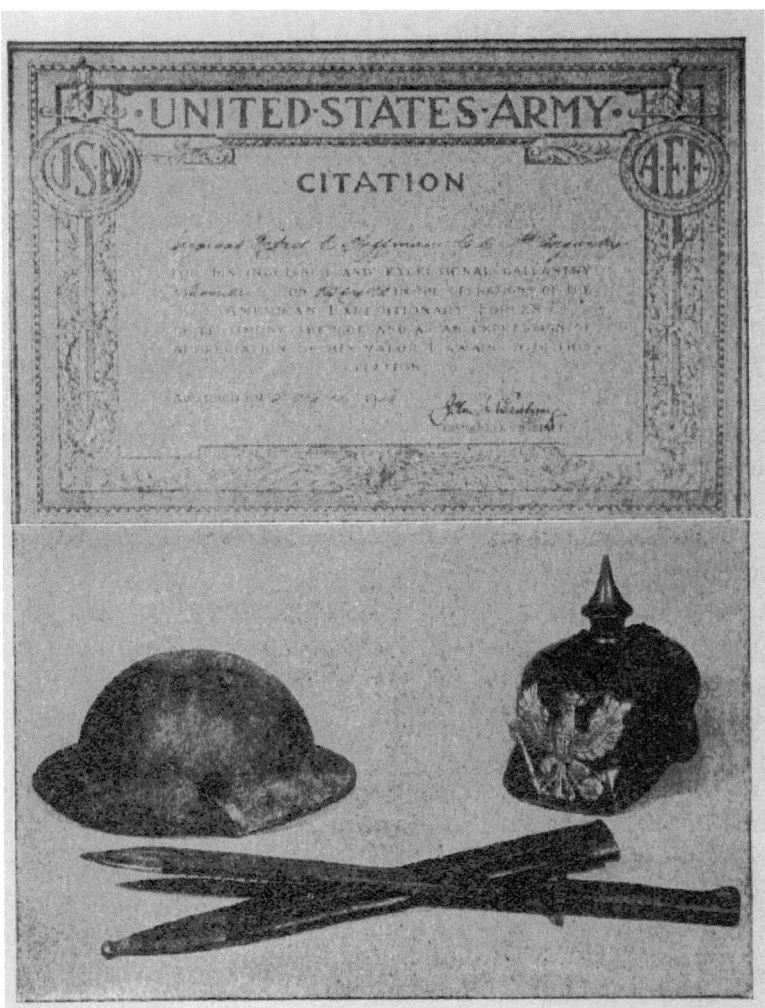

Bob Hoffman was awarded this citation in addition to those which accompanied his other decorations. It entitles the receiver to wear a silver star on his Distinguished Service Cross.
Helmet which miraculously saved the author's life in his first battle.
German saw-tooth bayonet which killed one of our men on Hill 204.
German dress helmet found in Fismette.

Battles in the Woods

It is a dismal day—the 25th day of September. It is unseasonably chilly, rainy, misty and gloomy—the sort of day which, in conjunction with my thoughts, gives me a morbid feeling. I have been sitting here in my study thinking about many things. Does the date, September 25th, mean anything to you? It would if you had been " Over There," for September 25th was the first day of one of the world's greatest battles—the final battle of the World War—the beginning of the drive in the Argonne forest. It was such a morning as this that we started out on that fateful day which was to be the end of the world for so many of us. The woods in which we fought for nineteen continuous days without relief was quite similar to the wood of fine oak trees I am looking at right out of my window.

I have this day acquired title to that thirty-two acre tract of woodland which for thirty-five years has been a picnic ground and park. It means that I now own over two hundred acres of woodland surrounding me here in one of the finest farming districts in the United States. It has been said that " man is an animal who cuts down big trees and plants little trees in their place." Too often man is an animal who just cuts down big trees, for there are many farms near here where not a single tree beautifies the farm home grounds or shades the house from the hot sun of summer or serves as a windbreak during the cold blasts of winter.

So it is nice to have woods and streams all around me, especially in as fertile and thickly populated a farming district as we have here in Pennsylvania. In many sections of our own country the trees have been cut down. In the middle west, and the southwest, not even a row of trees has been left. A row of trees along the fence would prevent the planting of two more rows of corn or wheat. Little thought was given to the protection the trees would offer, and now millions of acres of topsoil are being blown away because there are no trees.

Trees have a lot of uses. Aside from holding the top- soil, and holding the water, thus avoiding floods and barren lands, trees have meant a lot to me. I wandered in the woods as a growing boy. I hunted, fished, trapped, sought nuts, fruit, Christmas trees, wreaths, flowers, war relics, birds' eggs, geology specimens, fossils, and so many things in the woods near my home. And when I was grown to young manhood, I spent many weeks of living and fighting in the woods of France. In France, woods are appreciated. There are many of them. We camped in the woods, dug trenches in the woods and fought in the woods. Many of the events I will relate took place in the woods, and I would not be here writing this book if my boyhood training in the woods had not made of me a good woodsman. My work in the army was observation, sniping, scouting and patrolling. My life was saved many times by the trees in the woods through which I led patrols and advance guards. Our first big battle, Hill 204, near Vaux and Chateau Thierry, was fought in the woods. We fought in the woods around Fismes and Fismette and we were constantly in the woods during the weeks of the Argonne forest battle.

These woods were very similar to the woods on several sides of me here. How old is an oak tree? They are at their best when four hundred years of age. A few more venerable specimens live to be eight hundred or a thousand years of age. Sitting here looking at the trees across the way I realize that they were young and sturdy trees when Columbus crossed the ocean to " discover " our continent. Much of American history has passed by these trees at which I am looking as I write this. The road in front of the house was a game trail long before the dawn of written history. Early man, of thousands of years ago, must have passed here—particularly the Indians of a century and a half ago. The road is still a country road, but no longer a game trail or a path for aborigines. Now automobiles whiz by, but I cannot help but remember that it is ages old.

I have always been interested in relics. I found a flint arrowhead on a battlefield of France. For a thousand years they have used steel, first as knives and swords, arrowheads, and now for all sorts of machines designed to destroy mankind and all that it holds dear. An arrowhead such as I found must have been more than a thousand years old. They were fighting then—in those same fields and woods. They have been fighting through all the ages since, and no doubt they will continue fighting until the human race, through its inventive skill, designs and builds such ingenious machines that they can destroy modern civilization and the human race; destroy the great cities, all modern inventions and conveniences, and put man back into caves such as he lived in ten thousand years ago.

Our history here is not quite as old as that of France. France was a battlefield in Roman times. It was the Gaul we read so much about in our studies of Latin. Remember? Gallia est omnis divisa in partes tres, quarum unam incolunt Belgae. (All Gaul is divided in three parts; the first is inhabited by the Belgians.) I remember that much of it. In a shattered chateau in France I found Roman coins and other signs of the Roman expeditionary force of more than two thousand years ago. The young Romans of the legions, gathered from all parts of the world, fought and died in France. Throughout all the ages of history fighting has been going on over there. The ground has been drenched with the blood of innumerable mothers' sons—fine young fellows who desired to live, to love, to be happy, yet they were cut off prematurely before they had time to live.

Humans will never learn. Five times in the last eighty years the German empire has started a war—against Denmark back in 1868, France in 1870, France in 1914, and now Poland and France in 1939. We went over there to help fight a war to end war. But it only started war. War builds up hatred, a sense of injustice, which only waits " Der Tag " (the day) until it can boil over again. Since the war to end war, fighting has never ceased. The armistice was signed November nth, 1918, but the Russians and the Poles were fighting until 1921. That bred much of the hatred which has just resulted in the shattering defeat Poland has experienced, and in the loss of hundreds of thousands of their people. Even in recent years there has been the Ethiopian War, where Italy took from these primitive people one of the oldest Christian countries in the world; there has been war in Spain, long-drawn-out, bloody—millions died; the undeclared war in China—millions died and more millions—many more are still to die over there; Italy's conquest of Albania; Germany's bloodless conquest of Austria and Czechoslovakia; and now real resistance owing to their invasion of Poland. There has always been fighting in Europe and there will always be fighting.

But back to our own trees that I am looking at across the road. This farm was laid out in 1760, when George Washington was still a young man. Down the road a bit is a white oak tree large enough to have been a prominent landmark in 1760 and to serve as one of the markers in laying out the original farm. A bit farther down is an old gnarled, shattered oak that must be all of a thousand years of age. That is one of the main reasons I bought the first farm which has been added to by five successive purchases of additional land and woods in this tract. I have often walked through these woods. I like to look at them and see the small animals that make this place their home. I wouldn't harm one of them. Later in this book I'll tell you why. I want them to live, to be as happy as possible and obtain as much as they can from life.

I often like to think what these trees have seen. Do you ever feel that way about trees? I like to think of what has walked past them, camped under them; of the animals, the Indians, the pioneers. It is quite possible that George

Washington and parts of his Continental army camped here, for this part of Pennsylvania has figured in a number of wars. For a time the nearby city of York was the capital of the United States. The Continental Congress met here and some of its original members are buried in the churchyards here. The Indians left this part of the country for the west in 1768; they were driven out by the white settlers. They were still here when this farm was first settled and very likely many battles and skirmishes took place in our woods before they were driven out by a stronger people.

More years passed and there was another great war —the war of the rebellion, commonly called the Civil War. The southern troops, the Rebels, invaded our part of the country, advancing eighteen miles past here to the Susquehanna River. The bridge there was burned down; the Rebels turned back, travelling west on every available road. Some of them came this way and constant skirmishes took place in our woods. Towns near here were burned down, and finally one of the world's decisive battles took place a few miles from here, at Gettysburg—the Battle of Gettysburg, the high-water mark of the rebellion. The South had been winning up until that point. After Gettysburg they were weakened and it was a losing battle. They retreated to the Southland and finally capitulated two years later.

We find Indian relics around here. Civil War relics are in the possession of many people. So our woods could tell many tales if they could talk. I can't help thinking, " What would the trees think of us humans if they could think and reason for themselves? " Humans reason little enough.

The trees particularly at this time make me think of many things. They bring back memories, a great many of which are very painful: Of battles in the woods, friends killed in the woods, graves in the woods. Conditions were identical in those weeks in the Argonne forest to the conditions we have here—that is, as far as the woods and their appearance are concerned. Twenty-one years ago, when we fought the battle of the Argonne, I had thirty-two ugly blood boils on my body from eating a diet consisting almost entirely of meat and bread for some weeks—boils which made me swear more than I have all the rest of my life, as I constantly scraped them on the rocky ground while digging a new funk hole to protect my body each time we halted. I had French itch, and copious quantities of mustard gas; ugly burns which still leave their scars (they can be seen plainly enough on a cool morning like this); and the cooties—they lived on us; and we must not forget the rats, the dead and the wounded.

Scores of my friends—the men I had lived with, trained with, fought with, had come to like and admire—died in that woods in France, that woods that is so like our own woods here. It was only by a series of miracles—amazing escapes—that I did not die too; that I am here writing this book. I was young then— nineteen years of age at the time of the battle of the Argonne. I had been too busy to live, and because I had not found what a fine place the world can be, I did not mind dying particularly; had no actual fear of death. But now that I have lived and am living, I wish to do everything I can to prevent the death of thousands, even millions, of our young men who are on the threshold of life—men who will make their mark in the world if other humans do not make of them rotting, moulding corpses.

I have had twenty-one years of life since those days in the Argonne forest—busy years filled with the usual trials and tribulations all humans experience. I have been reasonably successful at several things. Now I have reached the heights in the work I like best—helping others to be strong, healthy, happy and successful. My escapes in the last war were so astonishing, so apparently impossible. Twelve bullets left their mark on my person or my equipment in the first short battle. I was one of thirty-two men of our two hundred and fifty strength company who marched out of the battle of Fismes. I was the only man to return of those who followed me on five patrols that I led in one day in the Argonne forest. These escapes, and enough more of them to write several books, made me wonder why fate saved me. What is my destiny? I have made the most of my life, feeling that it hardly belongs to me. I am not sure that I have done the proper thing with that life that God or fate saved for me, but I have done my best. I am pleased that I have been instrumental in enriching the lives of scores of thousands of people. And through my work, publishing Strength and Health magazine monthly, and writing books (every two months this year in particular), I have not only been a means of helping others, but I have received far more than a fair share of happiness and this world's rewards for myself.

I feel so much younger than I did in those days of twenty years ago when I came out alive from the fiery furnace of war. The photo which appears in this book, taken in March, 1919, still bears the marks of the horrors of war. You can see them in my face. I am far stronger, much healthier and have acquired enough of this world's goods to be able to help many people. I have often wondered what my destiny was—why I was saved when so many thousands of men around me died. I hope that the writing of this book is part of my destiny. If, through it, I can be of any assistance in keeping our own nation out of the mad maelstrom of war, I may have accomplished part of that for which I was saved.

I hope through this book to at least partially show the gruesome side of the war, bared from the waving of flags, the bugles, bands, the cheering; to show at least part of the ugliness, filth, dirt, evil, immorality and stink of war. I hope to persuade many to stay out of other people's wars. Be sympathetic, but remain aloof. Be strong, prepared to protect our own country against any nation or combination of nations which may attack our homes, our democracy, our American way of living. If our country was attacked the first hour would not pass before I would plan to enlist; and millions of other Americans would be in just as much haste to protect our wonderful country and our American way of living—by far the highest standard of living the world has ever seen.

During all the years since the war I have been urged to write a book about the war. I thought of it at times. In fact, during the weary months after the war until I could get home (war ended in November; I was not home and discharged from the army until the following September—ten months of waiting and planning for the future) I wrote long letters home, putting my experiences and opinions of the war on paper so that I would have the material for a book if I ever decided to write one. I don't have those notes now. I could get them easily enough, as my mother still has them, but I don't need them. Memories of the war are so deeply seared into my being, stamped into my memory, that I can write this book and a number of other books about the war entirely from memory of the happenings over there. I REMEMBER THE LAST WAR—every bit of it: every village and town in which we were quartered; nearly every turn in the roads over which we marched. I remember the names of the streets and the house numbers of the homes in which we fought. I know that in Fismette, much of my own fighting took place in a house at 35 Rue Cervante. I remember that we started into the Argonne battle on a compass bearing from the little town of Varennes of 10 degrees north of west. I could trace my path through France and the various battles just as easily as I could find my way through our own woods if I were over there. Civil War veterans came to Gettysburg fifty years after the war and found the very rock which had sheltered them as they fought there; the very trees which they had rested beneath or stood behind for shelter from the enemy bullets. We don't forget anything as important in our lives as the first war we fought. I believe you will agree that I REMEMBER THE LAST WAR as you go on with this book. After the war we wanted to forget it. I wore my uniform just one day when I returned home. I put away my medals and citations and started out anew. But now there is another war in Europe. Everywhere we turn the grim spectre of war constantly raises its ugly head. Men, women and children—noncombatants—are being killed daily by shell fire and the bombs dropped from airplanes. Ships are being sent to the bottom. The blasting of the Athenia, with its great loss of life, with absolutely no warning, is a good example of the ruthlessness of modern war.

Everyone is asking me about the war: " Will we be in it? " " Can we stay out? " " Will a man with a family or children be exempt?" "Why should I strive to build my body, to improve my health and strength, when a bullet may end it all? " " If we get in the war is it best to enlist right away? I guess the best jobs are to be had that way." " What is war like? " The newspapers are filled with war news. Regular radio broadcasts have been interrupted to bring the news of the latest war horrors right into our living-rooms, dining-rooms, bedrooms and kitchens. Everyone is talking about the war.

My friend, teammate and associate editor, Gord Venables, has just been visiting with me here. He only this day returned from Canada. He brought stirring news of the activities in our neighboring country, which is at war to the full extent of its resources. Our branch in Canada, The York Bar Bell Co. of Canada, Ltd., is turning its efforts toward doing its bit for the western democracies, Britain and France, the old allies. Instead of manufacturing bar bells and dumbells it will henceforth be manufacturing some form of munitions. We had a weight-lifting team in Canada, second only on the North American Continent to our own "world's strongest weight-lifting team" of the York Bar Bell Club. It has already been broken up. Many have enlisted; others have turned their full efforts to home defense or some other phase of war work. All activities in Canada are on a wartime basis. It brings the war rather forcefully home to us.

Through my work of publishing Strength and Health magazine, and my weight-lifting activities, I have friends all over the world. Each year I have sent a team to Europe to compete in the world's championships— at the Olympics of 1932 and 1936 in Berlin, and the championships of the intervening years at Paris and Vienna. We know intimately the lifters from Italy, Germany, Austria, France, England, Esthonia, Czechoslovakia and other countries. We have known them for years. Just a few months ago the German weight-lifting team were right here at my home. They were here in training for the International or world's team contest of last year. I can't help wondering where all these men are now. Are they in Poland or the western front? Where are the French champions—Hostin, Olympic champion of 1932 and 1936, Chas. Rigoulot, world's professional champion, Duverger and others? Where are Britain's lifters—Walker, Lawrence and Norman Holroyd? Are they still in England or have they crossed to France? Are they in service in the aviation, the navy or the land forces? These men were all friends. Now they must fight each other. They may come face to face some night in No Man's Land. They are not mad at each other. They have the same hopes and expectations of life. Yet a half-mad man who has come to power in one country has been able to precipitate nations into war—to cause the loss of hundreds of thousands of lives, perhaps millions (for in the last war 136,000,000 men were under arms; nearly ten million were killed, over 70,000,000 were injured, gassed or became casualties of some sort).

Consider our own team: men who have trained together, won national and world's titles, and made it possible for us to have the world's strongest team—Ter- lazzo, world's and Olympic champion, who was born in Sicily; Terpak, world's and national champion, whose father came from Russia; Davis, our colored world champion in the 181 pound class; Terry, another colored boy who is national champion and world's record holder; Stanko, whose grandfather lived in

Hungary, national champion and record holder; Grimek, champion of North America, and the most muscular man of the present (his people came from what was Czechoslovakia); Venables, whose parents came from England; Bachtell, of German extraction; Levan, whose ancestors are French. We have an array of nationalities on our team. Although my own name is German enough, the grandfather from whom I obtained the name was Swiss. My other grandparents were Scotch, Irish and English. Big Dave Mayor, national champion of 1937, record holder and America's strongest man, is Russian Jewish. If it were not for the fact that we live in "Lucky America," we could have the condition of all these friends at war among themselves. Bachtell, Terpak, Mayor, Grimek and Stanko would be allied on one side against Levan, Venables, Terry, Davis and myself. A sad condition, wouldn't it be?

War is so useless. Won't they ever learn? No one gains or profits by war. Millions of the best men of the lands engaged are killed. Think how much better the world would be if they had been fortunate like myself —come home to strive and work to better themselves, their nations and humanity. The ambition of a few leaders can get us into war. Germany, in the opinion of more than ninety per cent of the world, is the aggressor —is responsible for the war. Why did they need to start a war? Only to prove their strength, to satisfy their proud and arrogant nature, to satisfy their feeling of superiority. They had their years of difficulty after the war, but they had recovered to a fair extent. Through economic penetration of many markets they were becoming a greater Germany. They were spending fifty per cent of their efforts and their income on armaments. This is dangerous ground. When they have such a great force there is a well-nigh irresistible impulse to play with these toys, to try them out on weaker neighbors. And that's what they have done now.

What will come of it? Neither side will win. The last war gave us a crop of dead and crippled, of huge debts, of greater taxes, and this war will plunge the nations involved still deeper into the abyss. Modern war is so terrible that it will do nothing but cause one nation to break, to give up first. It is a question of staying power. Germany has been defeated before, but they rise and fight again. In the very old days when a nation was defeated (a nation which was constantly starting wars) all its men were killed. This can't be done in a modern world. If the country is broken up, a new leader will arise some day and unite the people—cause another war as Hitler has done. War will only end when warlike, war-lusting nations learn that it is futile. The power of modern defense is so great that a stalemate quickly results. Nations fight until they are so weakened that one must capitulate. The nation which apparently wins may be so weakened that it will not profit by the ultimate peace. The prostrate nations are susceptible to the germs of some of the isms which will in the case of the democracies eliminate our present system of living.

We are being warned by men who know, that if we send an army overseas to fight for democracy even if we win we have more than a good chance to lose our own democracy—our own preferred and much envied system of living.

Our only hope for civilization is to have no one win this war—to have it be a stalemate—and there is every good reason why it should turn out just like that. If we go over and win the war, at the high cost of hundreds of thousands or millions of our best young American lives, we won't gain a thing. After another score of years there will be another war. There are numerous countries who have lived in happiness and reasonable prosperity for long years—notably Norway, Sweden, Denmark, Holland, Switzerland, Finland and Belgium. There is no reason why nations cannot live in peace. War comes only through the unlimited ambition of the leaders. Controlled radio and press mould public opinion so that they can feel oppressed as their leaders wish them to feel.

If no one wins this war it will bring forcefully to the attention of many nations that war does not pay. Everyone loses. We must stay out. It is a proven law that the nation which attacks must have three times the force of the country on defense. The attackers lose tremendously. If we sent an army to another country, we would be the attackers and would receive the greatest losses. We should bend all our efforts toward becoming so strong that no other nation or coalition of nations will dare to attack us. We should build the physical strength of our manhood and womanhood, our mechanical equipment, our navy in particular, and our army, so that we can resist any form of invasion in the future.

This story of the folly and uselessness of the deaths, maiming of the flower of our country, in the last war, of the mistakes of wars, is respectfully dedicated to an effort to keep this country out of any war except an attack on our own beloved land.

Action on the Atlantic

I AWOKE to the sound of a series of terrific crashes. Pandemonium had broken loose. It was dark as pitch, for we were sleeping on G deck well below the water line of the fine old British liner Olympic. Twelve thousand men were crammed on that boat not unlike sardines in a can. Our hammocks were suspended from the ceiling; the tables on which we ate our meals were beneath us. The hammocks were staggered in effect so that more men could be packed into the depths of the ship.

I could hear sounds of guns roaring somewhere above and judged that there must be some sort of action with submarines. Hundreds of men from our deck were endeavoring to fight their way out of the room and up the stairs. I never even moved. If the ship had been torpedoed and would sink, there was little enough we could do about it—not enough lifeboats to go round. If the ship was sinking I would find it out soon enough. And if the damage which caused the stupendous jarring and rolling of the ship, and the firing on deck, was not really serious, then we would go back to sleep again. I had had precious little sleep on that trip, so I rolled over and tried to sleep some more.

The crash that awoke us was a collision between a submarine and our liner. It was coming up in the hope of launching a torpedo and perhaps sinking the huge troop ship. It came up directly in the path of the Olympic and was run over and sunk. There were other submarines around and the rapid firing that we heard was the sound of the efforts of the gallant British seamen to protect our ship. In a few minutes the attack was over; the Olympic was given credit for sinking an enemy submarine—and I had more sleep than usual.

Thus early in the war I displayed rather a fatalistic nature—believing that if I was to die, I would die when the time came. I had enlisted in the service immediately after the declaration of war, feeling that it was a man's duty to fight and die for his country. This had been instilled in my being somehow from my earliest childhood days. I had enjoyed above everything else playing soldier, receiving toy soldiers on birthdays and Christmas, reading war stories. My great-great-grandfather had fought in the Revolution. Newspaper accounts in old papers found in my grandparents' home told of our relative, Grandfather Shanner, who had fought in the War of 1812. Grandfathers Hoffman and Collins had fought on the Union side in the Civil War—my father in the Spanish American War. So I lost no time when war was declared in April, 1917, in an endeavor to live up to the tradition of our family. At last we were at war. The war had seemed far away in 1914 when it was first declared and the Germans burst through little Belgium on their way to Paris and the Channel ports. I had graduated from high school that year, and obtained my first position. I was door tender or assistant manager in a moving picture theatre. There were no radios in those days to bring us the war news even before it happens, as has been done on several occasions during the present war. But the newspapers carried full stories of the fighting. In an incredibly short time (that is, a short time for a day in which there were no transoceanic flights) the first war films reached this country and were displayed in the theatre in which I was employed.

The theatre was packed from early morning until late at night with a great mass of foreign immigrants. Hardly a word of English was spoken. The war pictures led to blows and some arrests; a great many of the men who saw the first pictures hastened to go home to their native lands to fight for what they felt was the right.

The summers of 1915 and 1916 went by with no disturbing thoughts about the war—no thought that we might get in it. It was far away. I lived chiefly for my great interest in athletics during those years. But in the fall of 1916 I felt that I would like to gain additional experience by performing some really hard work. I obtained a position in a shell factory, making eight inch shells for the British government, and the war seemed a bit closer to home.

Woodrow Wilson was President. He was reelected because " he kept us out of the war." But soon we were in the war. I wanted to do my part; and, much against my parents' wishes, I planned to enlist. My athletic sports had always consisted of swimming, rowing and canoeing. I wanted to enlist in the Sub Chasers, or " Mosquito Fleet," as they were familiarly called. My friends from the clubs of which I was a member were going into that arm of the service and I wanted to go too. But my father opposed my entrance into that branch of the service. He felt that I would not survive the war in such work. Seeing that I was adamant in my determination to enlist, he consented to permit me to join the old 18th Pennsylvania National Guard regiment. I was just eighteen years of age at the time and was expected to have parental permission to enlist. My brother had been on the Mexican border with that organization during the U. S. Army expeditionary force into Mexico, and Father thought I would be better off under the watchful care of big brother.

For some months we guarded bridges, munition works, tunnels and important public works. But finally we were taken off that duty and shipped down to Camp Hancock, Augusta, Ga., for additional training. We spent months of intensive training in the south; in fact an entire year of training had elapsed before we found ourselves on the Olympic crossing to France and what we hoped would be action.

During this period of training I had distinguished myself by constant study and application and had been sent to the first officers' training school at Fort Niagara to obtain a commission. They learned that I was just eighteen (it is necessary to be twenty-one to obtain a commission) so I was sent home in spite of my good showing. Nevertheless I had gained the stripes of a sergeant long before the beginning of our trip to France.

The Olympic was well camouflaged and heavily loaded. There were plenty of fights on this boat, for the i nth Infantry and the 59th Regulars were on board. We had a year's training back of us and felt like soldiers. The 59th was a skeleton unit of the regular army filled with draftees who had just come into service. Many of them did not know how to handle a gun, yet they ridiculed us for being tin soldiers, national guards, strike breakers, etc. Every afternoon for an hour or two boxing bouts were held and the fights between our organization and men from the 59th were rather bitter.

All sorts of men make up an army—good, bad, and indifferent. I found myself in lots of trouble for I had been fond of study, athletics and work when home. I didn't smoke, drink, chew, gamble, go out with questionable women or indulge in other diversions that some considered to be manly. There were men who thought that I was a sissy because I did not have " manly " habits. This led to a great many fights, and I thought at one time that I would have to beat every man in the company individually to prove that I wasn't a sissy. I did get enough practice that later enabled me to win the boxing championship in my bodyweight class of our division. This experience served me well on the Atlantic crossing, for I fought five three-round fights one day. Someone had to do it and the job fell to me.

Food on board was far from desirable, and the scrap money I won made it possible for me to supplement the rations with peanut brittle, which was about the only food we could buy on board. The principal parts of the British rations which were served on board consisted of bitter marmalade, frozen rabbit from Australia (of particularly uncertain age), and a concoction we learned to hate heartily, M. & V. (mutton and vegetables).

Days passed slowly enough and before long we were met by a group of destroyers who convoyed us into port. The courageous action of the German submarine (in spite of the observation balloons which were a part of the convoy and could detect submarines beneath the surface) very nearly spoiled our trip. It provided a place in Davy Jones' locker for the members of the submarine and its crew, for it was very definitely lost at sea. Great quantities of oil came to the surface and spread over a wide area of sea.

And one day in the distance we saw the barren hills of the British Isles. Britain itself was a beautiful country, but the hills one sees first are far from attractive. We finally were helped into the harbor at Southampton by tugboats, and after some hours disembarked. We were loaded into British trains. European trains differ from ours in the fact that they are made up of a group of small compartments which seat eight men. It was thrilling to be in a strange country. This brief trip from Southampton to Dover has been my only landing in England.

The countryside was beautiful. Every inch of ground was farmed or at least turned into gardens. All possible food was being produced. Men and women in uniform were everywhere. We passed around the great city of London, and finally pulled up in the city of Dover. We were billeted that night in improvised barracks. We saw our first British troops; had the opportunity to talk to them at considerable length. Almost without exception they had been in the war from the beginning, nearly four years before. Most of them had been severely wounded, and they were a hard-bitten lot. We were impressed with their optimism. They seemed sure that the winning of the war was only a matter of months. Such is the power of propaganda. Propaganda, you know, is not necessarily making misstatements; it consists of omissions rather than commissions, leaving out any part of the news that is not favorable to the side reporting. I was impressed from our first contact with the British and French that they were sure of winning—just a matter of months. Yet the actual fact was that the Allies were so nearly defeated early in 1918 that just a bit more would have put them over the brink.

Much bad feeling was created because we did not get in the war sooner. Many names were later applied to Americans that were far from complimentary. The British in particular greatly resented the fact that America could feel it had much to do with winning the war. True enough, we did not fight as long as our Allies, we did not lose as many men, but we did lend $13,000,-000,000 to the Allies—most of it to England and France —very little of which we got back. We didn't take a single colony or indemnity or reward of any sort for our aid in the winning of the war, while England and France derived all the spoils which are causing their difficulty at present. Land was taken from their ally, Russia, the Empire of Italy was not helped at all, and these nations tremendously resented being left out. The United States landed an army of more than two million men on French soil. A large part of this great mass of men was in action for a time at least. It was the ever-growing strength of the Allies through the addition of the Americans more than any other one cause which made the Germans finally surrender.

The entry of America into the war was the deciding factor, yet our Allies, who welcomed us so gladly in 1918 when they had met with great reverses through the powerful drives of the German army, soon forgot. And the mildest of the names they called us was Shylock. They felt at the very least that we should have cancelled the war debt. I am sorry to say that we didn't get along too well with the British. They were in a very tough spot, even if they didn't realize it, and at least should have been glad to see us.

We remained in Dover for two days and finally embarked across the short stretch of channel to France. The danger of submarines was far from over. The English Channel was well patrolled and mined, but submarines had managed to slip into the Channel with devastating effect.

We Land in France

IT is just a short journey from England to France, and in less than two hours we were ready to disembark at Calais. Here we saw our French allies for the first time—little fellows in ill-fitting blue uniforms. Our guide led us over to a camp on the beach. Circular tents, approximately ten feet in diameter, were to be our homes for a time. Two squads, or sixteen men, were allotted to each tent. I was the right guide, so was placed with the first two squads. That made seventeen of us in all. Half of us could not have slept in that tent. On the other side of a barbed wire fence was a camp of little Annamites—small Orientals, Chinaman-like in their appearance—who hailed from French Indo-China. They were small men, not over five feet in stature, and were quartered ten to a tent.

At one time I was the tallest man in our company, being six feet three inches in height. But we had received a draft of new men from Camp Travis, Texas, and they were huge fellows. Sixteen of them were taller than I. They ranged in height from six feet four to six feet seven inches, and seventeen of us were to sleep in one small tent. We tried it for a time with our feet extended well up the center pole of the tent. I quickly gave this up as a bad job and determined to sleep outside in the sand. Each tent was set three feet below the surface to escape danger from falling bombs. With such tents only a direct hit would cause fatalities. I was warned of the danger of sleeping in the open, but I was tired after the long ocean trip, the train ride, the rough billets in Dover, the Channel crossing, the waiting around for hours, and I slept outside in the sand like a log.

The next morning I was regaled with tales of the air raid which had taken place the night before. A bomb had been dropped among our small Chinaman-like allies in the next area. A great anti-aircraft battle had taken place with quite a lot of shrapnel raining down upon the beach. But I had seen nothing, heard nothing. Such is the sleep of exhaustion, for I am normally a light sleeper.

We spent two nights sleeping on the beach, and soon were ordered to prepare to move. Each of us had a pack, a rifle and bayonet, mess kit, condiment can, blankets, poncho, shelter half, tent pole and tent pins. In addition we had a barrack bag which in my case was completely filled with enough material to start a young store. We were ordered to take with us what we could, for we would have to leave our barrack bags until the end of the war. I had seventeen Red Cross sweaters, books, and many other things that I felt I could not do without. But it wasn't long until I did learn to do with out plenty of my belongings. We were instructed to roll our extra shoes in the packs instead of strapping them on the outside of the pack as we had normally done. I had a huge pair of square-toed English hobnail shoes— a very generous number twelve size. And when my pack was rolled it was a good foot and a half in diameter and bumped my heels.

Finally we were ordered to put on our packs and break camp. We spent hours getting out of Calais— going right through the business and residential district in single file; move a few feet, stand for a long period; move forward another few feet and stand for another interminable period. The packs hung heavily on our backs. Every man in the organization was woefully weak, due to the poor rations we had had from the time we had left the southern camp in Georgia weeks before (mouldy cheese, weak tea, marmalade and more of the M. & V. had been our diet while with the British, and little enough of that), strange water, and we had not yet become acclimated. We finally moved to the edge of Calais and started up a steep hill on the outside of town. Our men began to drop out like flies in front of the British rest camp, and they laughed uproariously and constantly ridiculed our men.

We had been strong enough in America. It was easy for me to hike twenty-five miles through the dust of Georgia, carry three or four rifles, two or three extra packs belonging to the fellows who were weak enough to be about ready to fall out, not drink a single drop of water all day long, and take a savage sort of pleasure in the experience. But here things were different. I dropped out several times on the way—dysentery and bleeding at the nose. But I finished the hike with grim determination. Only a paltry few of the thousand men in our battalion completed that hike. They came straggling in for the next two days. It was one of the worst hikes I experienced in France. There is one difficulty in hiking. The officers ride on horseback. The horses drone along on the level, holding the men back; but when the going gets hard for the men, the horses step out going uphill and leave the troops far behind. Then there is a lot of hurry, which makes it quite difficult for the men to keep up.

We finally pulled into the small town of Bouvlinghem. (That may not be the correct spelling, but that's the way it sounded.) It was a small town with a limited population. Men—that is, able-bodied men—were conspicuous by their absence. For the first time we felt that we were really in France. We were rather lucky in this town, for we had good billets, barns and quite a lot of straw. Other soldiers had been there, and had left their full quota of cooties, but we made the best of it.

There was a small cafe in town and I nearly lost my reputation for sobriety trying to bring home two of my sergeant former tent mates. They had imbibed a bit too much of drink. I was walking arm-in-arm with them, trying to steady them as we went down the street. As they staggered, I staggered too, and the report quickly went around that the three of us were intoxicated. But there was no punishment. After all there was a war on and the high officers knew that there would be few enough opportunities for this slight taste of civilian life.

The little town of Bouvlinghem was scattered over considerable distance. It was made up of two somewhat disconnected villages, with red-roofed stone houses set rather wide apart, with fields and orchards all around them. Our company was far down at the end of town, in a typical farmhouse. The men were quartered in every available building. At times it was necessary to drive out the cow or pig before one could sleep. Every house and shed, every home, had the number of men it could accommodate painted upon the door.

French houses were pretty much alike, so when I give you this brief picture of our surroundings at Bouvlinghem, you can obtain a pretty good idea how it was all through France. Every house, particularly on the outskirts, had an enormous barn and a generous manure yard. The financial position of any man was judged by the size of the manure pile in his yard. A bigger pile meant more cattle, horses, or hogs, and more servants too, for human manure was not permitted to go to waste. When we were in Bouvlinghem it was nearly time to harvest the wheat. But it was never harvested, for we did our training on the fields where the wheat had been. The United States government had to literally pay through the nose for everything it used. Later it had to pay rent for the ground used as cemeteries. Each barn and each home was built under government supervision with the idea of defense in mind. In the end of the barn toward Germany there were always openings for rifles or machine guns.

After my first night in the barn, I was invited to come into the house and sleep with a couple of sergeant friends of mine who had a feather bed. My heart leaped at thoughts of sleeping in a real bed after the trains, hammocks, hard floor, beach and barn in which I had recently slept. The French beds are very big, and one sinks far below the surface of the feather mattresses. There were three of us in the bed—rather crowded, but we managed. A comparatively young man, and his wife and family, lived in this house. He had lost one of his legs in the war and performed his chores stumping around on a peg leg. The wife was very nice, although sad, and we had a lot of fun with the two kiddies.

The French couple did all they could to make us happy, each morning insisting that we drink black coffee and cognac. It was intensely bitter. I didn't like wine or liquor or coffee either, but I could not seem to learn enough French to politely say no, and each morning I had to down this vile concoction.

After just two days in the feather bed it was decided to send one non-commissioned officer from each battalion to the British schools at Merkegham. I received the assignment from our organization. While on the subject of schools—I went to most every school there was. If one man went from a company, one from a battalion, one from a regiment, one from a brigade, I got the job; and sometimes I represented the entire division at a school. I was a good student and invariably finished with the highest possible rating at these schools. I had acquired, through my athletic work, a judgment of time, space and distance, which served me well in the observation, sniping, scouting and patrolling which became my work. I thought that I would soon be so smart that they would not want to get me killed. But it was just the other way when we got to the front. It was always, " Send Bob Hoffman; he's had that training," or " He's had that experience." I found that it doesn't pay to be too smart.

I was to leave on the morrow, so had to hustle to get my outfit in shape, and one of the ways to get ready was to boil the unwanted visitors in my clothes. After the evening meal I repaired to a place down over the hill with a wash boiler I had borrowed, and prepared to make myself a bit more sanitary. I stripped off all my clothes and put them in the wash boiler. About the time they commenced to boil, two of my friends went past. " Where to, fellows? " I asked. " Just taking a walk," was the reply. But about a half hour later they returned with two chickens. " What are you going to do with them? " I asked. " Cook them somewhere." " I'll cook them for you," was my hasty reply. I was hungry too. We weren't getting enough to eat. One thing about the army—rations were rations, and they didn't recognize any difference in the need of a big man and a little man; a man like myself who now weighs 260 pounds or a 120 pounder. Worse yet, we had a pint of coffee with each meal and I did not drink coffee. More than once it would have filled up my stomach to fit my dinner. So I was hungry most of the time.

The men of our company constantly complained of hunger, and I just as constantly reiterated that they weren't really hungry. It was just appetite, a desire to eat. They were accustomed to having a full stomach and the first time they didn't have as much as they were accustomed to they would complain. I urged every man to masticate his food more thoroughly, for that would stretch the food farther and fill the inner man a bit better. And I told them to apply this test to their hunger: think of ordinary bread. If the mouth watered they were hungry; if it didn't, it was just appetite. I don't know how much good my constant arguing with the men who claimed to be hungry did, but it helped a bit in my case.

I dumped the clothes out of the wash tub. Who knows anything about the history of a wash tub anyway? Water was very scarce in northern France. The French people depended almost entirely on the water which drained from the red tile roofs of their homes. This water, for washing purposes, was kept in enlarged sunken stone tubs in their yards. Month after month, year after year, the household clothes were washed in this same water. When it rained hard it was diluted a bit with clean water. I don't believe that baths were ever taken by the denizens of most of France, or other European countries as well. They thought we were very dirty people because we needed so many baths. The people rarely drank water, imbibing sufficient of wine and coffee to take care of the body's need of liquid. There was usually a town pump used by all the citizens of the town for their water supply for cooking. Little of the water in northern France was fit for our men to drink. The people who lived there drank little enough of it without boiling, but through the generations they had become immune to the germs it carried. The few people who had pumps of their own always had them right beside the manure pile, where it was easy enough for the material from that collection of fecal matter to contaminate the pump.

As I said, water was scarce and with the minimum of washing of the tub I put in some additional water. I didn't know anything about cooking chickens and neither did my friends. We took the feathers off, and removed most of the insides. We had no salt. I gathered some dandelion in a futile attempt to add some slight flavor to the chickens. They never would get soft—must have been before-the-war birds. But finally our hunger could stand it no longer. I bit into what I thought was a big piece of meat. It was filled with stones and corn. I couldn't understand what it was. The tub couldn't have been that dirty. And then it occurred to me that a chicken had a craw instead of just a stomach as did most animals. I had not removed it. It was the worst chicken I ever ate, but it was filling, and you would be surprised to know what you will eat when you are hungry. I ate many things later I don't like to think about now.

We stripped the bones clean enough. I put on my damp clothes. The cooties didn't bite. They were either completely boiled or at least weakened to the point, through their enforced bath, that they did not have pep enough to bite.

The next morning I was to be off to school.

At the British School

IT was not known at this time, whether the American army was to go into action in Northern France, near Belgium, with the British troops, or farther south with the French. We received training in the British style at this time. I had been sent to the infantry school at Merkegham. Our work was with rifles, bayonets, hand grenades, patrolling, and a great deal of engineering work—building barbed wire entanglements and digging trenches.

Trenches were being dug everywhere. Nearly every fifty yards along all the roads was a filled-in trench— filled in loosely so that the road could be used and yet could be utilized as a defensive trench in short order. The British were putting up a terrific resistance to the massed formations of Germans which were coming over. Considerable agitation was evident; much nervousness in the attitude of the men who were instructors at this school. They were trying to appear calm, but it seemed that the German drive would never be stopped. The British fell back from line to line, in many cases only a few yards apart. '

At this camp we saw many men who had been incapacitated for further action at the front from two common causes: trench feet—standing around month after month in mud up to one's knees in time caused a great enlargement, a painful swelling of the feet. The feet were more than twice their normal size and the men who contracted this condition could hardly walk. And there were a great many cases of mustard gas. This gas is used freely. It is not mustard—merely smells like it. It is quite popular with modern armies and anyone who enters the present war will receive more than his share of it. If a road or woods is sprayed with mustard gas it will be approximately two weeks before that road can be travelled by troops with safety. It attacks first the soft moist parts of the body: under the belt, between the legs, around the male genital organs.

Many men had it on other parts of their bodies too. It is very difficult to get rid of, for the instant it touches another part of the body a new burn appears. It is the easiest way to put men out of action. It seldom causes death, but will keep a man away from the front for ten weeks or three months. It makes no difference how hard he may try, no matter how angry he may be or how he desires to fight, he will be weak and sick and must leave the front. I talked to men who had been gassed three years before and their burns were still itchy and painful. Mustard gas caused burns; the burns were covered with scabs, and the affected place would itch; scratching would cause a milky substance to run out of the pores which in a short time would spread and form more scabs. Many men had mustard gas burns on theirfaces and were unable to shave, for previous attempts had spread the burns over the entire surface. They wore whiskers, like Robinson Crusoe, which in turn added to the itchiness.

I was to see a great deal of mustard gas during my time in the war. Hundreds of men were lined up on stretchers with bandages over their eyes when I returned to the front from my first trip to the hospital— all victims of mustard gas. There were hundreds of men suffering from this modern human invention in the base hospital at Blois, where I spent a couple of weeks. The poor fellows in most cases were so badly gassed they could hardly walk or urinate.

So many of these men had contracted gas during the greatest heat of the summer. Almost half of our original company was lost through gas during a particularly unpleasant experience they had in burying the American dead who had lost their lives in Belleau woods. These bodies had lain in the July sun for over two weeks before they were buried. Another particularly trying experience was the digging up of many dead Germans during July. One of the laws of war states that belligerents should remove the identification tags from enemy dead, and send them back through a neutral country so that the people at home will not suffer suspense. These Germans had been buried in a hurry, with their entire identification tags around their necks. It became our job to dig them up again and remove half the tag—far from a pleasant task and one which prevented our men from smelling the gas. Many died, others lost their minds and a great many of our original company were put out ofaction, due to these gas burns, for the duration of the war.

It is a most painful experience and something that any men who enter the war in Europe can look forward to, for mustard gas is particularly popular at the present time. A great many were burned with such severity around their genitals that they lost their testicles, and the penis was no longer capable of normal urination. It was necessary to make an opening through the side for urination.

We Americans who were in training spent many busy days at this British school. The Britishers seemed to have a rather poor opinion of our prowess so we worked especially hard to show that we were good soldiers and athletic, courageous men. We had many night patrols during this special training and it was there that I learned I possessed some sort of a sixth sense—a sense of direction which made it possible for me to orient myself in the inky blackness of the darkest night and to find my way through the woods to my objective. This was to serve me well in later operations in the woods, and certainly saved my life many times. We learned much here about sniping, observation, scouting, patrolling, and the many forms of activity which constantly took place in No Man's Land between the armies. The British soldiers had been performing this work for years as they had been firmly entrenched in the mud of Northern France. After the first great advances of the war of movement, the Germans had been defeated and had been driven back from the closest point to which they had approached the great city of Paris (within fifteen miles) and had dug in about seventy miles from Paris.

The British sergeants tried hard to do their duty. They told us constantly of experiences at the front and what to expect. I crawled around until my clothes were worn out—not as completely as they were to become worn in reconnaissance during our later battles, but made far from presentable. We had a great deal of practice with bayonets. Men were taught to yell as fiercely and horribly as possible as they rushed forward at the dummies to thrust their bayonets through them. We were particularly adept at yelling, for most of us had practiced some form of Indian yells in our youth, and the sound of other American platoons making a mock attack caused an involuntary shiver to go through my frame. We learned all the pleasant features of the long point, the short point, the jab, the butt stroke, the face smash and the cut down. The procedure in bayonet fighting was to try to parry the enemy's first stroke and make a long thrust to his body; if this failed and both came to closer quarters, the short point was to be used. And if you were really close, the object was to jab the bayonet upward into his abdomen, if you had fallen, or his neck if you were standing close to him. If the first long thrust missed, a blow was to be aimed at his testicles with a terrific swing of the butt of the rifle. If he missed that or an upper cut to the chin for which it was intended, the object was to smash his face with the butt. A rifle is not so heavy—just about ten pounds— but it makes a vicious weapon when swung by an expert. Assuming that the face smash did not put your adversary out of action, nor that any of your previous blows had finished him, then you were to cut down at the next man and go through some of the movements again.

At this stage of the war the Germans were coming over in mass formation—rows of men a hundred deep making a desperate attempt to break through the British and French lines through actual weight of numbers. When the defenders reached the hand-to-hand point with the enemy there would be rows and rows of them pressing forward and fast work was needed. In later hand-to-hand work, fortunately, we did not meet the Germans in dense masses, but had fights with their advance troops which I am pleased to say resulted favorably in my case.

I was studious by nature and I had read considerable about the war. I knew that the careless way in which they fired their guns and dropped bombs in France was hurting a lot of people. The average time in which a British soldier was still able to fight after he landed in France was three months. Killed, wounded, gassed, captured—something put them out of action in an average of ninety days. Some got hit with the first bullet; others went through the four years without a scratch. So I enlisted with my eyes open, expecting to get killed, but hoping to have done more than my part before I got mine. I was young enough that I had a desire to be doing something great when I died, so that my parents would receive a posthumous reward of some sort of medal and know that Bob had died bravely. But I did have ideas about the way I was to die if die I must.

And none of these ways was with a bayonet or knife in my ribs. I had an antipathy toward cold steel entering my body and I trained hard to learn all I could about bayonet work. In fact, all through the war I trained just as hard as I would for an important athletic contest. I often thought that I might be out in No Man's Land, or meeting some form of an attack, where I would come upon hand-to-hand fighting with a German, and he might be one of the great old German strong men of whom I had read (Swoboda, Steinbach or Turck of Austria; Arthur Saxon or his brothers of Germany; Strassburger, Wohl, Steinborn or some other superman). I knew they would have much more strength than my slender frame possessed, and in order to remain among the living I had to acquire skill to win such a battle. I not only worked hard during the training time, but I talked to every man I met who had experienced hand-to-hand work at the front, so that

I could learn any tricks there were. These tricks did save my life later in the war.

I must explain here that although I expected to die in the war, I knew that one army beat the other by greater courage or greater efficiency in fighting; the side that inflicts the greatest casualties on the other would ultimately win. Therefore I intended to sell my life as dearly as possible and see how many of the enemy I could take with me or send before. During the entire war I performed the work that was necessary (someone had to do it), but I was as careful as could be during all the months of the war. I never got careless; I always had my gas mask. I always carried a shovel and a pick with me throughout the war. Some men became tired and threw their entrenching tools away, but not I. I was the champion digger of the American army. Every time we stopped I dug a hole. We didn't know when we stopped whether it would be five minutes, five hours, five days or five weeks. And as long as we were there I improved my little dugout, and I can tell of many cases in which this digging saved my life. Aside from the fact that I believe I have a just claim to the title, " luckiest man in the American army in France " during the war, I owe much of the fact that I am here, to careful training, superb physical condition and being as careful as I could be.

The bayonet work was most important, but rapid fire was being taught and practiced a great deal. British soldiers told me of former attacks in which they had engaged. They would fire until their guns blistered their hands, but still the Germans would press forward. They couldn't stop. The men behind them would push them forward. We were equipped at this camp with British rifles which were somewhat different from the Springfields we had in the beginning of the war and the Enfields we used later. Our rifles held a shot in the chamber and five in a clip. The British rifles held five more shots, and two clips instead of one—eleven cartridges in all. It was necessary to carry the rifle sideways during close order drill, which is the reason for the different position of the British marching soldier as compared to ours.

We spent many hours learning to sight these rifles, to properly squeeze the triggers, and to fire as fast and accurately as possible. I had the happy faculty of learning things quickly and soon I was an adept with the British rifle. I remember the first time I attempted rapid fire on the range in our country; I was supposed to shoot ten shots in a minute, the whistle blew, signifying that the minute was up, when I had fired just five shots. But speed was needed at this camp. While there I set a record of thirty-two accurately aimed shots in one minute. The British army record was thirty-three, and was held by a major who had years of experience with that rifle. So the officers insisted that "no bloody, blooming Yank " could fire that many shots in a minute. But my sergeant was just as insistent in saying that I had fired thirty-two shots—he was standing right back of me—and twenty-nine of these shots had hit the small target at which we fired, and three others were very close to it.

There were air raids nightly at this camp. We were not far from Calais, and the German planes were constantly flying behind the lines. The Zeppelins in particular were trying to reach London. Every night we had sort of a Fourth of July. We were quartered in huts which would accommodate twenty men. They had round tin roofs and looked somewhat like a gigantic loaf of bread. Fritz was methodical, and we could expect a raid every night at ten o'clock. No lights were permitted; the days were long, and it was just thoroughly dark by ten. We retired at nine, but would not seriously attempt sleep until the nightly raid was over. We would lie on the hard floor (no bunks in these shelters) and stories were told. I heard more risque, or dirty, stories in my days at this camp than I had heard in all my previous life.

And then the fireworks would start. It is a funny thing about people—it has been proven in this present war—but it is almost impossible to keep them under cover. They never feel that the bombs will drop on them. They are sure they will fall somewhere else. And the stories we hear tell us of the citizens of Warsaw, the civilians of China, standing out with their faces in the air watching the raid. We were like that. In the many air raids I was in, I never had the slightest fear of them. I knew that men were killed but I never expected it to be me. I have been bombed in the daytime, when I could see the bombs falling. They quickly grew from a tiny spot to a terrific-looking implement, which seemed to be aimed directly at my right eye. When it seemed that inevitably they would hit me, I would dive down the mouth of a dugout, just like a prairie dog goes down its hole.

Not one of us expected to get hit with the bombs. We would lie in there and laugh and talk—occasionally walk to the door and stand outside looking up. The search lights would finally center themselves upon a plane high in the heavens. The anti-aircraft guns were going full blast and black and white puffs would form all around the plane. It was said that only one in ten thousand three inch shells brought a plane down. In the present war, they have more efficient guns and shoot down many more planes. The shrapnel from our own shells rained down upon us sounding like a gigantic rain storm as it hit our round sheet metal roof. The roofs were made round so that they would serve as a steel helmet did, to protect the wearer from shrapnel. Perhaps you don't know the difference between high explosive shells and shrapnel. Explosive shells ranged from the tiny thirty-seven millimeter, or one pounder, up through the usual three-inch shell fired by the French seventy-five and the German seventy-seven to the one-hundred-fifty-five millimeter, or six-inch shells. While many trench mortars of even tremendous size were employed by both sides in the war, there was little artillery larger than six-inch on most drives. It was too difficult to move the huge guns. But these guns were used on some of the fronts, and they did terrific damage. They would penetrate perhaps twenty feet before they exploded, and then lift huge blocks of ground into the air as large as a Ford automobile. They left a shell hole large enough in which to place an average two-story house. That is the sort of huge guns which are being fired over there now. What happens to men who are near such explosions? Later I saw hundreds of Germans lying dead; as they tried to retreat, they were caught by these huge shells and evidently killed by the force of the explosion; by concussion because there were no marks upon them. Shrapnel was usually enclosed in a three-inch shell, and instead of exploding with devastating force and making a huge shell hole, it was designed to explode in the air. A time fuse was responsible for this. The object was to have them explode over a group of men just as skyrockets explode, hurling their various colors of beautiful lights in a downward direction, and thus they would kill or injure more men than a shell of similar size which was high explosive. I saw many men in the hospitals with shrapnel balls in their upper body. Sometimes they had remained in the man for weeks before it was found that he had additional wounds. Then it was necessary to reopen the hastily closed wound, and dig out the piece of shrapnel and usually the cloth that clung to it—a piece of a man's uniform which had been driven into the wound with the ball.

But we were young and full of fun. War was serious, we knew, but it was a sort of game too, and I for one did not think of dying. I was at this camp just one Saturday, and that Saturday there was to be an athletic contest. The Yanks were invited to compete against the Britishers, and we managed to beat them in their own games in several instances; but they did win the majority of events. At this camp was Bandsman Rice, former British heavyweight champion of the British Empire. He was a famous figure and, naturally, the soldiers enjoyed seeing him in action. He needed an opponent and soon that job was thrust upon me, as men from our division told the sergeant who was making up the program that I was a fighter. I didn't think that I was enough of a fighter to take on a man like " Bandsman" Rice who, although never a champion of the world, was champion of nearly four hundred million British subjects. I was just a young fellow who had been forced into being a boxer. Someone had to meet men from other divisions and branches of service, or other armies, and when a man was asked for, one of our officers would say, " How about you, Bob? " A fellow couldn't say no. And after I had beaten the best in the company, the best in the battalion, regiment and division, I was constantly pushed in against better and better men—great old professional fighters, or comers who afterwards became great as did Gene Tunney. I was pretty fast, had learned to use my left, and had not been knocked out up to this time. I was in for a bad six rounds this day as I afterwards found out.

"Bandsman" Rice started easily enough. Then I don't know whether I had accidentally hit him too hard, or whether he felt that I was to be the victim of a Roman holiday, or whether he didn't like Yanks, or just the color of my eyes or how I parted my hair, but he soon waded into me, trying desperately to knock me out. I am not sure whether it was a pretty fight or not. I was still on my feet at the end of the sixth round and our fellows thought that was something of an accomplishment. I had done a lot of back pedalling, for I was a counter boxer. But I had gotten some good blows across and I think the last three rounds of the battle were pretty even. I was in splendid shape, and " Bandsman " Rice had grown a bit soft during the war. My superb physical condition was to serve me well through all the fighting, and save my life and bring promotion on several occasions.

Our busy days at this camp soon came to an end. I was sent back to our division with a letter to the commanding officer telling in glowing terms of the work I had done. It was quite an experience.

A Long Hike

WHEN I got back to my friends in the feather bed I was immediately informed that we were getting ready to move—up to the front, we were told. I wasn't quite convinced of this, although there had been the constant rumor that our Allies were having a pretty hard time of it and we might be thrown in the line at any time to prevent a break-through of the massed German forces. Rumors were the most abundant thing in France. Where they started from we could never learn. But through the entire period of training during the war and after the hostilities, we practically lived on rumors—usually of a favorable nature. Wishful thinking and hoping apparently gave birth to them. There was always the rumor that we were going to the front any minute. And after we were at the front there was always the rumor that we were going back for a really long rest; that we would be stationed in Paris for a long period; that we were to be sent back to America to help train other troops; even that selected men of the American army were to be mated with French women to help make up for the lowering of the birth rate due to the mortality and crippling of so many of the men. Many were the fellows who hoped that they would be found fit to serve their country and their Allies in the latter capacity. But it was just a rumor like so many.

Where there is so much smoke there must be some fire, the old adage informs us, and where there were so many rumors that we were going to the front, probably some day we would get to the front. And this most prevalent rumor materialized to the extent of bringing the order to roll packs and proceed on our way.

Where to, we had not the slightest idea. Little did we realize that we were to hike hundreds of weary, dust-filled kilometers through France to serve as Exhibit A. The morale of the French and English must be kept up. They too had rumors—that America would help only by lending money, sending supplies and materials; that they would not send men. They had been told that Americans could not successfully make the Atlantic crossing owing to the submarine warfare which had reached its peak in 1917. Even the Germans could not be convinced that Americans had really arrived in France. The first German I captured in France, seeing my brown uniform, instead of the horizon blue of the French, said " Anglais? " meaning English. I replied, " No, American."

So our work was to show the British soldiers, the French soldiers, and the French civilian population that we were really in France ready to help. We were to march from village to village, zigzagging back and forth across France, to show as many people as possible that we were there to help them. Anyone who took part in such a march in France, from the sea or the sands of the beach of Calais, by a long and devious route to the front (it seemed to me that we covered all of France on these endless marches), will never forget them. A glance at the map shows that Paris in a direct line is less than an hour's journey by plane from London, hardly one hundred and fifty miles from Calais in a direct line. I don't know how far we walked, but I completely wore out two new pairs of British field shoes on this trip. They seemed solid enough and had an imposing array of hobnails and iron reinforcements on the heel. Perhaps we walked the equivalent of hundreds of miles; perhaps the shoes were made of inferior materials. I have no way of knowing for sure. But it seems that we walked interminably.

Marching, marching, down splendid French roads—dusty roads—so dusty that one could not tell the color or nationality of troops which passed us in motor lorries, so heavily were they coated with dust. Lombardy poplars lined all the roads of France—two rows of trees and a white ribbon of road as far as one could see. We were always climbing hills and going down in little valleys; invariably seeing the steeple of the village church from a considerable distance as we approached the town; crossing the little bridges over the streams in the valley; marching for twenty minutes—the pound, pound of feet. A company usually led, and I was just a short distance behind the major's and his adjutant's horses. The packs got heavier and heavier in spite of the fact that they shrank at nearly every halting. United States equipment was spread from the sea to the front. My huge pack, which had bumped my heels in Calais, shrank to a shelter half, a single blanket, to one of the seventeen Red Cross sweaters friends and relatives at home had so patiently knitted, and still the pack was heavy. Strong as I was, far, far stronger and more enduring than the average, my back would ache excruciatingly after a few minutes of hiking. At every pause for a moment I would place my rifle under the pack to ease my back, and at the end of twenty minutes of hiking the bugle would blow and we would fall out for ten minutes. Normally an army marched fifty minutes and rested ten. But we had to modify that system by marching twenty and resting ten. We were strangely weak. I don't know whether it was the water or the rations but we could just stagger along. And each time when the ten minute halt was over, it was a struggle to fall in again and pound along for another twenty minutes. I began to appreciate why the South had lost the war during the high-water mark of the Rebellion at Gettysburg. Hiking along the dusty roads of France, I got thinking about Pickett's Charge across more than a mile of plowed field, up a hill, to the copse of trees they reached—since known as " Bloody Angle." I was looking at that battlefield just a week ago. Realizing how weak soldiers can become in war time, I wondered how they could run a mile loaded down with heavier rifles and heavier munitions than we had and with more cumbersome equipment. Certainly they couldn't be in very good condition to fight the fresh troops at the end of their long run. And that is why the South was defeated. A horse-riding officer had no means of measuring the lack of stamina and strength of the men he ordered to make that attack. And thus one of the few decisive battles in the world's history was won by the Union side.

Day after day as we marched we could hear the distant muttering of guns. There were few signs of devastation in the district through which we marched. We talked to civilians as best we could and found quite a few optimistic Frenchmen along the way—that is soldiers—who were very glad to see us. They were most friendly and told us that the war would soon be over. It was evident that we were not getting closer to the front as we marched, for the sound of the guns was always equally far away.

One day we spent most of our hiking time skirting a big city. It was the famous city of Arras. That night when we halted I borrowed a bicycle from one of the runners in our company and rode into town. There was little that could be purchased to eat even for someone who had money. I didn't, but the best crap shooters in the company (and there were plenty of them) had " beaucoup " francs. (My American army French isn't so good. It served there in war-time France and should serve now.) I mean they had plenty of francs. I formed a partnership with another fellow—he'd supply the money; I'd supply the motivating power to ride into town. A few mouldy chocolate bars and a half dozen lemons were just about the limit of the purchases I could make. In every store Gillette razor blades could be purchased, for that was one product which would be purchased universally. One could not eat razor blades and we were forced to be content with the mouldy chocolate.

But the lemons I turned over to my partner, and he was truly a profiteer the next day. Hiking along through the deep dust—it was June, beautiful weather, singing birds, blue skies, but no rain, and plenty of dust—the price of lemons went up. They were finally sold for a hundred francs each—just about fifteen dollars at the rate of exchange prevalent at that time. But if a man had money he didn't care.

We could never realize the value of the paper francs. Fifty or even a hundred meant nothing to us. If we had francs we paid any price asked; the French people quickly learned this and the price of everything went sky high when American troops were around.

Aside from the aching backs we experienced on the hike, there were the blistered feet (two heavy pairs of socks didn't seem to overcome this condition) and there was the pain of being constantly galled or rubbed from our equipment and where tender parts of our anatomy came together. Every night I sought a stream—if one was nearby—to take care of my injured parts.

I rode back to Arras after the first day's hike, after the second and after the third. I suppose we were making about ten miles a day on such a leisurely march, so I must have had a ride of thirty miles each way—sixty in all—to make on the last day's trip to Arras to purchase chocolate. It took me so long to get back the last day that the army had gone. I was informed that they had entrained for a part of the hike. Now missing a train in America can be serious, but anyone with a good bicycle can catch a train they have missed in wartime France. The trains stopped at every cow path and were sitting on sidings to let the other trains go by about half of the time. I had approximately sixty miles of riding, besides the ten miles of hiking back of me by this time, but I set out to catch up with the train. On the way I easily caught up with and passed a tiny motor car, " missing " along on its two cylinders. It must have been a 1905 or 1906 model. Few civilians could use autos in war-time France. In fact most of them had been commandeered by the army. About midnight I found my company upon the train and climbed aboard.

" 40 Hommes and 8 Chevaux " was the inscription borne by every French freight car—forty men and eight horses. And forty men such as we had was a crowd indeed; not room for forty to lie down or even sit down. Many had to stand. I found a place to sleep outside in the little cupola occupied by the brakemen on French trains. We rode on this train all the next day. French trains are small compared to our huge engines and freight cars. A man or two of average size and strength can easily push them around the train yards. A small horn is blown by the conductor when the train is about to leave. At every crossing is a sign, " Attention Aux Trains " (" Look out for the trains ").

A ride of a day and a night in this country, if it was a fast train, would extend from New York to St. Louis, a distance of twelve hundred miles. But in France we may have gone fifty kilometers. Why we got on the train I don't know, for soon we were off again and marching on our way. Perhaps the train ride was to serve as a rest.

Days later we saw that we were approaching a big city, and sure enough there was a sign, " Paris. 37 kilometers." We were quite close to the great and glamorous world-famous capital of France.

The Battle of Paris

We found ourselves stationed at Bonneuil, a suburb of Paris. It was only slightly different from the usual small towns with which we had become familiar—little more than a single street lined with houses built close together on either side; fields under cultivation to the rear of the main street; the usual manure piles; an occasional cow; and one huge Percheron stallion was quietly grazing in a field.

My particular home was on the third floor in one of the more pretentious houses in the town. There was a circular stone stairway which was flanked with a heavy bannister. Above it all were heavy, black oak rafters to support the attic in which a squad of us lived. The normal residents of the house were living there, but they were just children and an aged woman. The men were away in war service. She was a nice old lady, and did everything she could to help. There must have been thirty or forty men quartered in her house which was quite the largest family she had ever had. She deserves double or even quadruple consideration for her efforts to lighten the lot of all of us. Once she climbed the flights of stairs to see how we who were sleeping on the hard stone floor of the garret were faring. It was a mighty hard floor for a slender young man with prominent hip bones, but I managed, as did my roommates. I had a little warm water here to shave with, and I haven't forgotten the soft, soothing, thrilling feeling it gave me after so many weeks of cold water for shaving and bathing.

We drilled in the fields back of the village just as we did at Bouvlinghem. Days went by, and still we were not at the front.

One evening Terry Murphy (real name Trafelis, as he was a Greek; Murphy was his fighting name) said, " Let's go to Paris, Bob. Things are pretty slow around here. They won't give out any passes, but let's go in anyway. We can get a fight with a couple of Frenchmen, maybe make some money and see something of Paris."

I was willing enough. My service record had not yet caught up with me, and I had not learned to enjoy being broke and unable to purchase small delicacies which would make our usual fare much more satisfying. So we eluded all the MJP.'s (military police) and found our way into Paris. This was the first of sixteen trips I managed to make into Paris, all without a pass and all without getting caught. One had to be eternally on the alert and prepared to outrun the military police when they came over to interrogate one for pass and credentials. I was a pretty good runner and I did not get caught in spite of the fact that I believed all roads led to Paris. I didn't know my French geography, but I did get to know Paris. Later in the war I was asked to explain why it took me five days to go from Brest to St. Nazaire. The trip as I took it from Brest to Paris, and then to St. Nazaire, was not unlike starting from New York to go to Trenton, N. J., by way of Chicago. But I first went to Paris and then to the place where I should have been going.

A bit later I had a little friend, who became my particular pal after we met at one of the schools, who talked French and German like a native. The French people were always so surprised when he spoke to them without the slightest bit of accent, and I noticed that German prisoners were just as surprised and just as anxious to talk to him. His command of the language is the chief reason why I didn't learn more French. He did the talking. I helped out any way I could. We afterwards made several trips to Paris together. One time when we left the city we got on a train together. A military police officer with a sergeant came through the train examining the passes of all U. S. soldiers. When he found that we didn't have a pass he put us off, but we got back on, thinking that he would not come through again. But come through he did and put us off again. Then we stood on the platform waiting for the train to start. When it left the platform we hopped on; the lieutenant hopped on and we jumped off; then on again and off again. Finally the train had picked up speed, and as we got on at the risk of our lives the lieutenant, not being anxious to lose one of his limbs, let us go. Every trip to Paris was replete with excitement.

But we were on business this time. We made arrangements to fight two Frenchmen on the following Saturday. Terry had won the lightweight championship of our division as he had been a good professional before the war. He signed up to fight a tough-looking Frenchman who looked like one of the Apaches of Paris. Certainly he gave promise of being very capable. I was to fight a sergeant in the air force outside of Paris whose name was given to me as Jorjay Karpongteeaa. I afterwards learned that this hard-sounding name belonged to the same Georges Carpentier who fought Dempsey in the first " battle of the century " just three years later. Perhaps it is best for me that this fight never took place, for Carpentier was a clever battler, having already engaged in some five hundred bouts, fighting since he was a small boy. In the fight with Dempsey he showed his courage by unleashing an attack which jarred the great champion several times before he was finally beaten into submission.

We thought it best not to linger too long in Paris this first trip, but to get back to our organization before our absence caused too much difficulty or excitement. We rode and hiked our way back to Bonneuil only to find that it was strangely quiet. " Where are the soldiers, Terry? "[55] I asked. " Probably in eating," was his reply. " I don't believe so," I said; " looks to me like they're gone." " They wouldn't go without telling us," said Terry. " Of course they would. Do you think they're going to tell the world when and where they are going? No one ever knows anything for sure until it is time to go." " What will we do? " Terry asked. " Make sure that they are gone first and then go after them." I dashed up to the garret where I had been living, and quickly saw that it was bare with the exception of my pack and rifle. Someone had kindly rolled it for me. I came downstairs prepared to go, and asked the old French lady with whom we had been living (to the best of my French speaking ability) where the soldiers had gone. She shrugged and shook her head, but did make a sound like a motor lorry—honk, honk—turning an imaginary wheel, and several times said, " Meaux." I didn't know so much about the geography of France, as I said before, but I did know that Meaux was a town nearer the front which had figured in the fighting earlier in the war. As near as I could estimate it must be about halfway to the front, or thirty-five to forty kilometers. Perhaps you remember that a kilometer is three-fifths of a mile. They seemed like three miles sometimes.

" Come on, Terry, we must get going and find our outfit."

We hiked over to the little town where our regimental headquarters had been stationed. There was not an American around. We went still farther to where our divisional headquarters had been. They were just moving out the last of the equipment. I approached a truck driver and said, " Hey, guy, where's the army gone? " " Up front somewhere," he came back. " Can we ride up with you? " " Sure. I'm not going the entire way—just to the new divisional headquarters, but that will be a start."

It was the start—of a surprisingly long journey. We shuttled back and forth, at times perilously close to the actual front and the fighting. Finally, as it was just getting to be light in the sky, we found our company and I crawled into the tent my usual tent mate had pitched. I had barely placed my back upon the blankets when reveille blew. Boy, was I tired! But I had to get right up and at them, for I was a sergeant and had to maintain my reputation for being a good soldier.

I jumped into the head of the line amidst the surprised looks of those nearest me. And like Abou ben Adhem of the poem, my name led all the rest. As I answered " Here," in my best military manner, all eyes turned toward me. They thought that I was gone for good, but here I was.

Immediately after breakfast we struck tents and started on our way again. This time it was easy to note that we were heading toward the sound of the firing. The little town where we caught up to our part of the army was called Rebais. It wasn't a very long town, not far from the garden on which we had pitched our tents to the outside of the town. We went along the same sort of country roads we had always traversed. We stepped snappily along as our fine old colonel, Edward Shannon, stood at the side of the road with a group of officers to see us march by—uphill and downhill—but there was a difference here. We began to see for the first time signs of recent war. Arras had been subjected to many air raids and some artillery firing, but the damage was old. Here it was evident that the damage was recent. At some places the lines of poplar trees had been freshly cut down—probably to provide a clear field of fire if the enemy came that far. Far ahead we saw our first observation balloon. It hung there in the sky like a great sausage, moored to the ground, with waiting men ready to pull it down and try to save it in case of attack by enemy aircraft. Frequently we were so situated that we could see our own balloons and those of the Germans, but this was usually when we were at our own front. In the far-off distance we could hear first the whirring sound of planes, and then we saw several puffs about these distant (almost flylike in size) planes. We knew then that they were enemy planes trying to attack the balloon. A long time after we saw the explosion of the shell we heard the report of the gun and the explosion of the shells. We were getting there—nearer the front with every stride. It seemed that after these long months of training, of waiting and expecting, we were about to fulfill our destiny.

The colonel passed us riding with his adjutant. He looked stern, but kindly too. He lives just twelve miles from me now. He reached the position of commander- in-chief of all the troops in Pennsylvania, and the post of Lieutenant-Governor in a recent administration. He was a fine man then, a fine man ever since—a manufacturer from the nearby town of Columbia who really made his mark in the world. He seemed satisfied with his troops—the men he had brought so far and trained so long.

We passed through several small villages. Crowds of French people stood along the road and waved to us as we went by. The ladies dabbed their eyes with their handkerchiefs to wipe away the tears. We smiled and sang. It was hard to understand at that time why the French people cried. But they had seen too many fine young men walk by, singing and smiling—some of them never to return; others came back as wounded men, or at least with greatly decimated ranks. We were the first Americans to pass that way, and some of the French were seeing for the first time these men from that great and far-off country America. I could hear them murmur, speaking in astonished terms, as they saw the huge men who were in the forefront of our company. We had a real organization. There was a steadiness, a power, a confidence in the bearing of our men that showed their courage. The French people broke into cheer after cheer as we walked by. They were stirred for a variety of reasons. There was a uniformity about our army to which the French were not accustomed. There were a variety of uniforms and colors about their own troops—light blue, dark blue and brown uniforms—but our men were all attired the same. And they looked very impressive and capable. Even the children, who had seen many soldiers in the past, became excited as they pointed to the huge men who marched in line directly behind me.

We went down a long curving hill which at first sight looked not unlike some hundreds of other villages that we had passed through. But it was deserted—the first town we came to from which all the inhabitants had departed. The fighting had been bitter; the Germans were expected to break through and recontinue their march toward Paris almost momentarily. So the people had left. And French people don't leave so easily. They frequently remain in or return to badly-shattered towns. Later I was to try to evacuate old ladies who insisted on remaining. First they would tell me that they had lived there since they were " petite pickaninnies " (little babies); that they had nowhere else to go. But go they must and they would kick and scratch like little fiends as I carried out my orders to evacuate them by carrying them from the town.

This town was not shattered as were so many deserted towns, but there was not a soul in it. It gave us a peculiar feeling—not unlike that experienced when we pass through a graveyard at night. It was near the time of the noon halt, but we kept going through the town and up to the level ground on the other side of the valley before we halted.

And even before we ate, a runner came back and said, " Bob, you're wanted at regimental headquarters at once." I turned to Terry and said, " Here's where we get it for being A W O L (absent without leave), Terry. I thought they were going to forget it for no one said a word all morning. Hope I don't lose these stripes. I worked hard enough for them."

When I reached regimental headquarters along the side of the road, there was our colonel, his adjutant, Captain Arch Williams of our company, with Lieutenants Allen and Shenkel of B Company. The colonel didn't waste any time in preliminaries. He said, " The French general commanding the troops in this sector has asked for a small group of men from this division to make an attack with them at six o'clock tonight.

My regiment, I am proud to say, has been requested to furnish the men. I have decided to send one platoon from A Company and another from B Company. A great deal depends on this action. It is sort of a trial. The allied commanders or even our own officers do not know how well trained our American troops are. They insist that it takes years to make a soldier, and that soldiers are born as well as made. They seem to feel that we do not have the generations of soldiers back of our troops that the French and British armies have. In other words, I believe that they doubt our courage and our ability. The entire American army will be judged by what you men do. There will be more high officers— both French and American—watching you than there will be men in action. I want you to cover yourselves with glory, be a credit to the American army, the 11 ith Infantry and to yourselves."

With hardly a pause for breath he went on to explain that the attack was to be made at six o'clock that evening from the third line trenches on the edge of Hill 204. Hill 204, later to appear so often in U. S. dispatches, was a very high, wooded hill, quite rugged in terrain, about equally spaced between Chateau Thierry and the little town of Vaux. A terrific bombardment, chiefly trench mortars (although there would be some heavy artillery support), was to start at 4 P. M., and at six we were to go over the top for the first time. The French commanders had worked out the details of the attack, but we were to be under our own immediate command.

Lieutenant Shenkel was selected as the officer in charge of the platoon to go from B Company. He chose to take his own complete platoon, the second. I was asked to select the platoon from our company. Not a word was said about our trip to Paris. That was too trivial in the face of the impending attack.

Was I thrilled! The front at last! When asked by our captain if I wanted to go with the platoon, I said, " Do I want to go? That's what I've been yearning and aching for all these months." When I was just a youngster I would read books telling how anxious soldiers were to go into action. I couldn't understand how men could desire to go out and fight and die. But it is something that grows on you. You train and expect so long that finally you become anxious to get into it, to get it over with. Time was short. We went back to our companies on the run. Our company was assembled and I briefly explained that a platoon (fifty-eight men) was to be selected and that we were to make an attack with the French at six o'clock that night. My words fell like a bombshell. A brief cheer went up from our company. I asked all men who wanted to be the first in action to step forward, and, like one man, the entire company stepped forward. Men who did not get to go on this trip cried real tears—a direct contrast to the lack of volunteering for dangerous missions a few months later when they had become war-weary. Then they would go if assigned to any task, no matter how dangerous, but they did not rush in. They became fatalists, and said they'd go if they were chosen. They'd die if it were their turn, but they weren't going to overwork fate.

I knew every man in the company very, very intimately. I had been with them since the beginning. I had helped recruit some of them, for when I enlisted I was sent out for a time to help my brother who was in charge of recruiting the men for our regiment. Thus I had been instrumental in enlisting many of my very best friends. We had recruited these men near the club of which we were members. All sorts of ties of friendship, both before and during service, bound me to these men. The very best of the men recruited were sent to our company. Added to these was the wonderful group of Texas ranchers. Certainly our company had the cream of the cream of the army.

I knew everything about these men—to the inch— who could jump the farthest, run the fastest, shoot the quickest and most accurately, who were the best bayonet men, the best hand bombers, the best rifle grenadiers, the most skilled with an automatic rifle; in short, the best soldiers. I picked the very best men in our organization. It was done quickly, for in a surprisingly short time we had pulled out ahead. The men who were to remain behind shook hands with us and wished us luck; some told us that we weren't really going to fight—that we were just going up to observe life and fighting at the front, as had been done so much with other American organizations which had been in France.

For here it was June, 1918. War had been declared in April, 1917. The first American division had been sent to France a few months after war was declared and even in December, 1917, while we were still far down in the Southland, they had entered the trenches in a quiet sector. They had been in several raids, some of their men had been killed and others captured, and they had inflicted casualties on the enemy in turn. But they had not made an attack larger than a patrol or a raid. The famous Second Division was already at the front. It included the brigade of Marines who received more publicity than all the rest of the American army —a brigade of Marines, two regiments, seventy-five hundred men, a small part of the four million Americans who were in service during the war. But the publicity they received would make one believe that they had won the entire war single-handed. They had given a great account of themselves and had helped stop the Germans' march to Paris at Belleau Woods. They were holding the line there. But neither they nor the 3rd, 4th and 5th divisions, the 26th or the 42nd National Guard Divisions, which were already in France, had made a real attack upon the army. So it was falling upon us to be the first Americans to go forward against the enemy. We felt the responsibility and determined to acquit ourselves nobly.

We had been delayed somewhat before we left for we were not perfectly equipped. We had just received our " tin hats " that very morning. I still have mine. It was the luckiest hat in the American army and saved my life from the very first bullet which came my way. I had just received my forty-five pistol that day. I wore my white canvas leggings and white trousers, not yet having been issued overseas olive drab woolens. More than any other one reason this pair of white pants and white leggings nearly caused my death. I was a good soldier, always neat and clean and had frequently been held up as a shining example of how a soldier should look. Even when we guarded bridges and lived in a box car along the railroad track, many people had wondered how I kept my clothes so spotless. Later in Camp Hancock I always appeared in line for retreat with perfectly clean pants and leggings. I only had one pair. I would come in from drill at five-fifteen and had forty- five minutes to be ready for retreat. Most of the men were so tired that they would lie on their bunks and never move until six o'clock. I would run down the street, hurriedly wash and scrub my trousers and leggings, wring them out, hang them up in the sun, have a shower and put my clothes on as they were. I'd clean my rifle, even to applying oil on the strap and linseed oil on the woodwork of the gun, and get into line at six o'clock almost as neat and clean as a West Pointer on parade. And I still had those very white and faded trousers and leggings. I was the first man hit as I left the trench. I received more wounds and shots through my equipment than any other man. It was evident that the opposing troops must have thought I was some sort of a special officer, and all fired at me. Only a series of miracles brought me through the battle which you will read about in a few pages.

We took the best of the Chau Chat (pronounced Show Show) rifles, an automatic type of rifle that would " chung, chung, chung," about sixty shots a minute, if it didn't jam, as compared to the Germans' two hundred shots a minute from their machine guns. We filled out the cartridge clips and bandoleers of the men who were going, from the equipment of those who remained, changed a rifle or two, and were finally on our way.

The men marched away from their company flushed with pride and excitement. Only a handful of them were to come back. Over half were to lie and rot for weeks on Hill 204 before a detail found time to bury them. Many were to be crippled for life. But there they were—a well-trained, well-conditioned, courageous lot of wonderful young Americans; the kind of men who would have reached their mark in the world in their chosen profession if they had remained at home, and we had not been putting our noses into other people's wars.

I was to go to the hospital wounded after this battle. Not till long afterwards did I hear what had taken place on this hill after we had left, for we penetrated to the German third line trench, capturing the remnants of an entire company of Germans. But the French on either side had not kept up. All men who had reached this advanced trench had been killed or wounded, and the advanced position we had won was given up to consolidate our lines farther to the rear. All of our effort was in vain as far as gaining permanent possession of the hill was concerned. For some weeks this ground that we had won, and that was reoccupied by the Germans, was to be a strong point—a vantage position from which shells were ceaselessly vomiting and harassing our men.

The Road to Eternity

Little did we know it, but many of this handful of men who left their comrades that lunch hour were quickly going to eternity. The time of life for many was drawing to a close. We were just a group of young fellows far from our homes—going away from our faithful comrades of the inth Infantry to battle the enemy with strange comrades on a strange hill in a foreign country. The world is a peculiar thing. What combination of circumstances brought us young Americans to Hill 204 in France, and many young Germans to come there and give up their lives and take those of many of our fellows from us?

We marched along bravely enough, and apparently enthusiastically. But I feel sure that deep down in the being of many of us there were misgivings and unpleasant premonitions. With each step we went closer to the front—farther from our homes and comrades, closer to our destiny. We were being led by a French officer and several sergeants. As we marched along, it became evident that we could not reach the front and take our positions at four o'clock that afternoon. It would not be wise to approach the trenches after our bombardment had commenced, for the return barrage would no doubt catch many of us.

As we marched along we saw additional signs of war: a French cyclist, a group of French soldiers, a dead cow in the field (quite defunct, for we could smell it at a great distance), and finally two or three crosses at the side of the road. We paused there for a moment and I had the opportunity to read the inscription and see that they were men of our division who had died and been buried there—engineers who had been helping on the road.

Rather late in the afternoon we pulled into a huge " farm chateau," where we were to spend the night. We were urged to be careful—to stand close to the buildings or the wall, and never to move around when planes were in the air, or we might be the center of shell fire or the dropping of bombs. It was nearly time for the evening meal and there we had what I'll always remember as one of the best meals I have had in my entire life. Perhaps it was better; maybe it was only so good after the long period of poor and insufficient food we had had, that I so fully appreciated it.

While the meal was being prepared we sat around and talked. One of my friends was a little Greek acrobat, a professional, by the name of Pagamemos. He was quite the smallest man in our company, and compared with the six-foot, seven-inch Corporal Graves from Texas, he was a tiny mite indeed. But he had been a fine athlete. A man who has sufficient command of his muscles to be a professional acrobat in big time vaudeville can quickly learn to do anything else in the athletic line. We had long been the best of friends, for like myself he had an antipathy for having cold steel somewhere within him. We had both done a great deal of training outside of the regular drill periods. We frequently practiced fighting with trench knives and with bayonets, leaving our scabbards on the cold steel for protection. Pagamemos was far smaller than I, but he was no mean antagonist; he was strong, fast and light on his feet—could running broad jump over seventeen feet in the sand with his uniform on, and that's a real jump.

Pagamemos said, " Bob, I feel sorry for you."

" Why?"

" Because you are so big. You'll be the first to get hit. I'm so small they can hardly see me—certainly not shoot me."

Poor Pagamemos! I'm here (with perfect health, and all my arms and legs) pounding this typewriter, while he was actually the first man hit, losing both legs and one arm as a result of it.

Pagamemos and I decided to do a final bit of practicing for bayonet work, as there was more than a good chance that we might have some hand-to-hand fighting on the morrow. We gave the French an example of the sort of bayonet work we were capable of and as the action became hot, the foot work a bit faster and more dazzling, the enthusiastic Latin temperament of the French caused them to break into applause and frequently exclaim, " Bonne," or " Tres bonne." At the completion of our short bout, Pagamemos turned a few somersaults and handsprings, and startled our French comrades by running around the farmyard on his hands, going up and down stairs, jumping over boxes, etc. Poor fellow! It was his last exhibition of his prowess. He didn't have a chance to show his ability in action.

And then it was time to eat. That meal ranks very high among the best meals I have ever enjoyed in my entire life. The French cook was really a cook. We had just can openers in our company. Later, they were to send us twelve-pound cans of raw bacon to the front. Of course we couldn't fry the bacon or eat it raw. We went hungry, while other companies around us were treated to dainties such as cold steak and rice pudding that their cooks had sent up.

There seemed to be an ample supply of. brown beef stew for this meal, but the French cooks had made a poor estimate of the gastronomic ability of this lot of wild Americans. Half a beef was quickly sent for, and we were treated to as large steaks and as many of them as we could eat. I am sure that I got away with at least six of them. There was a-plenty of wine and cognac for those who liked it and soon our men were sitting on top of the world. They thought that war wasn't so bad after all. I thought this experience was quite like the condemned man who is told that he can have anything he wishes to eat before he goes.

After dinner, the sergeants and officers got together to plan our work for the morrow. From our company we had Sergeant Bill Felix of Pittsburgh, and Sergeant George Amole from Pottstown, Pa. The American Legion post in Pottstown is known as the Sergeant Amole Post, for Sergeant Amole was to lay down his life on that hill; Felix was to be very severely wounded —several rifle bullets tearing through his body, and the same bomb which injured my head and ruined my hair was to cut through both of his jawbones. I did not know the sergeants with B Company, but I knew Lieutenant Shenkel.

It was agreed that most of the officers would leave early in the morning and take up our positions on Hill 204. The two platoons were to arrive after noon, and take up their positions prior to the bombardment. The two platoons were to be separated—to attack with the French up through the middle of the woods, a platoon on each side of the woods, and more French troops on the outside. Probably not more than a thousand men were to make the attack, only one hundred and twenty of whom were Americans. It had already been a tough day, a surprising day; it was just twenty-four hours since Terry and I had been in the gay (gay even in war times) city of Paris. And here we were far up at the front preparing to go into action.

I should have been able to sleep easily enough, but the excitement kept me awake. I had not picked Terry for this trip. He was a good man, but there were plenty of good men, and he had been out all night. I lay talking to Pagamemos until far into the night, until someone yelled, " Pipe down, will you? " And then I was to sleep and dream—dream a too-realistic dream of men lying dead and wounded while I was able to walk and be around. It was there too that we had one of our first experiences with rats. Huge rats inhabit the front. Early in the war they found that there was plenty of meat up there to eat and they lived and bred in great numbers. That night a pack of them paid us a visit. I felt something apparently pulling my covers off bit by bit. I was dreaming of my stepmother—that she was pulling the covers from me little by little. I heard a yell from an Italian boy beside me. As I woke up I hurled the rat that was on my arm far from me where it hit the wall, squealed and ran off. What huge animals they were! There was no more sleep for us that night. We sat up fighting and driving away the rats. The nose of the boy who had shouted was bleeding profusely. We were as quiet as the dead. Perhaps the rat thought we were really dead, and started to eat the young man's nose. He carried that scar home with him.

We who were going up to Hill 204 early in the morning thought we might as well get up and start. The French cook had a good breakfast for us and soon we were off—just a thin line of us, six men and a guide. It was a quiet morning, beautiful, just like a July day at home. It was the first day of July. Were it not for the fact that we saw increasing signs of war, one could never dream that there was a war on. Everything seemed peaceful and beautiful. The army moved and fought at night to a great extent—slept or at least kept under cover during the day. All night, if we weren't too tired to listen, we would hear the constant sound of wheels, motor lorries, officers' cars, motorcycles and side cars, field kitchens, supply wagons, machine gun carts, artillery of all sizes—a blending of many sounds that sounded like a raging torrent, a river when it is at flood stage. But as dawn came, all of this noise ceased. The French and British got under cover. Our careless soldiers wandered around like it was a picnic, until they learned that moving was the cause of shell fire and bombing.

Our trip up to the front was so different from what we had always imagined war would be. We had read of and seen pictured so much of the trench warfare of other sectors. We expected to see row after row of trenches, barren ground, artillery, observation balloons. But we didn't see anything like that. This was a new front. The Germans had very recently been held up there and shell fire had not yet shattered the hill. We passed occasional fresh shell holes. Some of them were still steaming and the acrid odor of powder was in the air. At this time of the morning, no airplanes were in sight, and all was as quiet as one would normally expect in the country. The fields and woods basked in bright summer sunshine; the birds flew and sang as usual.

The few houses we passed were deserted and strangely quiet.

We passed a tiny stream, a tributary of the Marne, and in its shallow water lay a dead horse. Horses nearly always lie with their stiff legs in the air, their bodies swollen. They seem like statues or carvings of horses, not as if they ever could have lived. They are quite a problem to bury as we found out later. A bit farther on we saw more French soldiers. They were at breakfast and from what we could see this breakfast consisted only of beans. They rushed out and questioned us in French. They were surprised to see us. I didn't know enough of French to understand what they were saying, but I was informed by our French guide that they wanted to know if we were going to relieve them. They were pleased to hear that we were going to help them make an attack.

As we went along an occasional shell fell—not big shells, but they sounded big to us. We would hear them come with a z-z-z-z-z, getting ever closer and louder, and then finally a BOW, and the ground shot into the air with an occasional whiz from a piece of shell that ricocheted and went far from where the shell had landed. I tried to show how calm I was by not paying any attention, but my head involuntarily jerked with the falling of each shell.

Before long we started to cross a larger stream. There was a nice-looking young Frenchman (an Alpine chasseur, I judged, from the hat he wore), who was there gazing into the water. His bicycle was beside him. As he saw us, he vaulted lightly over the railing of the bridge so that he could come closer to see us. He was powerful and athletic—must have been a gymnast when he was home.

It suddenly dawned on me that this must be the famous Marne River. It was not large. I could easily have tossed a stone across it. We would have called it a creek in America, for it was no wider than the Codorus Creek, which passes through our town, the nearby Conewago, or the Conestoga which flows through the adjoining county to ours. There we were, looking at a world-famous stream, the turning point of the war. The Germans had rushed down to the Marne in a few short weeks after they started to attack in 1914. There they were met by " Papa " Joffre, famous marshal of France, and defeated by the " taxicab" army—the men that had so quickly been rushed out from Paris in taxicabs of about the vintage of 1912. The French and British were unprepared—almost as unprepared as are we in this country at the present. It took them as long to get organized as it would take us in case of attack. So the Germans found it comparatively easy sailing in the first weeks of the war. The hundred thousand contemptibles (who received that name because the great Kaiser called them a contemptible little army); the small regular army of Belgium; a few hastily gathered French troops offered the only resistance to the enemy. But the Germans had overrun themselves, got too far ahead of their support, and were defeated at the Marne. And here they were again— about to cross the Marne unless we could do something about it.

The part of the Marne we crossed here was quiet and blue. The grass extended down to the water's edge just below. There must have been a dam near to cause the water to so completely fill the banks and to be so tranquil. There was the usual small town here at this crossing, and above us rose the heights of Hill 204. As I looked along the stream I could see that it made several turns through the town, as it wound through the deserted village. Farther along I could see the more thickly-populated part of the town—white walls and red roofs, the usual church steeple and trees everywhere.

Soon we stood at the bottom of Hill 204. How steep it looked! Almost perpendicular! It seemed like a young Alps. Up the hill we went, following the guide, and as we passed we saw several piles of " flying pigs " (the name applied to trench mortars). They were big, heavy shells, weighing nearly one hundred and sixty pounds each. The hill was so steep that there was no way to carry them up except by man power. Placed in wicker baskets they were strapped to a man's back. Now I understood why the Alpine chasseur had been standing on the bridge. I knew where he got the athletic frame and those tremendously powerful calves I saw showing through his heavy blue stockings. The Alpine men, who were accustomed to climbing and carrying packs, were here to carry the ammunition and guns up the hill, and to assist in the fighting.

What a struggle they must have had, for I found it difficult enough to climb the hill with no impediment but my rifle and haversack. Our full packs had been left behind as we would not need them for the attack. We had made one mistake that was to be felt severely before that day was done. We had come to the front with just our shirts on—no coats. French soldiers wear their heavy winter overcoats during the hottest days of the summer. It is mighty unpleasant to wear them in the heat of the day, but there is no better way to transport them than by wearing them, and when the cool nights come along they have them. Especially, too, when a man is wounded and loses considerable blood an overcoat comes in quite handy. In the heat of the battle our fellows stripped themselves to the waist and rushed forward, like a lot of wild Indians, to the attack.

Near the crest of the hill we came to a deep dugout. Our guide stopped here and soon French officers came out to shake our hands one by one. The French were always friendly. They stood the war well, were smiling, kind, and generous to a fault. They would share their last crust of bread. We were invited into the dugout and there we saw the French major who commanded that hill. He was rather youthful, considering the importance of his post. He thanked us for coming—told us that what we were to do that day would have an important bearing on winning the war; that it would hearten the French, discourage the Germans; and, if we did well, all of us would get the Croix de Guerre. Wouldn't that be something! A decoration to take back and show to the fellows who said we weren't going to fight—just to observe.

As we walked up the more gentle slopes of the hill I looked all around me. I could see the cleverly hidden trench mortar emplacements which were to lay down a barrage before the attack which we were to make. I could see the Marne River far below us gleaming in the sunlight as it extended for miles and miles down the valley. Tiny villages were here and there. We could see a beautiful white city shining in the sun, a comparatively short distance away, and we knew that it was Chateau Thierry—a town that would ever be famous in the annals of the American army. There were several bridges in the town under which the Marne had passed. They were shattered and it seemed doubtful if they could be used in making a crossing. All along the hillsides were orchards, crops of one sort and another, flowers, especially poppies, and endless terraces of grapes. Little but grapes could be grown on these steep hillsides, and grapes were a necessary crop too, for wine and champagne were among the chief products of France.

Far to the left was another city, which turned out to be Vaux. We came to a freshly dug trench right on the crest of the hill. We were told that it was a reserve trench—the one from which we were to follow the barrage and make the attack later that day. On up the hill we went, through the woods. It seemed no more like the front than any one of a hundred woods in which I had been—than our woods across the road. Ah, I'll take that back. There was a rough cross—a German this time. He had come over on a patrol, lost his life, and had been buried in this still beautiful woods. He'd never see his Fatherland again. Then more crosses—this time marking the graves of the brave French defenders of Hill 204.

And then we saw the French soldiers, our comrades who were to make the attack with us. Some were still sleeping. They had been out on patrol or on guard all night. Others were writing letters home. Some were playing cards; others reading (I noted one with a Bible). The men smiled wanly. It was just one more battle to them, but one never knew when it was to be the last battle. We wandered around talking to the French, looking over the terrain, getting the lay of the land for some hours. Finally it was lunch time and we were royally dined in the French officers' mess. Sergeant Amole imbibed too freely of liquor. He was a fine soldier—one of the best—a great tactician, a man of many years' training, who would have held the rank of not less than a major if he could have left alcoholic beverages alone. He was to go over the top a few hours later far from his normal self, courageous and exhorting his men to do their best, yet not even knowing what hit him when he was killed.

Over the Top

THE hours passed slowly and finally three o'clock came. We retired to the supporting trench. Our men had moved up and occupied their positions a few minutes before. My position in the line was at the very end; the French soldiers were in the next bay of the trench. I went around to talk to them and found them not feeling much like conversation. Some were telling the beads of their rosaries and offer- * ing prayers; while still others sat grimly and waited. I found it a bit hard to put in the time. I had with me a book on tactics and battle formations which I kept studying. The hands of my watch crept around to four o'clock, and right on the dot the bombardment started. [v] The huge flying pigs went over our heads, turning over and over in the air with a swish-swish-swish which was quite audible during their entire passing. Each shell had its own sound. Big shells coming from the rear were called G I cans. They seemed to rattle-rattle-rattle as they went through the air, making a sound not unlike a collection of big garbage cans on a refuse or sanitary wagon in the city.

We watched the passage of the four big trench mortar shells as they went up and up in the air, and finally down with an explosive crash in the woods. You should have seen the birds—particularly blackbirds and crows—come out of that woods; rabbits and squirrels—even a fox—were seen to streak down through the brush. It was surprising to see a wild boar still up in the thick of things, but they were rather abundant in France, and a pair of them lumbered out of the wood and down over the hill. I could not help but think that the Germans over there must be wishing that they could run away and be safe as were the animals.

We were all standing up, looking over the parapet, watching the show like a bunch of kids on the Fourth of July. Retaliatory fire soon commenced; machine gun and snipers' bullets were zipping over our heads. An occasional shell was dropping well down in the valley. We were hard to hit, located as we were on the crest of the hill and well down from the high spots.

I saw a rabbit running along the side of the woods toward the German lines. The exploding trench mortars seemed to follow him almost as if he were the object of their attack. I thought of another rabbit I had seen at the British school at Merkegham. Toward the end of our schooling there a mock battle with real ammunition was planned. Prior to this time our practice warfare had been performed with no bullets or perhaps blanks. Observers were present whose work it was to determine which side occupied the most advantageous position and had won the battle. They would stalk around the mock battlefield, ruling out a man here and a man there, a squad here and a squad there as being out of action. They had been killed but didn't know it.

This mock warfare reminded me of our childhood days. We would point our guns or stab with our swords at the " enemy " and say, " Bang-bang, you're dead." " No, I'm not, you're dead. I shot you before you got here." And there was no way to settle who had shot whom and when, who was unscathed, who was wounded and who was killed. A bit later there was to be no argument. It would be known who was killed and who was wounded.

Here we were getting a bit closer to the front—big enough boys to play this time with real ammunition. Our troops had been spread along the crest of a gentle slope of more than a mile. The artillery was just at the top of the hill, and the various arms extended down from that point until we, in the position of the advance patrols, were ready to advance upon our mock enemies. Between us and the artillery were the trench mortar men and those who manned the deadly little thirty- seven millimeter guns. While the French and British arms were outclassed to a considerable degree in many ways, the Germans had nothing to equal the speed of fire, the accuracy and the all-around efficiency of the famous seventy-five millimeter gun which fired shells approximately three inches in diameter almost with machine gun speed. The French gunners were real experts and they could shoot as many as twenty shots a minute with these guns. When they found that they were on a particular target, it was just too bad for the group of men, the truck, or the laboring artillery horses who were trying to pull out under shell fire. The little thirty-seven millimeter gun was a miniature of the highly efficient seventy-five. It could be fired with great rapidity and unusual accuracy. Equipped with a telescopic sight, it could be aimed with just a little practice so that it was as accurate as a rifle in the hands of most soldiers. The little shells it fired were called one pounders, were approximately an inch and a half in diameter and seven or eight inches long. They could be used in action with devastating effect. Their principal use was to blast out machine gun nests and to put tanks out of action. They were at times used for direct fire against advancing troops, and had become a useful part of the equipment of the armed forces. Then there were the trench mortars, frequently called Stokes mortars. The guns from which they were fired looked not unlike stovepipes, open at the end; the mortar was dropped in from the outside; as it hit the bottom of the pipe, it was detonated, and hurled through the air by the explosive power of the charge of powder it contained. They were not nearly so accurate as artillery fire, but they were stationed right at the front where their action could be immediately observed, and the fire raised or lowered, turned to the right or left. The usual trench mortar fired a shell of similar size to those detonated with the seventy-five millimeter gun, but some mortars were tremendous in size—one hundred and sixty pounders, as were used at the attack on Hill 204, or much larger ones. While in operation they did not explode as terrifically as did artillery, would cough loudly and deeply as they were fired, and the path of the shell could be followed with the naked eye until it landed at the enemy lines.

In the mock war we were to have at the school at Merkegham, the action of all arms was to start simultaneously. We were to become accustomed to the roar of battle, to the big guns back of us, the trench mortars and one pounders with us, the machine guns firing over our heads. This was a step forward, for it requires time to realize that the hail of shells and machine gun bullets passing overhead will not harm our own troops but are meant only for the opposing forces. The most important lesson of all was being learned in this attack on Hill 204—how it felt to be shot at as well as to be under the fire of our own guns.

We had a Zero Hour at the school; our targets had been well planned. It is necessary to do this so that everyone will not shoot at the same target—perhaps at the center of the line, neglecting the men at both ends of the line. Our particular target was a small copse of woods far down the slope of the hill. The signal to fire was given. And as fire commenced a rabbit ran out of a clump of bushes this side of our target. Unconsciously every man turned his fire upon the rabbit and one could soon seen the dirt flying up back of it, for the rabbit was a good half-mile away and travelling with great leaps and bounds. Few realize the speed of a rabbit. For a short distance it can travel approximately forty- five miles per hour—about ninety feet a second. Although a bullet travels perhaps two thousand feet a second, it would take more than a second for our shells to reach the vicinity of the rabbit and it was travelling fast. That's why it is almost impossible to hit a rapidly-moving target at a distance. One must aim far ahead and trust to luck—good luck for the shooter, bad luck for the shootee—to score a hit. Soon the machine guns were firing at the rabbit, the thirty-seven millimeters, and the artillery. The rabbit hopped into the clump of trees, which was our target, to take a breath for a minute, but the artillery and a myriad of bullets searched it out there. It ran out and across the grassy meadow, with almost the entire army assembled there shooting at it, until it escaped over the crest of the small rolling hills of a stream down in the valley. I often thought what a tale that rabbit would have to tell to its grandchildren if it survived the war, had grandchildren and could talk to them.

The rabbit made me forget the realities of the war for a moment, but the shells were still flying fast— returning from the German artillery now, but zipping over our heads and falling in the valley below or on the hills on the other side. We could see the men in the valley and on the hill run for cover. Some of our men were laughing. It was exciting to them and they felt as if it were a gigantic game. What must the French have thought of these crazy Americans! I tried to study my book again—the long discussions about tactics, battle formations, advance guards, points, rear guards and flankers. I saw the formation we were to endeavor to follow—our platoon to advance in line of combat groups, four columns, each headed by the first gunner and the carriers of the automatic rifles. The men on the left column were to protect the left flank; those on the right to guard the right flank. My station was to be in the left combat group. I marked the little circle that would be me. It was hard to concentrate. There was too much excitement, too much at stake, but I had time to kill.

I crawled around the bay of the trench again toward the French and this time found someone I could talk to. The lieutenant in charge of the company or platoon there (I couldn't tell how many Frenchmen there were on our outside, or know what designation they gave to their bodies of troops) was a big, broad-shouldered young Frenchman—nineteen years of age, he told me; just my age, but so much older in experience. In the French army, age is disregarded when it comes to winning commissions. Manhood is usually considered to take place at twenty-one, just as in our country. But some males are real men when quite young, and some never become men worthy of the name man, regardless of their age.

This young Frenchman was an exceptional man, courageous and a powerful leader. His very presence strengthened the morale of his troops. They seemed to cheer up a bit.

The Frenchmen were fighting right in their own country. Although it was unusual, there were times when the fighting took place right in the villages or the farms of the men who were engaged in the action. The young lieutenant told me that he was. a native of Vaux—yes, that little town down there in the valley where an occasional shell was falling. He had been born there; had learned to swim in the Marne River right over there. He had roamed these fields and woods as a boy. To them, this hill that we called 204 was the mountain. It had been his ambition as a young boy to climb this mountain and one day he had slipped away from home and climbed to the top, to a position right in front of us. He had been soundly spanked for his escapade.

He warned me that great difficulties lay ahead of us in our endeavor to capture this hill. The Germans were particularly well informed; their high command seemed to know of our every move. Very likely they knew of our bombardment, the time of the impending attack, and they would be ready for us. It had not been possible to learn just how they got this information, but the participation of the Americans had become so generally known and talked about along the front that he was quite sure the Germans knew of it too. No doubt they would try to defeat us as decisively as possible to bolster their people's morale at home, and to give them something to write about in their dispatches. Yes, it was no picnic we were to go on this time—not like a picnic the French lieutenant had enjoyed on this hill even after the war had begun.

He told me that the hill was not as big as it looked— that the woods extended for perhaps half a mile, and then there was almost as steep a descent as there was on this side. It was believed that the Germans had a huge dugout there large enough to protect all the troops they had on this hill. He had at one time explored a cave there, and it could easily have been enlarged to an extent where it would shelter their troops during our bombardment. He called my attention to the fact that little shelling was coming from their lines. It was usual for the Germans to shell as intensively as possible when their troops were being bombarded. He felt that we were to have a hard time of it, and told me to be very cautious and to advance slowly.

Later in the action he was to rush over to me and tell us to slow up, that we were going too fast. But his advice was soon forgotten in the heat of battle.

The lieutenant told me that probably only a few machine guns were still on the hill to hold their lines during the bombardment. He warned us that there would be many dummy machine guns and emplacements and not to waste our fire. It was a habit of the Germans at this time to have dummy guns where they could be seen easily enough, apparently manned by dummy figures, while the real guns would be well hidden and camouflaged, so that they would be very difficult to detect. Even the snipers had camouflaged helmets and wore tree suits, which caused them to blend so thoroughly with the trees that they were very hard to detect.

I asked him about some of the rumors that we had heard. Frequently a dead German had photographs of stout and smiling German women. Usually these women wore clothes of about 1912 vintage. The German styles were well behind the times and of course during the hostilities money ordinarily spent for clothes and butter was being spent for bullets. We had heard so many reports of regiments of women, of Amazons, who had vowed to fight to the death. This was always of interest to the soldiers. Many of them thought that it would be nice to capture and try to tame an Amazon. Usually we had been away from women for so long that even a woman behind a machine gun would add interest to our existence. Then there was a lot of talk about women who were fighting with the men.

The French lieutenant said that these were just stories; occasionally women were at the front, or rather behind the front in the big dugouts, but they were entertainers of some sort—singers and dancers, not unlike the American actresses who entertained the American soldiers in advanced points at the front with singing, dancing and comedy; or the WAAC's Queen Mary's Women's Auxiliary Corps, of the British army, who entertained the soldiers and tried to make their lives more livable. Sometimes too the female costumes which were found in reserve dugouts had been worn by female impersonators. There were shows held by our own division after the war in which all the chorus girls were men, and many of them made good imitations, too. He said that the women who were dressed as soldiers evidently belonged to some organization, served as ambulance drivers, or workers, and had their pictures taken with guns just for fun.

About five o'clock I heard a terrific jarring report in the next bay of the trench. It sounded like a sixteen inch naval shell at least. I crawled around to see what had happened, expecting to find that all were dead. Everyone was covered with stones and dirt. They looked a bit frightened, and I saw that one was hit— little Pagamemos. There was little we could do for him. The stretcher bearers came quickly and took him down to the first-aid station which was ably supervised by a French doctor. The smallest man in the company hit first—such is fate!

All during this time the Frenchmen were working like mad with their trench mortars. They kept shells continuously in the air. There was a bit of help from our own artillery, but not much, as it was difficult to hit the enemy lines when they were so close to ours. The clock crept around, and finally it was five minutes to six. I had been watching everything that occurred and reading my red book at times. At three minutes to six Sergeant Felix walked along the parapet informing all our men that we were going over in a few moments. I urged him to keep down, not to make a target of himself, but he disregarded my advice.

Finally as our watches, which had been synchronized before the bombardment, pointed exactly to six o'clock there were whistles and commands, and climbing men leaving the trench all along the line (the gunners who had been working so desperately with the trench mortars to pave the way for us) cheered and cried out to us, evidently urging us to sweep the Germans from the hill. I couldn't understand just what they said.

And soon we were in the thick of things. Bullets were flying merrily by this time from the German trenches, perhaps a fourth of a mile away. I was hardly out of the trench until some great force pushed me, knocking me over and over for a distance of perhaps twenty feet. I didn't know what had hit me, but I felt blood running down my right eye, and then I did a peculiar thing, considering that we were in the midst of the battle. I took out my trench mirror that I carried in my pocket and examined the cut I had received to see if I had enough of a mark to make a scar to show the fellows when we got back to our regiment.

In the Heat of Battle

I NOTED even then that a miracle had occurred. A bullet coming direct for my right eye while I was running with my head down—a bullet which would have meant the end of the world for me if it had been seven-twelfths of one thousandth of an inch lower! The tiny point of the bullet struck an infinitesimally small distance above the triple edge of the tin hat, or steel helmet. It turned up, and ran around the helmet, leaving a mark of the bullet's rifling. No one with whom I came in contact during the remainder of the war ever saw anything like it. A high-powered bullet will go through five feet of solid wood, or through three- quarters of an inch of steel. The hats are lightly constructed, designed to deflect shrapnel, but my hat had deflected a high power bullet.

After that knock down I forgot the line of combat groups and we fought just as our ancestors had always fought—instinctive rushing forward, stopping to shoot, rushing again, and shooting again. I don't remember all the battle—didn't when it was over. We went over the top at six o'clock. I was in the first-aid station at twenty-seven minutes after twelve, midnight. I had three rings on my fingers when I went over. I never saw them again. That is one thing which was difficult to understand.

Immediately after I replaced my helmet, I looked well ahead and saw apparently where the bullet which had struck me had come from. I saw this German working his machine gun. I prepared to fire my first shot in the war. Although I had not been nervous during the preliminary bombardment, I was especially surprised to find that I was as steady as a rock. Usually before an athletic event of any sort I would be a bit nervous; involuntary thrills would chase up and down my spine and through my stomach. Even on the rifle range I was quite nervous until the first few shots were fired. Some athletes never get over this preliminary nervousness; some screen and radio stars never entirely recover from their early nervous feelings and are always upset when they start a program. I marvelled, as I prepared to fire, that I was as steady as the Rock of Gibraltar. It is difficult to know when you hit a man in action, for many men are shooting. At least the gunner went down and did not rise again. He was either killed, wounded or so nearly so that he decided to keep under cover.

Meanwhile we were advancing, remembering only the moving pictures we had seen of the soldiers fighting in the Civil War, and fighting the Indians in the old pioneer days. I saw big Corporal Graves directing the firing of his squad kneeling to observe the effect of the fire. That's nice in theory but it's a sure way to leave this world in a battle with efficient enemy snipers to pick off any man who behaves a bit differently from others. They constantly try to pick off the leaders. In fact after the first skirmish or two, even the high officers dressed exactly as did the lowliest private. It prolonged their usefulness and their lives.

Suddenly a small group of Germans rose up out of the deep weeds and grass a bit to the left of me. Apparently they were the crew and guards of a well-hidden machine gun which I saw there. They had run out of machine gun ammunition and were not firing, so we had not noticed them until this time. The resulting fight was of short duration, too short for me to get into it from the point where I lay. It was my closest view of hand-to-hand fighting. It is not a bit pretty to look at. Men have fought with knives and spears since the earliest cave man days when Cro-Magnon man defeated the Neolithic man who was still fighting with thrown stones and clubs.

Fighting with spears and knives is such an ingrained characteristic of the human race that it was impossible to persuade the savage races who fought on the side of the Allies to use their guns. The French had considerable help from the black fellows from far off Senegal in Africa. Even the Germans came to fear these black men. Fighting was second nature to them. They seemed to like nothing better than to go on patrols at night with a knife in their teeth, crawling silently along, until some unsuspecting German lost his life's blood through a severed jugular vein.

And in the actual attacks they seemed to completely disregard rifle bullets, but would rush forward laughing and shouting until they came to grips with the enemy and fought hand to hand. Naturally many of them did not get that far, for the age-old method of fighting they used was not the best way in modern war.

A great many native Indian troops fought with the British. And they could never feel well equipped with a rifle which could kill at a mile or two away unless they had their curved chopping knife or kukri—a terrible weapon not unlike the famous bowie knives of early American history. Modern war should no longer be a matter of chopping axes, swinging swords and embowelling with knives, but such fighting is an inherent tendency with every man—particularly of the races where men had fought with swords and knives not so many generations in the past. A man quickly forgets what he has learned in this modern world and reverts to the position his ancestors occupied a few generations or centuries ago.

The hand of fate directed these Germans to a most unfortunate place—a meeting with supermen, for they rose up right in front of a group of the huge Texans. It wasn't so many years ago that the ancestors of these Texans had created an epoc in American history that won undying fame for them and the men of their breed. Greatly outnumbered in the siege at the Alamo, fighting against an overwhelming mass of superior troops under the Mexican general Santa Anna, they had resisted until the last man had fallen. They used the rifle as long as they could, and then fought at close quarters with their bayonets and their curved knives. These Texans were hardly more than two generations removed from such fighters.

There was Indian fighting in Texas sixty years ago. The fathers of some of these men were in such fights as young boys. They had grown up on the prairies where a man lived or died, survived or perished, chiefly due to his courage and his physical ability. The Texans were great fighters, as were so many other troops from the former outposts of America. But all Americans have a legacy which has come to them from courageous, fighting pioneer ancestors. The American soldier is a good soldier. He has not had the centuries of drilling to make his own individual self subservient to the will of the commanding officer; he does not like to salute the brass bar of Lieutenant John Brown unless that lieutenant has won his respect through his deeds; he does not like to be regimented, turned into a mere robot; he can think and act for himself; and when a battle has passed the initial stages, he's the best soldier in the world.

Wars of the present are fought largely with machines, but those machines must have the guiding of human hands. Americans are particularly fitted for this, for they live and work with machines every day of their lives. Even the rancher has his light plant, his tractor, and all its equipment, his truck and so many other mechanical appliances. So the American is a good soldier while guiding machines, and he's even a better man in actual action.

This unfortunate group of Germans found this out to their sorrow. I wonder what they must have thought to see this wave of huge men, gigantic men, approximately six and a half feet tall, almost as broad as barn doors, for they were built to proportion. Perhaps the Germans were too startled at the size and evident ferocity of their antagonists to fight well for a minute. But it seemed like a group of big men who had met a lot of boys playing soldier. One push, and the German's rifle was knocked from his hand; a long thrust and that unfortunate man had reached the end of his life. I can still see the faces of these men—their evident terror, their astonishment at the number of men who leaped at them from the grass, at the size and power of these men, their evident helplessness. There was not time for them to surrender. They had jumped up with bayoneted rifles and in a moment or two it was all over.

The entire action was like a gigantic Indian fight; pausing to fire, at one time one of our men complained that I had fired my gun too close to his ear. We sniped, rushed forward where we could, crawled through the grass over the more exposed portions; rapid fire, running forward, and soon the Germans would run back, with us getting some of them as they ran. Somehow I worked over near the woods from what had been my starting position at the left. I looked up in a tree and there hung a man as if he were a gigantic bird. And what a man! A sniper, attired in a mottled suit not unlike the clown suits we are familiar with, so that he would blend with the green and brown of the trees. From where I lay I could not tell whether one of our men had killed him or whether the preliminary bombardment had put an end to his life.

Imagine eating raspberries in the heat of battle. But that's what I did. They were growing along the edge of the wood and the field. I crawled under the bushes and for a moment had a delicious feeling of safety, protected by the shade of the woods and the thick white branches of the raspberries above me. July first. Raspberries were always ripe on the Fourth of July where I had lived. And momentarily I thought of many other trips I had made after berries during my life. What luscious berries they were! Huge black ones with just a tinge of white. This was not the last time I was to eat berries under fire, for later, in the attack toward Fismes, the blackberries were ripe and I ate my fill several times.

I kept reaching up for a handful of berries time after time, until finally a bullet struck the ground right beside me. Some sniper had seen me. I lay still as death; and then when he fired at another point, I saw him. The blue smoke was drifting slowly out of his rifle as he ejected the spent shell, placed another in the chamber and looked for his next target. But there was to be no next target for that sniper. As he looked from the wood to the men in the field I had ample time to aim very carefully, and down he came just as the sparrows had done from a shot from our air rifles as boys, but with a much greater crash.

I lay under the raspberry bushes for a minute to note how we were going. Our advance troops had passed me by. I could see dead Germans lying here and there. Right near me were two of them, close together. One of them was a big, older man with a Prussian mustache. It seemed that he had tried to protect the younger fellow—he may have been a relative, a lad from his own village, but he had been killed just the same. His hands still clasped the point in his stomach where the bayonet had gone in and been withdrawn. The youngster lay all twisted up; he too had been bayoneted and it seemed that his bones were broken from the strokes of the butt of the rifle. A rifle is a wicked weapon when swung by a powerful man, and there were many strong men in action that day.

Far, far off to the left I could see blue specks advancing up the hill beyond Vaux—little men two inches high with what looked like toy guns in their hands. It seemed that I was a witness to a toy battle. Men fell, got up and ran forward. I could see them fighting hand to hand. The French were terrible antagonists at this sort of fighting. I would rather have faced the Germans in a bayonet fight, although they were no mean antagonists. But the French had a round bayonet three feet long which, added to the length of their rifles, gave them a two-foot advantage over our own rifles. Of course we had leverage in our favor to parry, but if we failed to parry, a lot of steel would have gone through our bodies.

It seemed that the Germans over there had driven the French back; then a group of French rushed up and soon the Germans were retreating over the crest of the hill as fast as they could run. But we had a war on our side too, and it was time to get back into action. Fresh from the respite, I caught up to the front waves of our attack just as they reached what had been the German second line trench. They faced us for a moment, tried to fight us hand to hand, but they had no chance against our giants at close quarters. At a distance a gun makes all men the same size. The big man can be killed just as easily as the small man, but in hand-to-hand work, strength and weight count. Of course the big man must be fast too, or a smaller, quicker adversary will win the battle.

The Germans weren't giving up without a real struggle. We had read a lot about chained machine gunners, but these men weren't chained, and they were fighting to the bitter end. Our men were constantly rising and falling—some of them never to rise again. Our ranks were becoming rapidly decimated and there were few of us still going forward at this point.

I saw Sergeant Amole fall and lie still. Men were dropping all around me. Our casualties were especially heavy, for we were rushing forward like a lot of Indian fighters. We got far ahead of the cautious French. At each halt the careful, battle-wise Frenchmen would throw a parapet of dirt up before their faces to fire around. But we didn't spend any time digging. We went forward. I could see the men attacking far off on our left and well behind. We couldn't see what the French were doing in the woods. But they were being held up evidently, for we got far ahead and suffered a great many casualties on account of it. We had fire from the men in front of us, and from both sides.

I have never seen an authentic list of the casualties of A Company that day, but I know this: I never saw a single one of those fifty-eight men of our company, who went over the top that night, again at the front. I saw many of them in the first aid station, the field hospital, evacuation hospital or the base. I saw several in Pittsburgh after the war. But not one was still with our company when I returned a few weeks later from the hospital. Most of them became casualties on Hill 204; those who escaped were killed or injured in the defensive work along the Marne and the great offensive which started there July 18th.

We had passed two advanced trenches which were not at this time occupied by the Germans. We kept going on, giving no thought to the manner in which we were overrunning our objective, or our failure to keep in contact with the French troops to right and left of us. As I went along I had been hit several times— once on the left knee, once on the right knee. Either bullet could have left me a cripple for life but both glanced off the bone, only leaving a scar which is noticeable to this day. One grazed my arm, leaving a scar at present an inch long and three-quarters of an inch wide. I had a variety of feelings as these bullets struck or scratched me. The first which hit my helmet gave me the same sensation as if I had been pushed by a gigantic hand. The bullets on the knees stung like I had been hit with a whip, the bullet that cut through the arm and the one which left its mark on my face felt like a drop of hot water had hit me.

About this time the battle had become very hot. We fired at every enemy we could see, and they were firing from every direction—from the front, left and right, and even from behind, because we had gone so fast that we had not dropped the snipers who were firing from the trees. Our position was not greatly unlike Custer's last stand when they were surrounded by an overwhelming number of enemies.

Up to this point one of our Chau Chats had been working near me with the regularity of clockwork. A lad by the name of Mike Vanish was the first gunner on that gun. He had been our regimental baseball pitcher, was shot repeatedly through the chest, lived, but was put out of action for the duration of the war. Charlie Hall, of Pittsburgh, was the first carrier. He later lay beside me in the hospital and I could easily see the wound he had received as I watched the doctor dress it a number of times. A piece of flesh had been torn from his arm, easily as large as the saucer of a teacup. I don't know what other than an explosive bullet would make such a mark. The second carrier picked up the gun and almost immediately was killed. The operators of machine guns of any sort are the targets for all riflemen. Their vulnerability in action gave rise to the term suicide squad.

    Sergeant Felix called to one of the runners to bring him the gun. The runner dropped dead as he handed the gun to Felix. We had advanced to the German third line trench, fighting desperately meanwhile and driving the Germans before us. I had not reached any of them with my bayonet, but had been doing deadly work with my rifle. As we rushed to the German trench expecting to jump down into it and fight hand to hand with the enemy we saw that we could not do this. The trench was covered thoroughly with barbed wire so that nothing much larger than a humming bird could get in. We lay down outside the parapet to fire at close range. Someone shouted, " Look out, there's a bomb." It went right off in my face, but all my parts seemed to be present immediately afterwards. It was that explosion which caused me to lose my hair. I had hair so thick when I went overseas that I could hardly keep it out of my eyes. The bomb blew some of it completely loose and the nurse who shaved my head with a dull razor in the hospital didn't help any. The fact remains that I came home with very little hair.

    I saw Felix lying there sprawled out, groping for his pistol. I said, " What's the matter, Bill? " He couldn't answer, but turned weakly to me, and I saw that half his face seemed to have been torn off. The potato masher bomb—sort of a tin can on the end of a stick, bearing considerable resemblance to an old-fashioned potato masher from which it had derived its name— had split open with the jagged metal going through the face of Felix. That wound looked terrible at the time, but I saw Felix after the war and the scar it left had not greatly marred his manly face.

I picked up the automatic rifle and as I turned it into the German trench, they got up and ran back. I was the only one firing; I saw many of them drop with the sixty shots a minute I was pumping at them. So I knew that I was getting enough of the enemy to make up for our men who had been killed and wounded.

For a time there was nothing to shoot at, so I took stock of the situation. So far back that they were hardly more than specks I saw tiny men in blue digging in. It must have been all of a half mile. I knew that we should not stay out here in such an isolated post, but what were we to do? I never thought for a minute of abandoning the wounded, so there we stayed. The snipers far off in the wood were still firing at us and there was no way that we could reach them or entirely escape their bullets.

I couldn't get into the trench, so I crawled around it, well over into the woods. Shell holes were everywhere. I saw for the first time what havoc could be wrought by shell fire. At places the shell holes were connected solidly to each other. The trees and bushes were shattered; men were blown up and blown up again—they were in pieces. It would have taken a bushel basket or a G I can to have gathered up those Germans for burial. Many of them had gone back to the dugout during the bombardment, but there were plenty of them killed right here on the line.

For some reason I had never liked Germans. Germans had lived across the street from us when I was at home and were constant visitors to our house. From the very beginning of hostilities in 1914, old Mr. Schenck liked to talk about the war, and go on at great length about the superiority of the German people, their courage, efficiency and ability as soldiers. Perhaps I did not like them because I had come to fear them. To me they had become sort of Frankensteins; like huge insects, or men from another planet. I admit that they were the finest of soldiers. After four years of war, they fought to the death before they would give up a position.

They were so well trained that it was second nature with them. They had been regimented for so long that they never questioned an order, put up with all sorts of privation and suffering and were cheerful through it all, during most of the time. The majority of them were in very good condition when captured. It showed that they could take it. I often wondered if our own men would be as good soldiers as they after four years of war.

Germans are nearly all of one race. The men of our country are made up of every race on the globe. America has been a melting pot, but some of the nationalities have not completely merged with the contents of the pot. (When the German weight lifters were here they considered the roster of our team and said that it was Germany against the whole world. We had a colored man, John Terry, in the 132 pound class, Tony Terlazzo, born in Italy, as our 148 pound man, Johnny Terpak of Russian parentage as the 165 pound lifter, Stanley Kratkowski, a Pole, and Steve Stanko, an Hungarian-American, as our heavyweight. Our team, which went to Vienna that year, had a Czecho- slovakian and another young colored fellow.) The behavior and endurance of some of these men after years of war would be doubtful. We have a great many men as brave as the bravest; we had others who were not naturally brave, but had a rarer kind of courage—the sort that drove them forward to do their duty even when frightened almost out of their wits; and of course we had the slackers—the men who always managed to skulk out of battles, to hide somewhere until the drive was over. We did not have the discipline, but we had private soldiers as well as officers who could think for themselves.

All of us could not be brave. Bravery is sort of a fixed quality—something that some men have and others do not. Only physical collapse or death stops the brave. Some will be brave when they must—when they, like a mother animal, are driven by the instinct of self- preservation to protect their own lives or that of their offspring. I once saw a moving picture of a goat that had been tied with its kid as leopard bait while a moving picture was filmed; the mother goat knocked the vicious leopard down time after time until finally it gave up and slunk away. A man who naturally has courage is fortunate. It is the ability to control his mind, to prepare it, so that he feels nothing. Courage is the product of physical strength and mental strength combined. Proper training will make men more courageous. And certainly these Germans were courageous—no mean antagonists.

In spite of the terrific trench mortar bombardment they had held their ground and continued to fight back until they were overwhelmed by our advancing troops, which, in the beginning, had outnumbered them.

It seemed that the Germans had made themselves very much at home here. It was intensely interesting to see the things that they had left. Leaving in such a hurry as they did, their most intimate belongings were left behind. I had heard so much of traps that I was very careful what I picked up, pushing it with a stick or my rifle first to make sure that it was what it seemed to be. But I need not have been so careful. They had left in such a hurry that there was no time for traps.

The Germans always made themselves much at home. They had names for all the paths and the openings in the woods. One was named Hindenburg Strass; it led first to Potsdamer Place, which seemed to be the area in which they had sat around, talked, smoked and ate. And in back was their latrine, which they had named Tipperary. Truly it had been a long way to that Tipperary.

The loss of life here during the days of the fighting had been terrific. It was evident that they were determined to hold their part of the hill at most any price. Whereas I had seen a few graves on the French edge of the woods, there was a small German cemetery here. I examined some of the crosses—Fritz, Hans, Adolph— all some loving mothers' sons. The Germans here had overrun their supplies and were very short of heavy munitions, which accounted for so many more German dead than French. The Germans were especially tenacious in holding their positions all along this front, even when they were retreating. Everywhere they defended the woods, thickets, and curves in the roads with carefully-placed machine guns, until it was time to fall back or until the last man had fallen. Sometimes it took direct fire from the seventy-fives to blast them out, and even then bayonet work to really take the places they had held.

It gave me a peculiar feeling to be apparently entirely alone back of the German third line trench. What series of circumstances had brought me alone to this advanced point—in a strange country, behind the lines of a strange enemy? I shivered for a moment. I believe it was the dead and the German equipment which gave me that feeling. Somehow it seemed to carry a scent of fear, of danger. I wanted souvenirs, but I almost feared to take them. It was too much like robbing a cemetery somewhere.

This little woods, which had looked so innocent on the outside, contained unbelievable quantities of warlike material. Everywhere I looked I saw refuse and trash of one sort and another: German newspapers and magazines, cast-off boots worn through at the toe or heel, many of the little round Boche hats which were used when the helmet was not worn, rifles, bayonets, a broken machine gun, a leather haversack, shrapnel- damaged helmets, pistols and ammunition. Probably little they had left behind was worth anything.

When the Germans remained in a place for any length of time they made their quarters quite livable. They even built bungalows with bomb proofs extending back into the hills for their protection during shell and artillery fire. They planted gardens, raised rabbits, and lived the best life they could. Of course this was not possible on an active sector such as this. But they had constructed little rustic bowers and seats, cleverly woven in a style similar to that used in rustic porch furniture. The paths were lined with seats and white stones, and across from Potsdamer Place was a little beer garden, with bar, tables and chairs all made of roots and saplings.

At times I felt that the Germans weren't quite human, but this little homelike touch to the places they had left showed them to be men like ourselves who could enjoy the simple pleasures of life.

I soon left this part of the deserted woods and crawled back to my comrades on the outside of the wire-covered trench.

I noted that Sergeant Felix was badly wounded and Jim Early had all of thirteen wounds in him when he got to the field hospital. One of the Texans whose name I did not know was lying there dead. A chap by the name of Danuel, whom I met in 1926 in Philadelphia where he was employed on the new subway, the dead runner who had brought the gun, and a dead Italian boy by the name of Vochona were all who had reached this advanced point. The others had dropped somewhere along the way, killed or wounded, and in a few cases had remained with the attacking French and were well behind our post.

German Prisoners

WHAT to do? That was the problem. I knew that we could expect the Germans to come back to their trench if they learned it was manned only by a skeleton crew of dead and wounded. We lay still with our heads turned toward the parapet of the German trench, and were safe from that direction. I pulled the dead bodies around to protect us from the fire on the right and then used my shovel to pile dirt over them as partial protection. The sniper whom we could not locate kept pumping bullets into the piled dirt as fast as I could put it up. One bullet came close enough to sting, the next tore my trousers, the next made a black and blue spot, the fourth drew blood—getting too close for comfort.

I tried to do something for the wounded. They were very cold by this time, suffering from loss of blood. They were lying there stripped to the waist. I reached for the canteen of one of the dead men. There were two bullet holes through mine and it was empty. Just as I turned, a bullet from far off to the left tore through the flesh of my cheek. If I had not turned that very instant it would have gone through my head dead center, either killing me or sadly maiming me for life. I am sure that some of the bullets—five in Felix and thirteen in Jim Early—were inflicted by the sniper or snipers who were firing at us. Bill and Jim were men of such great determination it could be expected that they would be able to carry on with several bullets in them. I saw their wounds dressed in the field hospital and I don't believe that any man could run with all the wounds they had. One bullet had gouged more than a foot along Early's big back muscle. A number had gone through his leg around the knee. Thirteen in all.

They did not offer a single complaint about their wounds—only that they were so cold. Bill got thinking of home and said, " Bob, if you get back, tell my mother the last thing I thought of was her." There was a girl at home who had come to visit Bill at camp, but he didn't say a word about her. And Jim Early got worrying about the few francs he owed Captain Williams. " Tell the captain, Bob," he said, " that I will pay him what I owe him when I get back from the hospital." I never saw Jim Early after those first hours in the field hospital, but I am told that he played football in the fall of 1919. These men were made of stern stuff.

Little Vochona who lay there was just sixteen years of age. He was the first of a dozen youngsters whose ages ranged from fourteen to sixteen who had enlisted in our company. They had lied about their actual age, enamored with the appearance of our fellows in uniform; they too wanted to be soldiers. Some of them lost their nerve before they reached the front and tried in many ways to get out of service. The Spencer brothers, fifteen and sixteen years of age, were to be killed by shell fire as we went into Fismes to stop a counter attack. But there was no fear in this little Italian boy. He had always been a hothead, wanting to fight with a knife, fork, or anything he could lay his hands on when someone antagonized him a bit. He was dashing forward, with bayoneted rifle in hand, so fast when the bullet which killed him hit him that he lay well out on the barbed wire covering the German trench.

There were German souvenirs all around and I was collecting a good pile of them. I was still determined to show the men of our company that we had been in a fight. I gathered German guns, knives and bayonets, a field cap or two, a shovel, coal bucket helmet and a few miscellaneous items. When I heard shots from the woods on the right, I would shoot in the direction of the shot. Still no way to get back! French soldiers far to the rear digging in! I saw a brown uniform a bit closer to the lines than the French. I crawled back and there was one of our men crying. I asked him why, and he replied that so many of his friends had been killed. I told him not to worry about the killed, that we had living wounded to be concerned about, to get back; that he had better go for help and stretchers, and see if we could not evacuate our fellows.

Shortly after I regained my place outside the parapet a German plane flew over so low that I could see the face of the pilot. We all lay still as death, and as some of the men were in the grotesque attitudes of death it was natural that the aviator would go to the rear and tell them that the opposing troops were digging in far to the rear with only dead men near their former trench. I knew that we could expect an attack. I asked Felix if he thought he could fire a gun. He thought he could, so I loaded and lined one up for him. I had a gun in front of Early too, and had managed to procure a full semicircular clip for the Chau Chat rifle.

I had no other thought than that I should die as bravely as I could for my friends or country or something—so I prepared to sell my life as dearly as possible. In a surprisingly few minutes there came a crashing through the woods, the sound of voices, and a large body of men came into view. I lay still, waited until they were quite close, and then jumped up pointing the automatic rifle at them and was prepared to go into action. I suppose it was very startling to have a dead man jump up, for I certainly looked dead. When a young nurse in the field hospital held a mirror so I could see how I looked, I must admit that I never saw a human being who looked half as bad. I would give much for a photo of myself that day so that all could see what a few hours of war can do to a man. I was a mass of blood from head to foot—mostly my own—but I had been trying to dress the wounds of my comrades, and had some of their blood on me. Where the bullet had hit the helmet the eye was cut, bloodshot, swollen and had bled profusely. Where the bullet had hit my left cheek, it was swollen much worse than if I had the mumps, and it was some weeks before the swelling went down. The bomb which had gone off in my face and the great amount of sand and gravel which had peppered against me had caused my face to be swollen, bloated, discolored and appeared like nothing human. My clothes were torn. In short I was a mess.

I pulled the trigger and as soon as one man fell the others all shouted, "Kamerad." It is like holding up a train. No one wants to be the first killed so a crowded car permits one man to hold them up. When the Germans found that I stopped firing they were very anxious to surrender. Their officer was as nice and polite as any head waiter in a high-class restaurant. He knew a little English and understood when I told him to have his men pile the arms one place, put their packs another, and make improvised stretchers to carry back the wounded. This all took just a few minutes and soon we were starting back. I was gathering up souvenirs as I went and had quite a lot of them. As we went well to the rear, several other men, who had been nowhere near us in the advanced post, joined in the procession. That's why my citation reads (a citation issued by Marshal Petain, who is still a great soldier and leader in France) that I " had led my men gallantly in action, had remained at the front although severely wounded, and HAD ASSISTED in the capture of thirty-eight Germans."

When we arrived back at the support trenches, we were greeted by the major and his staff, a few men from our company who were unwounded, and quite a few French soldiers both from the Trench Mortar Battalion and the infantry who held the hill. They were laughing and patting us on the back and some of them tried to kiss me. The major was talking French at a great rate, telling us what bon soldats (good soldiers) we had been.

One of our men came up with a German identification tag which had been given to him by one of the young Germans. Noting that the German's name was Hoffman—Paul Hoffman—he gave it to me. I still have it. It was the twentieth birthday for that young German, and at least he was to survive the war and return to his native land after the hostilities had ceased.

When the excitement had died down just a bit, someone said, " Bob, you'd better go down to the first- aid station and get your wounds dressed." I thought that only soldiers with arms or legs off went to the hospital—that the wounds I had would respond to self- applied bandages or salves of some sort. But they told me that blood poisoning might set in, or lockjaw, and I had better have the wounds properly taken care of.

Very reluctantly I said, " Well, all right, but watch these souvenirs for me. I want to take them back and show the fellows. I'll be back here in about ten minutes." But I never did get back to Hill 204 again, or even to my company for a period of weeks. They put enough bandages on me to give me a startling similarity to an Egyptian mummy, gave me two hypodermic injections to ward off possible lockjaw, and put me upon a stretcher, refusing to let me move from it. I was supplied with some hot coffee and for the first and only time in my life it was welcome. I drank it with relish, but have never cared for it since.

There were quite a number of our wounded in that Red Gross dugout. One was a friend of mine from Pittsburgh. The bullet that laid him low had hit where most men fear to be hit, right through the genitals. It was just a gob of stuff. " How does it look, Bob? " he asked. " Do you think I'll be all right? " " Sure," I said, " it'll heal up all right." But I knew it wouldn't. Later I became quite an accomplished liar in endeavoring to relieve the fears of wounded men. It was particularly unfortunate in the case of this young fellow for he had been married just as he enlisted. Only a week before he had received word that he was the father of a pretty little girl. And here he was destined to spend the remainder of his life as only half a man. I saw him on the main street in Pittsburgh shortly after my return, and he said that he was still living with his wife. It would have been quite a sacrifice for her. They tasted very little of the joys of married life. I don't know how he fared after that for I have never seen him since.

At this time I noticed that it was twelve twenty-seven, six hours and twenty-seven minutes after we went over the top. It didn't seem that we could have been out there on the hill so long. It seemed like just a few minutes.

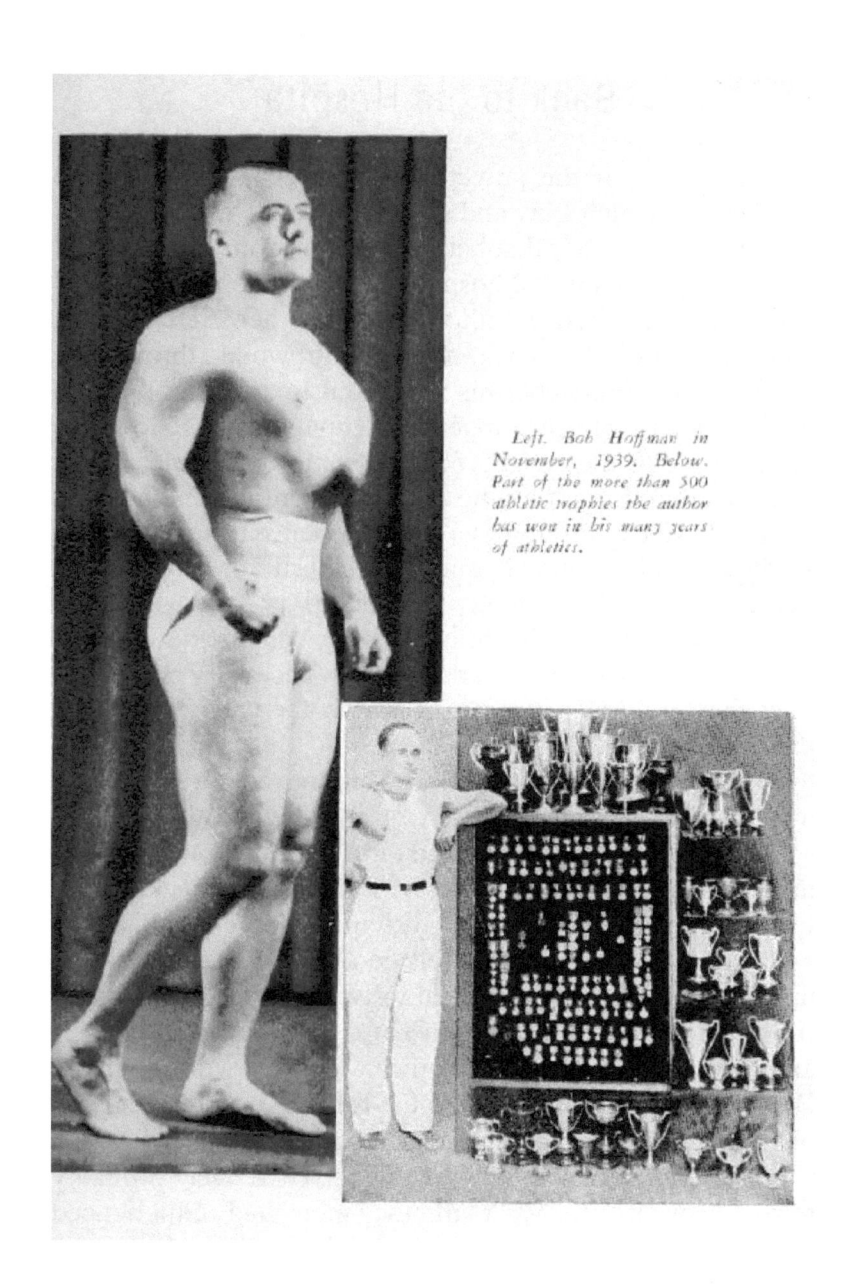

Left. Bob Hoffman in November, 1939. Below. Part of the more than 500 athletic trophies the author has won in his many years of athletics.

Back to the Hospital

SOON four of the powerful Alpine chasseurs took the stretcher on which I lay and started down the hill with me. I wasn't so heavy after that battle. I weighed one hundred and sixty-five pounds in the hospital. At the bottom of the hill I was placed in a Ford ambulance, with another stretcher case, and one of our fellows who had a painful wound through the elbow. I can't remember his name, but I remember the man well. He was a tall, fine-appearing, young Italian fellow. We bumped along the rough road for some hours and finally were quartered in a field hospital, in a tent which had been pitched beside a hill. It was a sad experience to see the many suffering and wounded, but it was thrilling too, for the nurses were rather young and attractive American girls. Anyone who has not been away from women and children for a long period does not know what a necessary part of our lives they are. Later in the war, after some weeks at or near the front, we would yearn to see people, other than soldiers, to an extent which would make us anxious to advance to the next town, hoping that people would live within it. We were so disappointed when we found only piles of stones. One of my best memories of the war was after some weeks at the front, when an American girl, driving a French ambulance, waved at me and smiled. I felt good for a week. Between battles we often walked fifteen to twenty kilometers just to find a place where the Red Cross was giving out sandwiches and chocolate and to see the ladies who were working there. Being away from children and the feminine gender was one of the hardships of war.

The tent was filled to overflowing. There were probably thirty beds in it. Most of the men had experienced emergency operations and were horribly sick as they came out of the ether. I was especially pleased to learn that my wounds were only superficial—required dressing only, no operation or cutting. All the hair was shaved from my head with a razor so dull that I could hardly keep from shouting. But I saw the nurse shave around the wounds of Felix and Jim Early, and they didn't murmur, and they were hurt so much worse than I, so I smothered an involuntary exclamation and was perfectly quiet. Most of the men in this tent were Americans—men whom I knew, although some few were from B Company's platoon and I did not know them. They couldn't keep me in bed, for I was too anxious to talk to our fellows—to learn of the severity of their wounds, to ask what had happened to so and so and to answer their many questions. There were several Frenchmen in this field hospital and quite a number of Germans. One of the Germans was particularly laugh able. He was a small German Jew, just the sort we had known since childhood, for so many of them had become peddlers and hucksters in the places where I had lived. He had no shoes and was much perturbed about it. There was one very sad case there—a nice-looking German boy about eighteen years of age. His leg had been amputated. Gangrene had set in and it had been cut several times. Now it was so close to the body that the advance of the poison could not be arrested and he was sure to die. I believe he knew it too. But he lay there quietly, smilingly, with a patient answer to any question. We began to feel at this point that war was what Sherman said it was, " Hell," multiplied to the nth degree.

One of the men looked over my equipment which I still had with me and found more bullet holes. " Here's one through the shovel, Bob—from the front. How did you get that? " There it was, right through the center of the shovel. The shovel is worn on the outside of the haversack, in the exact middle of one's back. The bullet hadn't gone through me. Finally we decided that it must have gone past my head while I was running forward and the shovel was bouncing around. I then took inventory and learned how lucky I had been. Forgetting the bomb, bullets had left their mark upon my helmet, the left side of my face, left knee, right knee, my left arm, four through the trouser leg—one of which had drawn blood and the other caused a great discoloration—one through the shovel, and two through my canteen. How many others must have come quite close we could only conjecture.

Soldiers always felt that they were lucky. If they lost one leg, it could have been worse; they might have lost both legs. If they lost both legs, it could have been worse; they might have been killed. It was always " If it had come a foot closer it would have killed me," " If it had come an inch closer it would have killed," " Three inches farther up and I wouldn't be here," " Lower down it would have been through my heart instead of my shoulder," " The fellows all around me were killed and here I am with just a few wounds," " Everyone else who reached the advance point is dead, but here I am," etc. But I had marks which would have killed me if they had come a tiny fraction of an inch lower or higher or to the right or left. My comrades decided that I had been the luckiest one of the lot and many times later during our period of service at the front we were to agree that I was superaaturally lucky.

The Germans in this camp were all nice fellows—young, fine-looking men. They were happy to be alive and talked to the best of their ability as we exchanged souvenirs. Later in the war we were to encounter so many of the older men, the stiff-necked Prussians who would not even speak to us—said they didn't talk to their enemies. Youth of all nations seldom reckons the cost. They make the best soldiers because they will go out and try to die bravely for their countries as I expected and tried to do. Older men are more cautious. They have homes—perhaps families—positions; they know about life; they usually know the folly of war. They are careful, and battles are not won by being careful. The impetuous, youthful soldiers are the best fighters. That's why war will always take the flower of the manhood of the nations involved—the strongest, most intelligent, most useful of men.

Two days at the field hospital and we were on our way again—this time to the evacuation hospital at Collumieres. Here again we were quartered in tents. There were some permanent buildings but wounded had been coming back rather rapidly and all beds were filled. The first night at this hospital we were subjected to an air raid. Bombs fell not far away and the antiaircraft guns put up a terrific battle. I did what seemed to be a peculiar thing here—put my head under the covers. I knew that it would do no good. If the bombs were to fall, the canvas roof, the sheet and blanket would not stop them. But it was comforting to have my head under, in an ostrich-like manner. I learned here that men who are the bravest of the brave at the front with their guns and bayonets are just little boys when they are wounded and in bed with their pajamas on. That's why later in the war I spent so much time trying to reassure the wounded, to cheer them, to build up confidence in them, for I knew how I felt.

Two more days and we were on our way again—this time a long train ride to the farther south city of Blois. There for the first time since arriving in France we were free of air raids. After the long journey we found ourselves in the Mixed Hospital at Blois, a city on the Loire River. It was called the mixed hospital because aH sorts of people were there—a few Russian soldiers some Germans, even women and children, as there was a maternity ward and a venereal ward. I heard much shouting and screaming from that department and it taught me to be careful. In the ward in which I was placed were mostly Americans—not all white fellows, however, for there were some of the colored troops who were a part of the 93rd Division. One of these had been shot through the shin, which is particularly painful. While most of the wounded suffered in silence he could not refrain from screaming when his wound was probed and dressed.

On one side of me was Charlie Hall from Pittsburgh, the first carrier on the automatic rifle as I mentioned before. On the other side was a man who had been wounded with shrapnel. After some weeks in the hospital they discovered that all the shrapnel had not been removed from his body. The doctor probed right on the bed beside me; the flesh had grown over the piece of shrapnel and had to be cut again. Finally cloth and a big piece of metal were pulled out.

I hadn't given much thought to my part in the war up to this time and here I was surprised to learn that I was a hero—that the papers had been filled with my exploits on Hill 204. I felt that they were just part of the battle, what anyone should do. But war news had been scarce of the American soldiers' participation in actual fighting, and the papers both in France and in America made much of this capture of the first fairly large body of enemy troops. Later in the war it was easy to capture Germans. They had learned that they would be well taken care of as prisoners if taken by the Americans, would be well fed and safe, and many of them were only too glad to be captured. There was talk about the citations and decorations I was to receive.

The entire platoon was given Croix de Guerres, the French cross of war. I was to receive additional citations for particular deeds other than just participating in the meritorious attack, for which I received citations and was authorized to wear two palms and a silver star upon my Croix de Guerre ribbon. The lieutenant in charge of the B Company platoon was given the Croix de Guerre, Distinguished Service Cross, was promoted to a captaincy and sent home to train troops. There he was a great hero, was kissed by the mothers, wives and sweethearts of the inth Infantry, so I was informed.

Later I was to receive a number of other decorations besides the three Croix de Guerres. The Belgian Order of Leopold, the highest Belgian decoration—only eight given in the American army—the Italian War Cross, the Order of the Purple Heart, an extreme gallantry citation which entitled me to wear a silver star on my Distinguished Service Cross. Eighteen years after the war, at the instigation of one of my competitors, I was to receive one of my rewards for having participated with some valor in the American operations in France. I received much unfavorable publicity through the efforts of the powerful Federal Trade Commission to prove that I did not possess the Distinguished Service Cross. The record of the awarding of the Distinguished Service Cross, better known as a D S C, appeared on my service record and honorable discharge; the papers while in France carried a record of my citation, and the award of the cross. I was asked to join special societies to which only those who have won the D S G are invited to be members. I received the silver star to wear on my DSC ribbon, which was the equivalent of winning two D S C's. And then, years after the war, the records in Washington disclose the fact that there is a mix-up on my DSC; that I was recommended for it but it was never awarded. It made me wonder which army I was in—the Italian, the Belgian, or the French; they thought enough of me to give me awards for valor. The government body—the Federal Trade Commission—gave me my award for service in the U. S. army by considerable unfavorable newspaper publicity.

Tales of the Wounded

THE ward of the hospital I was in was a huge affair with row after row of iron beds filled with wounded. I believe there must have been five hundred wounded in the huge room in which I was placed. It is doubtful if this building was originally a hospital; it had been pressed into service for that purpose. The song " Madelon " was popular at this time and a boy about fourteen came daily to sing for us. He thought that he was doing his bit to cheer us up. At the age of puberty which he was passing through, any boy will have far from an attractive voice—an occasional near bass, alternating with a high falsetto, and all degrees of tones in between. But this young fellow had a particularly terrible voice aside from going through the period of changing voices—a piercing, penetrating, rasping voice which would have done credit to an east side fishmonger.

It was very trying and the fellows who were less badly wounded would chase him out every day by throwing everything they could find at him. Singing was one thing; his type of shouting was another.

In my first few days in the hospital I walked around quite a bit to see what I could see and to get acquainted. Later I was confined to my bed, when I had the fever, by the simple process of taking the lower part of my pajamas. Even a young man who had passed through what I had already encountered could not walk around with only a pajama coat. But the first few days things were quite interesting.

I walked down into the inner court or garden where soldiers of several nationalities who had been severely wounded, and had been at this hospital for many months, were convalescing. They told me many tales of the fighting of former years. It was truly a league of nations there. No wonder it was called the Mixed Hospital. At least a dozen different races were represented. French, German, American, Turkish, Russian, Belgian, Roumanian,

Montenegrin, Austrian, and a French Senegalese warrior or two were there.

There were men badly enough wounded in my ward. Most of them were wounded only in the arm or the leg. I knew there were more seriously wounded men somewhere. I wandered one day into another ward similar to the one we occupied, but with much more seriously wounded men occupying its beds. There were men who had their faces marred almost past recognition as anything human. Some had lost noses, jaws or ears. The records prove that men who lived had been shot through every single part of the body, every organ, even all parts of the brain. Men normally die who are shot through an important internal organ—heart, intestines, or liver. Usually a head shot kills the man instantly; but many have lived when shot through the head.

Few have any idea of the horrible cripples left by the last war. Even in the years which have intervened since the ending of that war, hundreds of thousands of men have been kept in hospitals—some of these men so severely wounded that they are never permitted to be seen by others. While it is no harder to lose a nose than a finger, what a horrible thing it does to a man's face. I could not help but think how I would have looked from the bullet which left its mark on my cheek if I had not turned my head just at the right instant. I might have been here with these men, having only half a face of my own.

There were many good surgeons in the war, but there were others who found in it an opportunity to try experiments, theories of their own, on sorely wounded men—men who did not have strength enough to argue back. Some worthy work of plastic surgery was done, but most of them, when the operation was ended, were no better looking than Frankenstein. There were doctors there who thought they could cure flat feet. They tried their experiments on any men who would submit, and certainly they didn't do them any good, but did harm to many. There was considerable faulty setting of bones and rebreaking of these bones, in an endeavor to do a better job of setting them the next time.

Surgical skill improves. In the time of the Civil War amputation was the chief method of treating the wounded. I often pass a point on the Lincoln Highway two miles this side of Gettysburg. That is one of the first stone monuments the interested person sees when passing the battlefield. This stone monument marks the site of a field hospital which was located there during and immediately after the great battle. Years ago an old man who was in that battle, and at that time lived In Gettysburg, serving as a battlefield guide, told me that there was a pile of arms and legs outside of that hospital six feet high and ten feet across the base. I can believe it too, for sanitation and medical skill had not advanced so far at that time (nearly eighty years ago). Amputate the limb first, think about it afterwards seemed to be the plan.

There were constant operations in this part of the hospital. But most sinister of all, and perhaps most important of all, was a small room, which contained a few beds, in which the very worst patients were placed. Many called this the morgue, the " dead room," or the " dying room." Men were dying every day in spite of the fact that the more seriously wounded usually died before they reached a base hospital. In spite of all medical skill, tetanus—lockjaw—would set in; gangrene could not always be prevented. Some of these men had lost a great amount of blood, and many of them, even during the summer season, already had contracted Flu, which in their weakened state was fatal.

When a man was dying they would move him out. It was bad enough for him to die without his comrades, who did not know when their own turn might come, having to watch him die. Some of the men went out screaming when they were moved. The nurses would try to ease their going by telling them that they were only going to the operating room for minor treatment or to the dressing room, to have their bandages changed. The fellows soon learned to observe whether the little bag which held their personal belongings—sometimes a helmet or a coat—came with them. If it remained behind they could expect to come back; but if it too was moved, then they were sure that worse was in store for them. Some begged to be left there to die with their friends around them, not to be placed with a lot of near corpses who were complete strangers.

The more pitifully wounded did not wish to live. They constantly begged doctors and nurses, sometimes at the top of their voices, to put an end to them. Some made attempts to end their lives with a knife or fork. It became necessary to feed these wounded and never leave a knife or fork with them. One of the orderlies told me that a blinded man who was suffering greatly and did not wish to live had killed himself at one time with a fork. It was hard to drive it deep enough through his chest to end his life, and he kept hitting it with his clenched fist to drive it deeper.

There was a limit to how many pain tablets could be given to any man—how many his heart would stand. But most of them begged for another tablet the minute they recovered sufficiently from the former tablets and once again felt severe pain.

Most of the nurses back at the base were older women. I am sure the long hours they had to work and the demands of their patients shortened their lives considerably. The younger and stronger girls were up nearer the front, where even more labor and more difficult duties were encountered. It was interesting, although somewhat gruesome, to stand in the lobbies and watch the traffic going by: wheeled carts containing men who were going up into wards such as mine; men who were hurt worse than they had expected and were going downstairs in the ward with the worst cases; many men expecting to die being moved to the living morgue and men who had died being taken out for burial. Some of them were better off; at least I would rather be dead than as horribly crippled as many—a lifelong dependent upon others—living dead. I have always felt that life would not be worth living if constant pain and suffering, being confined to pain-ridden beds and wheel chairs, was to be one's lot until death. But humans cling to life. They want to see loved ones, their home, the sun rise the next day, see the spring again. They seem willing to live in spite of all suffering. It is a good old world, after all. So we may change our minds if we must face the stern realization that death is finally at hand.

Five or six men a day were dying. They were taken right out in the fields back of the hospital and buried. Bugles sounding taps, and the firing of guns, as each man was buried with military honors, became familiar sounds. Normal death is not so bad. I've seen a lot of death of one sort and another. I've really died several times myself—by drowning, unconscious four days after an automobile accident, knocked to unconsciousness in the Argonne; not a bit different than actual death as far as one's feelings are concerned. The difference is the fact that in real death one never wakes up, never opens his eyes to the light of the world again. But I was brought back each time to life. I am sure that I experienced real death at one time; although in my prime, my life before me, everything to live for, I had absolutely no desire to live. I felt this way when I first became conscious four days after an auto accident in which I was involved. Dying under those circumstances could not be so bad. And dying of old age must not be so bad either. Under those circumstances one has lived his or her life. There is a slow losing of the faculties, a dulling of the mind; finally one has no realization of whether he is alive or not. That would be a nice way to die. Some of my relatives died that way, really of old age. But others died horrible deaths from cancer, Bright's disease, dropsy, or diabetes. Sudden death from heart trouble would be quick—like a bullet that ends things.

But many of these men were doomed to a life of slow and painful death. The doctors and nurses, of course, told them that they would become completely cured in time, but the fellows talked among themselves and didn't quite believe it. I admired their courage, for many of them were smiling and calm under the circumstances. I wondered if they were not more deserving of medals for bravery than was I. It is one thing to be brave when one's body is whole, one's comrades around, and a stirring fight is in progress; but still another thing to be torn to pieces, in pain, little more than half a man lying in a hard bed, in dark and miserable surroundings, without one's friends and loved ones nearby. But I suppose it is worse to die, as so many died, in the mud, in front of our lines, unable to get medical attention as so many were to die a bit later in our part of the war.

These brave young fellows, like the young German I had seen in the field hospital, knew that they must die, were soon to leave this world, friends, hopes, prospects, many of them never having had the opportunity to live. They had been studying, working, training, striving for better things to come. But there were to be no better things for some. Their lives were all but ended, their candle of life had all but burned away.

Far from pleasant moments I spent in this ward below ours. It was bad enough in our section, and I could tell even the most sorely wounded of the men whose beds were around mine how lucky they were. It is hard to feel lucky when a rifle or machine gun bullet has gone through the bones of the shin; when it has gone entirely through the huge muscles of the thigh (for there it is difficult to heal. It must be kept open, forced to heal from the center first. Drainage tubes must be constantly kept in it, so that it will remain clean within and not become infected in any manner. It was necessary to reopen so many of these hastily cared for wounds that had grown shut while not quite clean inside); a shot through the elbow or the knee, a wound that would usually leave the bone stiff for the remainder of life; or through the hand or the foot. Such wounds might take years to heal. The men who merely had a hole in an arm or a shoulder were lucky enough.

And I was so lucky that I was ashamed to be in the hospital with men who were really hurt. But the doctors had insisted that I go there. They must have known whether it was necessary or not. I believe that they thought some of the bits of iron, sand, and gravel, which had made my face so terrible to look at, might have penetrated the flesh or even the skull to a point where they would be removed some time later. But it turned out that my wounds were only superficial. You can be sure I was pleased when I saw what the doctor was doing to other men around me. I was lucky.

It is not pleasant to lie on one's back with a leg suspended in the air high above one's head—perhaps to have it enclosed in splints for long weeks and months; or to have closed eyes, as so many hundreds in that hospital had, from gas; to lie there in absolute darkness, having no idea whether they would be able to see again or not. There were no radios in those days—nothing to do but lie there in darkness until the doctor and the nurse made one of their two trips a day; until the orderly brought a bed pan or one of the meals.

And speaking about meals—they were mighty poor in this hospital. They may have sufficed for a small man who was sorely wounded; but I was perpetually hungry. I became a pest in the kitchen—until my pajamas were commandeered. Then my only redress was to complain orally. During the entire war I wondered what became of the food that was sent to France. The people at home were doing without it so that the men who were doing the fighting would have it. The men in the rear didn't have it; they said it was at the front. It wasn't at the front; we had just enough to exist on; it wasn't at the big camps. Where could it be? I often wondered. Later I was to learn that much of it was at the base ports. The marine guards at those ports, even the colored stevedores, lived royally—it not being unusual to have roast beef and chicken, five or six kinds of vegetables, one or two desserts besides ice cream— and not on Christmas either. That's where the food was—in the hands of the men who took it off the ship. The more desirable portions stayed there; we at the front got only what was left.

The days dragged along. I helped where I could— talking to the more seriously wounded, helping the orderlies feed a badly-wounded man, even aiding the nurses in making beds. I wasn't a pretty sight as I went around in my pajamas and with slippers of the Oriental type. With my head shaved in front, with my face still swollen and bloated, I looked like an accident that had happened or at least a cross between a Chinaman and a misspent life.

I had been getting out of bed too much, and it did seem about this time that comrades, doctors and nurses who had warned me to go to bed and take things easy had been right. I broke out with a fever and a rash, and then I was kept in bed. I could look out the window and see the French people fishing for a tiny flat, sardine-like fish. They frequently popped these fish into their mouths and ate them raw. There was a rowing club near, and soldiers who had been invalided home due to wounds would row along the river in a four-oared shell. I had been an oarsman at home and longed to be out there with them.

We heard stories of what was going on at the front.

Our own Fourth of July had passed while we were at the evacuation hospital at Collumieres. And now came the equivalent in France of our Fourth of July— Bastille Day. The Germans had selected that day as the beginning of their big drive to Paris. Things looked gloomy at first. There was talk of the possible necessity of moving the wounded in this hospital still farther south if the German drive continued. Then came the Americans' counter attack on July 18th. We soon learned that they had driven in on the flanks of both sides of the large pocket which extended to Chateau Thierry and in a surprisingly short time had caused a great German retreat which was to continue until the cessation of hostilities. It was the turning point. Nurses, doctors, patients and visitors were elated.

The hospital was already filled. Great numbers of men were dying and being wounded in the terrific battles at the front. A place had to be found for them. Doctors came through examining each bed case carefully to see which of them could be moved or were able to get out of bed and perhaps be conveyed to some other location—other public buildings, or the homes of French people. I told the doctor when my turn came that I was anxious to leave and get back to my comrades at the front. He refused to even let me out of bed. I was particularly chagrined, for I yearned to go out in the yard and walk along the river. He told me that I would be required to remain in bed for at least a week. Then he would see.

Many men were evacuated. Comrades I had come to know were gone. That's one thing about the war—you meet people one day, come to know them well, and to like them, and in another day they are gone, never to appear in your life again. I am carrying some scores of fellows around in my memory that I came to like and have never seen since. While our original company was made up entirely of men who lived in Pennsylvania, notably Pittsburgh and Pottstown, many of our men were from the smaller cities around Pittsburgh—men who had enlisted while we were guarding bridges, factories and tunnels—Beaver, Beaver Falls, New Brighton, Elwood City, Wampum and other places. We had men from Texas, from Montana and from other parts of the West and South, men who, if they survived the war, lived so far away that I could never see them again.

The fresh wounded started to come in about this time, and by some coincidence in came a man from my very own company who was placed in the next bed to mine. He had been shot through the leg and was to spend many long weary weeks lying upon his back, with his leg in splints, suspended in the air, with a pulley-like arrangement to raise and lower it, with a drainage tube to keep the wound open. He was able to tell me what had happened to our organization in the days of my absence, and as he was unable to sleep much, we talked about the war.

The wounded that came in now were particularly serious cases—men who had been wounded by tremendous shells. There was much screaming and anguish displayed by these sorely-wounded men. Seldom was it quiet at night. Men whose nerves broke would be screaming all night. There were many cases of shell shock—men who had their maniacal moments when they felt that they were still at the front, being subjected to shell fire. They were out of their minds and there was nothing that could be done about it; but it made it most unpleasant for the other wounded. Horrible cases of mustard gas were everywhere. Some of these men were blinded and had to lie for endless days with their heads covered with bandages. Some of the men later were able to walk spraddle-legged down the aisles. I was told that their testicles had in some cases shrivelled up like dry peas in a pod. Certainly they were in a bad way.

I Rejoin My Regiment

About the 21st of July the doctors at the base hospital decided that I was fit to go back to the front. It was nice to have my uniform again after several weeks in pajamas. I bade all the nurses, doctors and patients good-bye and was off to St. Agnain for equipment and shipment to my organization. A single day's trip, two days at the camp, new uniform, rifle and complete equipment and I was off again. But this time I went through Paris. I spent two days in the great city and saw the sights.

And the next day I was to have one of the busiest days of my life. Early in the morning I entrained for Chateau Thierry. It wasn't a long trip—perhaps three hours with the slow French trains. Long before I reached Chateau Thierry I saw signs of the war— chiefly shattered trains, which had been used to haul troops to the front. The windows were smashed; there were holes in the roofs—principally from shrapnel; but there had been considerable machine gunning of these trains by the German aviation. As usual the Germans had control of the air and could do as they willed. I could see the blood on the cushions of the cars as we passed, and knew that the men who had occupied those coaches had had a bad time.

About eleven o'clock I arrived at the station in Chateau Thierry. I disembarked and was met by a transportation officer who examined my pass, looked in his book to see where our organization was, and made arrangements for me to ride toward the front in a French truck. There were hundreds of cots lined up on the station platform, chiefly gas patients, waiting their turn to be sent to the base hospitals. They lay there as if dead, with bandages covering their eyes. There were a host of gas casualties on this front.

This was my first time in Chateau Thierry. I had seen it at a distance from the heights of Hill 204, when it was occupied by the Germans. Now the Germans were many miles away. The people were already coming back to the city. There were a few women and children, a few elderly men, and soldiers in abundance —both from the American and French armies.

After a reasonable wait the truck on which I was to ride drew up to the station and I was off. Apparently I was the only one going back to the front at this time. I saw something of Chateau Thierry as we drove through it. It must have been a beautiful town before it had been shelled and occupied by the Germans, for even in its partly-shattered state it still showed signs of beauty. In a short time we were out on the country road, going north. Before long I could hear the muttering of the guns. There were plenty of signs of the war that had passed. In the first stages of the journey, the dead had been buried. Crosses lined the roads and the edges of the fields. A great many of our engineers were working on the road, trying to make it passable for large bodies of troops as soon as possible. There were many places where we had to detour through the fields as a shell hole had made the road impassable. The bridges along the creeks had been destroyed, and temporary bridges had been set up so that we could cross.

In a surprisingly short time, at about two o'clock, we were close enough to the front that we started to see the dead soldiers of both armies along the way. The American soldiers had been buried hastily in the holes they had dug along the road as they were advancing. But there were still many of them lying in the fields. I could see their khaki uniforms and their white faces as we passed.

As we went along we came to many dead Germans. Some had been pulled off the road. At one place we saw many of them lined up for burial. They smelled quite dead, but the driver of the truck insisted upon stopping to look them over. " Boche, mort, bon," he said over and over. I would translate this as " dead Boche, or German, is a good German." French soldiers standing alongside the road held their noses and laughed and said, " Tomorrow." They weren't in a hurry to put their enemies under the ground.

Sanitary crews and engineers were cleaning up as fast as they could, but a bit farther on we started to pass dead soldiers—Germans—still lying upon the road. They had remained too long in their endeavor to stop the forward progress of our troops, and they had paid with their lives. I saw German soldiers sitting beside the road quite dead. Their arms and heads were bandaged. They had had a bit of attention but had died anyway.

My driver had a hatred for the Germans and a strong stomach too, for he ran over every dead German he could reach with his truck. He zigzagged along from dead German to dead German, driving his huge truck over them and smashing them as completely as the rabbits and skunks we see killed along our own roads so often. Then he would stop and look at them and laugh. It was a rather trying ordeal for me. For days I had been back with human beings, in reasonable comfort and safety. Only that morning I had left one of the world's gayest cities (although Paris in war time was a great deal quieter than usual, it was still a gay city); the night before I had visited the Folies Bergere, had strolled down the Boulevard Italians, and out of the thousands of—how shall I say it—femmes de nuit (I hope that no masters of French read this book, for my American army French is twenty years behind me. But I am trying to say, " ladies of the evening," as they were called in Paris) I had found a very nice little girl and had enjoyed being with her.

And here I was back at the front with a vengeance. The truck drove perilously near the front, finally stopped and let me off. I asked a military policeman on guard at a crossroads where the 11ith was stationed. He told me that they were up at the front and directed me. I asked everyone I saw along the way for directions and about four o'clock I was so close to the front that I could see the action up ahead. Machine gun and rifle bullets were whizzing overhead. Seventy-sevens were falling all around, and the stretcher bearers were coming back in bunches. I walked, and then I crawled, to get back with my outfit. And when I got there I found it was not the inth, but the 112th regiment of our division. I admit frankly I was relieved and pleased to learn that our regiment was not at this time in the lines. I went back, glad enough to get away from the raging inferno I had found at the front. Three or four kilometers away I found our regiment, and our company camped in a wood. Everyone was glad to see me and I was glad to see them. They had not expected me back—had heard that I was much more seriously wounded than I actually was. The captain told me that he had heard great things about me, and was glad to have me back as casualties had been so heavy that few capable men were left. It seemed to me that I hardly knew the men in the company. Most of the original members were gone. New men had joined the company and I had to get acquainted all over again. It is difficult to understand why men who have been at the front—who had been, perhaps, badly wounded—are so anxious to come up again. People may wonder if it is an irresistible impulse like that which draws the moth again and again to the flame when it has already been burnt, or is it the same feeling some people get to jump from a high place? Scores have jumped over the brink at Niagara Falls. The magnet that drew me back to the front was the desire to see my friends again—to see what they were doing, to learn what they had done, to find what had happened to so and so, to be glad that another friend was still alive and well. All the men had had narrow escapes and were glad to be alive.

I learned here what had occurred in my absence. After the two platoons had marched away, the regiment had continued to a small town named Le Petit Villiers. This little village was well behind the front but there was considerable air activity nearby. Bombing squadrons constantly passed as well as observation planes. It was believed that the Germans were preparing for a big drive. What was left of the two platoons came back to their companies at this little town. Prior to their return there had been many rumors about them, but now for the first time there was firsthand information. While most of the wounded had passed through the French first-aid station, some had gone through our own regimental hospital as they were sent to the rear. Only a few men from A Company had returned, and they received a tremendous ovation as they arrived.

The entire company stayed up that night until very late listening to the wonderful stories of the " veterans." Excitement and enthusiasm remained at fever heat all during that evening. And from hearing of the exploits of these men—the first to engage in battle—a new spirit was born which was to carry our troops to heroic exploits in the weeks and months to come.

The story those who returned told was a wonderful story, a story of mad adventure, of wounds, pain, death by bombs, bayonets, snipers and machine guns. Any man who returned was alive only through a series of miracles. The survivors' faces were still flushed, their eyes wide and starry from the excitement which they still felt. They were enthusiastic concerning the behavior of our troops in action, of the long-remembered meal the French general had given them after the battle, of his praise for their fine work, of the decorations which had been promised to them. They told particularly of how certain men had died, and of Jim Early, Bill Felix, and Bob Hoffman who had reached the farthermost point; of the prisoners who had been captured. And they showed a great number of souvenirs to commemorate the first experience in battle. The men were proud of their organization.

There was drilling for the next day or two at this place until one day a group of officers from the regiment climbed into a light truck and journeyed forward several miles to look over a new position to which our regiment was to move. A hike of five kilos nearer the front was made at this time. It had started to rain and the next day there was a march of more miles. At that point the colonel called the officers of the regiment together and read the message of congratulation the French general had sent concerning the action of the two platoons, and a citation from divisional headquarters concerning their fine work. Our regiment remained a full week at this point and then moved up to positions at the front. There was a great deal of gas at this point, constant gas alarms, many of which heralded genuine gas attacks. Our organization lost men heavily from gas near here for they had two rather unpleasant assignments to perform. One was the burying of the dead soldiers who had lain for two or three weeks under the July sun, and the other was the digging up of dead Germans to remove their identification tags.

In a woods nearby the soldiers were still lying who had helped stop the German advance toward Paris. They had sold their lives dearly in many cases, for a great many Germans had died too. Three weeks these men had lain in the sun and our troops set out to bury them. Americans and Germans alike were put under the sod. There were horses too and they were a problem. Horses are huge when they become bloated, swell to twice their normal size. Their legs are thrust out like steel posts and it requires a hole about ten feet square and six feet deep to put a horse under. If the legs were off, a hole hardly more than half that size is required. At times we succeeded in using an axe and saw to cut off the horses' legs. It was a hard task and an unpleasant one, but it had to be done.

Finally the fields were cleared but there was still another gruesome task to perform. It is a law of war that the names of enemy dead be sent back through a neutral country to their homeland. The identification tags had been taken from the dead Americans but the Germans had been buried just as they were. There was the task to dig them up again—enough to remove half of their oval-shaped identification tags. That was a much more disagreeable job than the first. Gas came over and owing to the terrific odor even the powerful-smelling mustard gas could not be detected. Our men were working hard in the mid-July heat, perspiring, just in the right condition for mustard gas. Nearly half the remainder of our company, sixty-seven in all, were gassed badly enough to be sent to the hospital. Many of them died; most of them were out for the duration of the war—all reasons why I never saw any of the men who made the attack on Hill 204 at the front again.

Did you ever smell a dead mouse? This will give you about as much idea of what a group of long dead soldiers smell like as will one grain of sand give you an idea of Atlantic City's beaches. A group of men were sent to Hill 204 to make a reconnaissance, to report on conditions there as well as to bury the dead. The story was a very pathetic one. The men were still lying there nearly two weeks later just as they had fallen. I knew all of these men intimately and it was indeed painful to learn of their condition. Some had apparently lived for some time; had tried to dress their own wounds, or their comrades had dressed them; but later they had died there. I was especially pleased that the capture of the German soldiers had made it possible to bring back all the wounded in our sector. Many of the men had been pumped full of machine gun bullets—shot almost beyond recognition. A hundred or so bullets, even in a dead man's body, is not a pretty sight. One of our men was lying with a German bayonet through him—not unlike a pin through a large beetle. Bayonets are hard to remove when once they have been caught between the ribs, especially the saw-tooth bayonets many of the Germans carried. To dislodge them it is usually necessary to shoot once or more to loosen the bayonet. This German had not waited, but had left his gun and passed on. The little Italian boy was still lying on the barbed wire, his eyes open and his helmet hanging back on his head. There had been much shrapnel and some of the bodies were torn almost beyond recognition. This was the first experience at handling and burying the dead for many of our men. It was a trying experience as I was to personally find somewhat later. The identification tags removed from the dead were corroded white, and had become imbedded in the putrid flesh. Even after the burial, when these tags were brought back to the company, they smelled so horribly that some of the officers became extremely sick. One huge man—a giant of a man—who was shot cleanly between the eyes was lying among a group of dead Americans and Germans (that must have been Corporal Graves); and a middle- aged sergeant, who must have been Sergeant George Amole. There is nothing much more pitiful than a battlefield after a battle.

There are two chief reasons why a soldier feels fear: First, that he will not get home to see his loved ones again; but, most of all, picturing himself in the same position as some of the dead men we saw. They lay there face up, usually in the rain, their eyes open, their faces pale and chalk-like, their gold teeth showing. That is in the beginning. After that they are usually too horrible to think about. We buried them as fast as we could—Germans, French and Americans alike. Get them out of sight, but not out of memory. I can remember hundreds and hundreds of dead men. I would know them now if I were to meet them in a hereafter. I could tell them where they were lying and how they were killed—whether with shell fire, gas, machine gun or bayonet. In the town of Varennes there were scores of dead Germans lying around. They had held their positions until the last moment. Many of them had been killed by the tremendous bombardment as they tried to leave. Others had been killed by our advance troops. I spent three days in this town as our battalion was in reserve and I came to know all the dead Germans as I walked around. Later perhaps a hundred of them were laid out for burial. I saw them lying there and I am sure that I could have taken every one of them back to the point where he had died and put him in the exact position in which he had lain.

In the beginning we had a fear of the dead. We hated to touch them. Some of the hardest experiences of my life were taking the identification tags from my dead friends. The first dead man I touched was Philip Beketich, an Austrian baker who was with our company. He was wounded in the battle of Fismes. I had tried to save his life by carrying him through the heavy enemy fire and putting him in one of the cellars of the French houses. He was shot in my arms as I carried him. A few hours later I found time to go round and find how he was. He was dead—stiff and cold. He had quite a splendid development of the pectoral muscles— the big muscles of the chest. Working as a baker had apparently been responsible for that. I had to remove his identification tags, and they had slipped down between his collar bones and the flesh of his chest. They were held there, and it took an effort to get them out. I thrilled and chilled with horror as I touched him.

Just a bit later I had to touch my very good friend Lester Michaels, a fine young fellow who had been a star football player on our company team, and a good piano player who entertained us when such an instrument was available. He had been walking past me in Fismes, bent well over. " Keep down, Mike," I said. " There's a sniper shooting through here." Just then Mike fell, with a look of astonishment on his face. "What's the matter, Mike?" I asked. He replied, " They've got me," shook a few times and lay dead upon his face with his legs spread apart—shot through the heart. He lay there for more than a day. There was a terrific battle on and we had no chance to help the wounded—certainly not the dead. I was running short of ammunition and I needed the cartridges in Mike's belt. I tried to unfasten his belt, but I could not reach it. Finally I had to turn him completely over. It was quite an effort owing to the spread-eagle manner in which he lay. His body was hard and cold, and I saw his dead face—difficult to describe the feeling I had. But necessity demanded that I unloosen his belt and take his ammunition and still later his identification tag. After the war I heard from his relatives who wanted to know exactly how he had died.

There are many people who sought this information. They liked to know whether the soldier was killed by shell fire, whether while fighting hand to hand, while running to the attack, or in some phase of defensive work. It was hard to touch these dead men at first. My people at home, hearing of what I was passing through, expected me to come back hard, brutal, callous, careless. But I didn't even want to take a dead mouse out of a trap when I was home. Yet over there I buried seventy-eight men one morning. I didn't dig the holes for them, of course, but I did take their personal belongings from them to return to their people— their rings, trinkets, letters and identification tags. They were shot up in a great variety of ways, and it was not pleasant, but I managed to eat my quota of bread and meat when it came up with no opportunity to wash my hands.

One night I was hiking along through the darkness going into the Argonne battle. We fell out for a moment at the side of the road, and I sat on what I thought was a partially buried sand bag. After resting there for a time a comrade told me that I was sitting on a dead man. I didn't even move. I didn't think he would mind. At times men died in such a position that they were hard to bury. The ground was hard; there was danger of shell fire as long as we were on a burial detail. We'd try hard to make the graves as shallow as possible. So often men were buried in the holes other men had dug along the side of the road as they advanced. A rifle or bayonet would be thrust in the ground at the head of the grave, and a man's identification tag placed upon it. Soon the remainder of the army would be moving up—the machine gunners, the artillery, the supply trucks. They would have to pass on a narrow road. The truck would run over the grave and knock down the improvised cross; there was no further way to identify the dead man. For this and a score of other reasons it was folly to bring back the men who had died in France. I am sure that few of them had been properly identified and were actually the men they were supposed to be. Later in the war we always left one tag upon the dead man and turned the other in to headquarters after making a report of the death. A cross would be erected and marked. These men could be identified. We had a coordinated position on the map so that the body could be found. But earlier in the war when both tags were placed outside the grave, and later lost, the body could not be identified.

When a man died in a sitting or kneeling position it was impossible to straighten him out—difficult to dig a deep enough hole to cover him. More than once I would try to straighten out the body—stand on the legs and the head would come up; stand on the head and the legs would come up; finally compromise by burying the upper body, letting the legs stick up for a cross, and hanging the helmet and gas mask to the human cross. Other times it was necessary to put a big man in a comparatively small hole. We would step on his middle to bend it sufficiently to make him fit the hole.

One of my most poignant memories of the war took place in the battle of Fismes, which I will get to presently. For several days we had been crawling around the town, firing from windows, cellars, attics and from behind the stone wall in the back of the house yards. This got tiresome, and finally the fellow next to me—a candidate by the name of Vaugn (a man who had qualified for a commission through a special course of schooling, and was waiting only a vacancy to receive it)—raised up, laid his gun upon the top of the wall and started to shoot over the wall. That was more comfortable and it was much easier to see what was being shot at. It was the method used by the old Indian fighters as they fired over the stockades of their forts. I should have known better with my previous battle experience, but I thought, " If Vaugn can shoot over the wall, I can too." Soon we were banging away merrily. But after several shots each I suddenly saw Vaugn's helmet go sailing down over the slight hill. I looked at him and the entire top of his head was off— apparently a dum dum type of bullet (one in which the lead had been cut so that it would spread the instant it struck, tearing a terrific hole in the object it hit) had flattened against his helmet or tin hat, and had taken off his head to a level with his eyes and ears. He had been kneeling; his buttocks went back a bit, his head forward and his brains ran out there in front of me like soup from a pot. I did not fire over another wall. The sniper had his choice to pick one or the other of us. For some unknown reason he chose Vaugn. I'm here and he's gone. Vaugn lay there for a couple of days; finally he was carried down and stored in the room where we had the other dead piled up like logs of wood; but he had to have his own place in the corner. It was gruesome enough.

Moving Toward the Front

THE nerve strain of the constant gas attacks was severe. We were wakened up at every hour of the day and night to stand to in preparation for an attack, to prepare to move on, or to at least put on our gas masks. The Germans were expected to start a new drive most any minute, and we were in constant readiness. The next night the false alarms ceased to the extent of really bringing us an order to move. As we went up we passed an outfit coming back from the front who were so tired that they didn't even answer when we asked them to what outfit they belonged. There was intermittent shelling at this point and many of us had narrow escapes from death. About twilight we started off in single file, turning and twisting as we went forward to relieve what we were told was the 30th Infantry.

We learned for the first time that there was really a war on. One of the greatest barrages in the history of the war was being put over. The earth and the air constantly trembled with the force of the explosions.

From this point we could see the flares at the front. Flares were being constantly fired to prevent a surprise attack. It was hard to keep together going to the front. Confusion was everywhere. There were innumerable false alarms about gas. The high explosive burned one's throat so it was easy to believe that gas was near. At this point machine gun bullets were droning through the trees overhead and cut branches were constantly falling.

It was pitch dark, and each flare would show us details of the No Man's Land between the lines. Dead men were lying everywhere in the most grotesque positions. Some of them lay as if sound asleep. One man's head rested so comfortably on his arm that I could not believe he was dead. Others had been blown to pieces several times, and some were just arms and legs or torsos. This night approach to the front made us sick. (I could not help but think how much nicer our first trip to the front at Hill 204 had been.) There were many dead horses lying around. We had difficulty in finding our positions. It was beginning to turn faintly light in the east, and we knew that in a short time we would be targets for German machine guns and artillery.

The artillery preparation had been terrific. We were told that it had been the greatest barrage of the war. For miles the shell holes almost touched at every point. The Germans were preparing their way for a drive through Chateau Thierry and on to Meaux and Paris. Regiments of our men who had been billeted in the woods had been caught in the barrage and practically wiped out. It was one of the hard-hit outfits that we were going forward to relieve.

There was only one encouraging feature about this whole phase of the war. The allied espionage force had learned every detail of the impending attack, and just one hour before the Germans were to start their drive to Paris, the Allies started their drive to Berlin. The allied artillery caught the Germans all prepared to march in columns of squads, and thousands of them were killed right there. The frightful fire of the Allies changed the entire course of the war. We were told that the men of the 39th American Regiment had been responsible for stopping the Germans here. They had pulled the French seventy-five artillery guns forward with man power, and fired them directly at the ranks of the advancing Germans, breaking up the attack. To this point the Germans had been advancing. Now the tide had turned, and the ebb was to flow back toward Germany with ever-increasing speed; but not without a great struggle. The least we can say for the Germans is that they are good soldiers and tenacious fighters. They follow instructions, and if they are told to hold the line, they hold it until they are killed.

As we finally found the men we were to relieve we were all thoroughly sick. The ground was rotten with tear and vomiting gas. Mustard gas too was all around. War is bad enough without the constant torture of gas. (In this newest war, and wars to come, human ingenuity has made even more horrible gases which will be used, in addition to the old gases, of a most devastating and terrible nature.)

Shelling continued bitterly all day from both sides. The German shells were falling a bit short but we had a number of wounded each hour during the day. Toward dusk, when the volume of artillery increased, there were three or four wounded men every little while. It was bad enough while most of the shells were falling short, but about eleven o'clock that night the range lifted and the shells were falling right among the men. Some were evidently Austrian eighty-eights, a shell with such speed and so flat a trajectory that it arrived before the sound of it was heard coming. Others were the German seventy-sevens and still larger shells. There was a constant cry for stretcher bearers, for the Red Cross—the most diabolical screaming and moaning that could be imagined. Human beings, lying helpless, no way to fight back, not knowing who would be killed by the next shell. It is hard to be brave at night. We could be brave in the broad daylight, rushing forward on an attack like that one on Hill 204. But shelling at night saps the courage from the bravest. Everyone lies there and shakes. Only the strongest can keep in their right minds. It is on such nights as this that men go out of their heads.

. (The same thing is taking place along the Western Front now. The communiques say that all was quiet last night along the front except for intermittent artillery duels. We read about the artillery duels daily, and wonder why the French and English don't really attack. How many of us can imagine what the soldiers in the advance posts are going through—the French and Germans between the Maginot and the Siegfried lines.)

One never knows how he will behave under such an ordeal. Some men weep; others shake; some stand up, nonchalantly, apparently not caring whether they get killed or wounded; some tell crude jokes; but mostly the men dig and dig, so that only direct hits will get them—grimly enduring the torture that human beings subject each other to, not knowing who will go next. " C'est la guerre " was the favorite expression at times like this. We spent five days in that place which was popularly called death valley. I don't know whether there was any real object in staying and dying there, but we were ordered into that valley and there we stayed. .

There were always a few maniacs around—men who had lost their minds through shell fire and had to be overpowered and bound. Some men were buried alive and we were constantly busy digging the live ones out. Many smothered before we could get them out. At times we would have a group of wounded and stretcher bearers making their way up the hill; a shell would fall among them and nearly all would be killed. So many men were wounded—wounded again—and were still under fire. One sergeant in our company was blown up three successive times—each time wounded still further but not killed. He did die prematurely sometime after he went home, and this may have been the cause of it.

I had endless narrow escapes. Later we were to go out through the lines with shelter halfs and pick up all the arms, legs and other human parts we could find— parts of the men we had known and trained with for months. That would have been the right time for us to go over the top. We could have torn the enemy to pieces, not realizing that they were men just like ourselves, who were just as anxious to live, just as reluctant to fight and kill—men who only followed the instructions of the men higher up. Sometimes we found two or three men dead together and so badly mixed up that we could not tell whether we got the right parts in the right grave or not. The men suffered and so did the horses.

The horses—poor dumb animals, a rival of the dogs for the honor of being man's best friend. Men were drafted, taken from the midst of their work, homes and families, their hopes, desires, and expectations, and sent to this distant country to die as their part in " making the world safe for democracy." But they could think, they could reason, they could listen to the words of their superiors, be sold on the idea that they were fighting for the right. But the poor horses—they were taken from some quiet pasture on a peaceful, remote, American farm. They were drafted into the American service as artillery horses, to pull supply wagons, kitchens, or even light machine guns. And if they survived the war they were not sent home to their pastures from which they had come, to their familiar surroundings and their friends (for even a horse seems to have the ability to recognize its friends and to be glad to see them again).

The men who lived went home to their families, started life anew and have obtained a fair measure of happiness and satisfaction from life in the majority of cases. But the horses and the American mules remained in France. They were sold for a song to work in French cities and on French farms. I saw many of them after the war. While in our service they became accustomed to the " Giddap " of our drivers. They had to learn enough of French to know that " Allez vite, vite, vite " meant to pull out in a hurry or be lashed with a huge black snake whip. That was their reward—a life of servitude, of scanty rations, of hard work, if they survived the war.

Horses cannot be dispensed with even in the present wars. There are not enough roads. Particularly in France and Belgium the mud is deep, gummy—impassable for tanks, nearly so for trucks—during much of the year. They are doomed if they must leave the road even for a short distance to pass a broken truck, a hole left by shell or bomb. But horses can pull the guns, the supplies and the equipment through the muddy fields. Horses will always be required in the fighting of wars.

They have always been a necessary part of war. The cavalry has been all important from the days of Genghis Khan, the conqueror, down through the wars of history—Greece, Rome, Persia, early France and England. British and French horses carried their masters to the Holy Lands to fight during the Crusades. They died there. During the middle ages they were killed in all sorts of horrible ways. They were used by the Spanish conquerors who visited this country and devastated entire tribes of natives in the sixteenth century. Later even the Indians came to depend on horses, to use them in their battles. In all the wars in which our nation has been involved, horses have played a most important part. They died by the millions during this time.

Uncomplainingly, courageously, striving, until they met their deaths, to do as their drivers willed. Life at the front was a particularly difficult one for the horses. Most of the water in wells or streams was unfit to drink. Usually a reasonable amount of water could be brought up for the men, but the horses too frequently had to go without. And a look at the gaunt, rib-showing horses near the front was pretty good proof that their rations were frequently scanty too. The drivers of the horses took great pride in their animal helpers but it was not possible to give them proper care while at the front. A horse could not talk, tell when it was sick, would continue on until it dropped never to rise again.

Men could get under cover during shell fire or at least lie flat, or in a shallow trench. But the horses had to stand, to be the target for any shells or shrapnel which came their way. In those days of 1918 gas masks had not yet been devised to protect horses from gas attacks. Many of them died from gas, but still more of them lingered on for weeks or months with their lungs half eaten away, continuing to do their duty as long as they were able. No decorations for these animal heroes, who made war possible throughout the ages. If they fell, others took their places and they were forgotten. They were buried if there was time, after they had been killed, for horses, like men—only on a larger scale—were not things of beauty when they were dead. They would swell up to twice their normal size, their powerful legs would extend out straight and stiff as steel rods, and burial was a problem. The Indians in Nebraska had accomplished it by covering the men and horses with dirt. The Indians believed that the warriors would need their horses to carry them through the battles in the Land of the Great Spirit, and would bury a man's horses with him. This was a custom of the Egyptians too—to kill and bury a warrior's horses so that they could travel with him in the hereafter. In an Indian mound which I saw being opened were an equal number of human and horse skeletons. Men and horses have been inseparable since the horse has been large enough to be of service. And no one knows how many hundreds of thousands or millions of years that has been. The horse is believed to have been descended from a dog-like early type of animal, which had its beginning way back in the Pleistocene age. And they have served man almost since there has been man.

One of my most painful memories at the front was seeing a shell drop near two artillery horses. The horses broke away from the tree to which they were secured and galloped up through the field. One of the horses was hit in the abdomen; its intestines dropped out, dragged on the ground, and soon its feet were entangled in its own intestines to the point where it fell down and could not run any farther. It lay there with its head up for what seemed to be an endless period. It seemed to be more surprised concerning how it had become entangled in its own parts than to be in pain. We were sorry that it was so situated by this time that it was difficult to put it out of its misery.

It is bad enough for men, who can think and reason, to continue to fight throughout the ages, but it isn't fair to take poor dumb animals and force them to work and die in the fighting. They went on suffering, willingly performing their duty, in spite of gas and minor wounds; in spite of being ill, starved, sick and exhausted.

In just a few more days that company, and our battalion in particular, was to have as stirring and as horrible an ordeal as any battalion in the entire war ever experienced. Few of this full strength company, including replacements, were to walk out of the inferno in which we were to be sent. Our splendid captain, Arch Williams, was to be wounded. Captain Lynch of B Company was to be killed and lie for days in front of our line, as a number of men were killed or wounded in an endeavor to get him back. Captain Law of our battalion was to be killed. Captain Haller, who became acting major, later a lieutenant colonel who spent his time as acting major, deep in the safety of a dugout, was our only captain to survive the coming action. Captain Thompson of M Company was to be killed and many, many others of our friends and comrades.

Following the Battle

THAT night there was little return fire from the Germans. Our artillery was going in full force, blasting the Germans out, giving the poor devils over there as much and more as we had suffered the preceding nights. The war that night was a tremendous thing. For miles and miles the guns winked, the reports roared, and the sounds of shells filled the air. The next day we saw dead men or parts of them in every imaginable position. Most of them had died suddenly with their eyes open. One man had apparently been struck right in the stomach by a direct hit. We saw one aviator who had been brought down here. His plane had crashed. It had burned up and there was a burnt skeleton still in the plane, but little more than buttons to prove that it was an American.

There were many horses about killed by gas. (The poor horses did not have gas masks in that war.) They would be puffed to enormous size and the white mucus had run from their eyes and noses. Near there I saw a broken down German wagon; the driver was still on the seat but he was dead. Nearby was another German who was headless. Apparently his head had been carried away completely by a shell.

We usually rested during the day, but this day the enemy had moved back and it was our work to follow. Our company was now about one-half of its former strength, there being just a few over a hundred of our original strength of two hundred and fifty-eight men left. (There should have been two hundred and fifty men in this company, but there were a few more than the usual quota.) At one time as we marched along, two enemy planes rushed toward us, flying very low. Everyone rushed off the road just in time to escape the machine gun fire he had aimed at us. The plane came back and although we knew it was folly to try to hit such a rapidly-moving object, nearly the entire company stood up and fired at the plane—of course to no avail.

Here our company was still further decimated by men who had recently been gassed. Some of them were really sick; others were gold brickers who wanted to escape the front and pretended to be gassed or at least to be gassed worse than they were.

Many of the farmhouses and some old mills were scarcely damaged. We passed occasional dead men where German machine guns had been, a dead horse, and even saw a dead German floating in the still water above an old mill.

We paused in Varennes only briefly and soon marched north. Signs of the war were everywhere. The artillery became more and more insistent and we felt that a great drive was about to start again. We could see that there had been a fight just a few hours before. The holes where the men had dug in along the side of the road were everywhere. We passed improvised field hospitals with great rows of wounded lying on stretchers outside the walls. There were far more men than they could possibly care for. Many of them still wore their bloody emergency bandages which had been a part of their own Red Cross kits. Some of them were highly nervous and screamed when our own batteries fired. Little did they know it, but some of them were lucky. They were still alive—out of the war—while many of the men who marched by with our troops were soon to die. Up to this time we had lost only a handful of officers, usually lowly second lieutenants. We had not lost a captain or a field officer. But soon, in a matter of about two weeks, we were to lose eleven of our captains in the fighting in the town of Fismes. Our own captain went along, laughing and joking with the men, keeping up the morale to the best of his ability.

We were thoroughly weary at this time; had hiked all night and nearly all day. We were getting closer to the battle, for we began to pass many dead soldiers. They had held on as long as they could and sold their lives dearly. For what? I often wondered. They had but one life to live and they had lost it before they really began to live. We passed a wrecked field ambulance. The driver was dead, and one of the wounded was still in the wreck. It was evident that he too was dead.

All night long it had rained—a nasty, cold, penetrating drizzle. Many of the men had thrown away every available bit of equipment and did not have coats, shelter halfs or ponchos. They paid for their error this night. It was brutal to slop along through the mud, hardly able to see the back of the man in front of you—so easy to get lost, in spite of the fact that men were stationed at every fork or crossroads to direct our march. Many times during the war sections of our troops were lost because some man would fail to keep contact—would wander off at a tangent. The men behind, having no idea at all where they were going, would follow along, and the company or half a battalion might be kilometers away before they found that they were travelling the wrong way. And then the weary march back to the place where we had gone wrong, and forward again! We marched far enough in France, but so much of the marching was unnecessary. Someone must have known exactly where we were going, but the line officers and their men had no idea at this stage of the war where our destination might be. We stopped when we were told to stop; we packed up when we were ordered to pack up; we went forward when we were told to go forward—no idea why or where or when we would catch up with the Germans who were moving fast at this time.

All along the way were signs of their passing. A broken wagon was beside us at one halt. It was minus one wheel. The horses had been unhitched and taken forward. Usually there was nothing to eat on these wagons, but here was something—and different too— black bread and apple butter. Fall was approaching, and it was quite likely that the regimental cooks with

the German army before us had picked the partially ripe apples in some French orchard, and had made this apple butter. It was packed in big crocks, open at the top; it would not have remained preserved for long in that condition, so it must have been intended for immediate consumption by the German troops.

Not knowing what minute the whistles would blow again, we hastily filled our drinking cups with apple butter—a full pint each—helped ourselves to some of the bread and were enjoying a late midnight supper when we received the order to go forward. The apple butter was good—the black bread hard and quite unpalatable. I covered the bread with apple butter and managed to get it down. But that wasn't the last I knew of it. It remained in my stomach all the next day as a lead-like, indigestible mass. I had a cast-iron stomach, and could barely keep this bread down; what digestions the Germans must have developed to eat this sort of food for years! Perhaps they had gradually become accustomed to it. Our bread rations during most of the war consisted of the big round French loaves which were quite palatable. The bread was brought up to the front, piled high in open trucks. It was handled, time and time again, by men who almost never had the opportunity to wash. It was piled along the road, fell off the trucks to roll through the excrement of animals, then back on the trucks. But we ate it with relish when we received it. Dirt seldom kills.

It was beginning to get slightly light at this time and we knew that soon our hike would be over. In a few minutes we left the road and pulled into a woods a short distance away. The Germans had been here, apparently, for some time, for as usual their refuse and their equipment were everywhere. There were a few deep dugouts—not quite enough for everyone, but our platoon was lucky, and found one in which we could spend the day; a day of as much rest as we could get before starting another weary night march.

German dugouts were quite German. Deep in the bowels of the earth, they were refuges of safety which must have been occupied by the Germans for months at a time. There were numerous pictures on the wall, nearly all cut from German magazines and German newspapers. There was the Kaiser, helmet, mustache, beard and all. His short arm was particularly noticeable as he sat upon a white horse. The German troops were goose-stepping by. There were many examples of German humor in the cartoons upon the walls. I could not read the inscription but I could see John Bull, Uncle Sam, and Marshal Foch being chased by a little dachshund wearing a German helmet. And there were scores upon scores of German postcards which were quite lewd to say the least. There was a big chap in our group by the name of Tiedeman. He had been studying for the ministry and apparently was the only man among us who understood German. I asked him to translate some of the inscriptions of the postcards. I could see him blushing, and then he would say, " You don't want to know what it says; it's not nice."

The days were long in these dugouts, for actual night extended only from nine-thirty or ten until about half- past three in the morning. It was rather hard to put in the hours. Considerable of the time was spent in reading—not reading of books and magazines; we rarely received newspapers at the front. The London Mail and the Chicago Tribune came to us at times, and when they did we eagerly read every word of the advertisements as well as the news stories. We heard here first of the hot fighting of the Americans who were a bit in front of us; of the terrific fighting in Fere en Tardenois. The Americans had taken the town from the Prussian guard and repelled attack after attack, counter attack upon counter attack by the Prussian guard.

There was intense fighting at a place called Sergy— and the usual atrocity stories. We heard many of them. They went something like this: " At Malines, a two-year-old child got in the way of the marching column of German troops. A soldier bayoneted it and carried it away on his bayonet." " In Tamines, children were slaughtered for no apparent motive. The soldiers tied up civilian prisoners, prodded them with bayonets, put lighted cigarettes in their noses and ears and shot them. Eyes were burned out with red-hot pokers. Civilian snipers were tortured in every possible way. In Vomille they had been spread-eagled in the public square; a rat would be placed under an iron kettle upon the man or woman's bare abdomen, then a fire built upon the top of the kettle. The victim was tortured first by the frantic running around of the rat on his or her bare abdomen when it became nearly smothered and terror-stricken and pain-filled from the smoke and heat; then it would eat down through the human living flesh to escape." " We found the dead body of a girl. Her arms were nailed to the door in extended fashion; her left breast was half cut away. A young boy of five or six years of age lay on a doorstep with his two hands nearly severed from the arms, but still hanging to them. At another place were the dead bodies of a man and a woman, a girl and a boy; each of them had both hands cut off at the wrists and both feet above the ankle. Child of seven beheaded. A whole family killed, including a young girl, because the girl would not give herself to the Germans. Burned to death in their houses. All the women violated. The entire German regiment drunk," etc.

The above are exact quotations from the Bryce report which specialized in outrages against women and children. They are samples of the sort of stories we were always hearing.

I never saw any examples of such torture, killing and mutilation. I later talked to many French and Belgian women. Perhaps a thousand of them worked in the salvage dumps and warehouses outside of St. Nazaire the summer after the war. My special friend in that locality was a medical officer, a captain, and I spent considerable time with him. The German prisoners who worked in the salvage department were reporting in considerable numbers with venereal diseases. Certainly they weren't in a position to force their attentions upon the French and Belgian women. It might be thought that the women were passing the disease on to the Germans as a matter of revenge, but more than likely it was just carelessness on their part, and a generosity with their persons which was characteristic of most of the women in this part of Europe.

One never knew, when he went out with a French girl after the war was over, whether she last had been with an American general or a black Senegalese trooper. It seemed to make no difference to them. Horses were black, and red, and white, but they were horses, and we used them to pull our vehicles. What then was the difference between black, yellow, brown or white men?

I asked a number of them, who had been in France or Belgium behind the German lines, how they were treated. They would laugh and giggle endlessly and tell me that they got plenty of loving. They seemed to enjoy it—were willing enough victims.

But the atrocity stories never ceased. It is the method still used to stir up the soldiers to fight—to persuade the civilian population of the necessity to fight. Chancellor Hitler informs Ambassador Henderson that the Poles are torturing the German minority—that they are castrating the Germans. Henderson admitted that he knew of one case of the castration of a German sex maniac. Hitler insisted that there were more. These stories are multiplied, stretched, distorted, magnified, and believed by many people. It gave Hitler the excuse for all of his expeditions into other lands which he annexed.

Other nations used similar methods. It was the carefully arranged and distributed propaganda—particularly the horror stories—which got us into the war. No doubt there was considerable shooting of civilians. It has happened in Poland. They resent the invasion of their native land. They fight back in every possible way. Women, so the papers informed us, recently, in Poland, "fought like tigers." They are particularly vicious and stop at nothing when they find wounded upon the field. Torture and emasculation is only part of what they do when they find wounded enemy soldiers. They take pot shots at the invading troops, and the invaders—the Germans in this case—retaliate by ordering what seem to be minor massacres. They order all snipers or those found with arms in their possession to be shot. The stories grow with the telling, and soon wholesale murder and rape are reported over the entire world.

We didn't know what to believe. But we didn't want to be crucified if we were captured, and I planned to never be captured—to die if need be, but not to give up. And before going on with my story, I should mention that I talked, personally, to practically every American who had been captured by the Germans. They returned through the huge replacement and casual camp, St. Agnain, while I was there. And the worst that any of them received, so they told me, was a good kick in the pants to make them hurry while they were loitering along hoping to be captured by our advancing troops. The Americans' treatment may have been better than that of the other Allies. The Germans knew that they were losing; they weren't particularly anxious to fight the Americans, for most of them had relatives here in our country. Many of them planned to come to America after the war, and thousands of them did come. They knew that their treatment of Americans would be an important factor in the sort of peace terms they would receive when they were finally forced to capitulate. So perhaps the treatment our men received was not a good sample of what had happened to the usual prisoners of war. I know that there were many times when there was no opportunity to take prisoners back. They couldn't be permitted to run around loose. It was customary to disarm them, remove their leather belts with the big Gott Mitt Uns (God with us) belts and cut off the buttons of the trousers so that they would be forced to walk holding up their own trousers. There was little chance to fight while engaged in holding up trousers. I had frequently heard that guards were started back with prisoners with the orders that they should take them back ten miles and return in half an hour, which was really an order to get rid of the prisoners. I do not know whether there was truth in this constantly-recurring story or not.

Death From the Sky

WE did a lot of reading besides reading the newspapers. " Reading our shirts " —for all of us were infested with a variety of cooties— huge, hungry, grey-backed body lice. There was the constant insistence that the Germans had a different kind of body lice than the ones we carried on our persons. It was said that a German louse could always be identified by the stripe down its back and by its oversize feet. I seemed to have several kinds of lice on me nearly all of the time. I say nearly, for there was a time in the Argonne forest when I had mustard gas, French itch, and blood boils but not cooties. My blood finally became so bad that even these hardy insects, which almost plague the life out of the soldier at the front, found me unpalatable. Many hours were spent reading, or closely examining the seams of our clothes in our search for the huge grey backs. When German dugouts had been unoccupied for a few days or a week the lice were particularly hungry and pounced upon us with such enthusiasm that sleeping was difficult.

But this day there was to be more excitement than " reading our shirts." Early in the afternoon we heard the roaring of planes, the barking of anti-aircraft guns, and finally the dropping of bombs. One young fellow in our dugout was pretty badly shell shocked; he had refused evacuation to the rear, thus demonstrating the rarest and finest kind of courage; but he became terror- stricken anew at the sound of the airplanes and the bombs.

I tried to reassure him, held him tight with my arms around him, talking to him as fast as I could. " Jim, don't let it get you down; it's nothing—just our planes going over to bomb the Jerries, to give them a taste of what we have received so often." " But, Bob, you must be mistaken; those are bombs I hear—German bombs, I bet." " No, Jim, they're not bombs, just our artillery over there in the woods firing at the Germans." He would be quiet for a time, but tremble and shake every time he heard a falling shell or a bomb somewhere near.

I climbed up the stairway, which was little more than a ladder, to see what was going on. It had been comparatively quiet in the dugout; only the sounds of the bombs which fell near had been heard. Pandemonium had broken loose up above. There must have been a dozen German planes. A smaller- number of allied planes, either French or American, were trying hard to stop them. At one point I saw two planes going round and round in a circle, each trying to catch up sufficiently to get on the tail of the other and to shoot him down. I could see their tracer bullets. The Germans had the best planes at this stage of the battle. We had heard rumors of Baron von Richthofen: that his circus was opposite us, sweeping the skies clean of allied planes. The Allies were getting quite the worst of this battle. I saw three of their planes come down one after the other. Only one German plane headed back with smoke issuing in great clouds from somewhere within its mechanism. Perhaps it made the German lines; it may have landed and burst into flame on our side of the lines. One of the allied planes fell near, coming down with a tremendous crash in the nearby woods.

Meanwhile the German bombers went rather methodically at their task. Their objective was a group of one hundred and fifty-five millimeter artillery which had been emplaced near, and must have been creating considerable damage, as the Germans were so anxious to destroy them. The German planes circled low, with the machine gunners and the anti-aircraft men firing desperately throughout. To the everlasting credit of that small group of artillerymen I must say that they fired with redoubled fury, realizing that they were doing important damage to the enemy. They disregarded the planes, their machine guns, and the falling bombs. They were rewarded for their efforts, for far off ahead we heard a sound not unlike that of many guns and saw huge clouds of fire and smoke extending high into the air. Our guns had made a direct hit upon a huge German ammunition dump—ammunition that had been moved forward to assist in the Germans' drive toward Paris, and which they had been unable to remove as yet during their retreat. It was precious to the Germans. They needed every shell of it. But that little group of our brave artillerymen had managed to blow up enough German munitions and supplies to require an entire bond issue to replace.

I could see the bombs falling. They would seem to come directly toward me—seemed to be aimed exactly at my head—then I would drop down the mouth of the dugout, only to find that the bomb had fallen a quarter of a mile away, near the battery. One bomb did fall close enough to cause considerable of the ceiling of our dugout to fall down. I was glad, when this almost direct hit landed, that the Germans had been good mechanics and had done a good job of reinforcing the ceiling of this dugout, or there would have been an end to all that was left of our platoon.

The hours of this day slowly wore away, and soon we received the order to pack up. Ready to move again! We went up a hill, past endless woods, with occasional cultivated fields on either side which could be seen by the light of a thin, cold-looking moon. Occasionally we passed ruined towns, occupied by advanced groups of our troops. Blankets over the broken windows nevertheless permitted a little light to filter through. There were halts every little while, as the officers who were leading held a conference concerning the road we were to take, or stopped to examine maps to be sure that they were going right.

This endless starting and stopping, falling out and falling in, travelling along in single file with a line which extends for miles; catching up to the troops ahead at times, falling back when the road was narrow; going off into the fields to let a truck or an ambulance pass; thick mud from the rain of the night and the day before—the memories of the trials and tribulations are a bit dim at present, but I do remember that we hated and loathed them so much, the men grouched and grumbled about them so much, that we became almost anxious to get to the front and stop this endless hiking and dilly-dallying along. We were often told that we were to halt for an hour's rest only to be aroused again in five or ten minutes—to move on another hundred feet before we stopped again. Why couldn't we have been permitted to really rest for an hour?

None of the men were so strong at this time. Some were slightly gassed, many had dysentery in greater or lesser degree, all were weak and discouraged. It had clouded up again and now began to rain—first a thin cold mist, and finally, with ever-increasing tempo, it came down in torrents. Why did it always have to rain at night? we thought. There was an excessive amount of rain this summer—rain which was to flood streams and make a quagmire of the roads we traversed on the long weary march to the Vesle River. We staggered along this night in the rain; stopped once or twice in shattered towns. The order was given that all should remain beside the road, not to go into the ruined houses. But everyone disregarded the rules, and there was great difficulty getting the men up and off again when the order to move came. A moment's relaxation was a big help. I felt constantly fatigued; my back ached, my feet hurt; life was at a very low ebb at this time. But I cheered myself up a bit by remembering that I was stronger than the rest. They must all feel so much worse than I did. The going became ever more difficult and finally we were ordered to halt. Off the road we went—right into a quagmire of mud. Was this where we were to spend the day? Evidently so, for we were still sitting there when dawn came. Mud everywhere! Not a dry spot on us, we were cold, and most uncomfortable. I had the thought there that if we were so desperately cold and uncomfortable in August, how must it be in the actual winter months? I could appreciate why the British and French soldiers had trench feet—why their feet became swollen to nearly twice their normal size after months and months of being in the mud up to their knees. My feet were tender and sore already. I wondered if they would ever be clean and dry again. It made me almost long to go back, even to the horrors of the hospital. At least we were clean and dry back there.

I was sore all over, partly from the mud, partly from the constant hiking and the rubbing from my equipment, the galling of tender parts of my anatomy, but also because of mustard gas that seldom left us entirely free for a moment. A chance to wash would have helped it somewhat. With the coming of broad daylight, I could see a narrow-gauge track down over the hill with abandoned cars lying and rusting beside it. Apparently it was part of a coal mine which had been unworked for years. But there was a small stream of fresh water below the tracks, and that was my chief interest at the moment. I took the best bath I could without soap, washed every stitch of clothes I wore including the shoes, and left them lie upon the grass while I took a swim. I was joined by some friends and we forgot the war for the moment. Comfort at last! Feeling the comparatively clean water against my skin, being free from the bites of insects at least for a time, freedom from the discomfort and the burning of the mustard gas and the galled flesh! The attempts of the sun early in the morning seemed rather futile in its efforts to drive the mists and the clouds away. But now it was out in full force, transforming the quagmire of the night into more of a normal world.

There was a sadly demolished farm up the stream a bit. Some of our fellows went up there to sleep. Up there were mud, dirt, filth, dust, tiles from the roof, glass and stones, horse manure, cast-off material in general, and more than likely cooties. I preferred to stay where I was, in the fresh sunshine, lying on the clean grass after my swim. It was safer where I was, for about the middle of the afternoon a single gun of the Germans started to shell the farm. Perhaps two shells a minute came over, crashing into the already shattered walls. Before our men could evacuate the farm there were cries of stretcher bearers, first aid, gas, and the war which seemed far away for the moment was on once again. I heard a shell coming my way, with its " z-z-z-z-z" ever growing louder and closer, finally a BOW, close enough that pieces of debris fell over me. I reached for my shovel and pick, and started desperately to dig in. The ground was soft. I was making good time, loaning my shovel or pick to my companions but commandeering it again when I wanted it. On one hike there were just eight shovels and picks in our entire company of over two hundred and sixty men at that time. I had two of them. Each man should have an entrenching tool. They tired of carrying them and threw them away to lighten their load. But I realized their value and always carried both the shovel and a pick. I was well rewarded for carrying them and being a close competitor for the title of champion digger of the American army.

My companions were digging in with their fingers, helmets, lids of their mess kits, their bayonets and borrowing my tools at times. I had a hole as long as my body, but only about four inches deep. When I heard a shell coming, I threw myself into the hole; the shell struck head on against a big tree which was near—a tree perhaps a foot in diameter; shattered the base of the tree, cutting it as easily as a scythe cuts through a stalk of grain. The tree, slowly at first, so slowly, started to fall my way, then it came down with a great crash right across my back. The force of it was terrific. I was pinned down so tightly I couldn't move. Had I been a bit slower in digging or not had my entrenching tools, my back would have been broken or the life knocked out of me. As it was I merely had a sore back for a day or two. My comrades lifted the tree off my back, and we continued to dig until we were well under the ground.

I can cite a score of times when being a good digger saved my life. Time spent in digging was time well spent, for when one's body is beneath the ground only a direct hit or one very close will cause damage. Luckily for us the Germans were either short of ammunition or found some other target to shoot at, for the shelling soon ceased.

I slept quietly for a few hours, and was well rested when night came again. That night we were not to move far, for we were already close to the front, being held in reserve while some other outfits tried to break through the stand that the Germans were making a few kilometers away. We remained near the artillery most of that night. The battery closest to us were very long French guns which were placed in a field nearby. They had not been there for many hours and so far had not had the opportunity to hide or camouflage their guns. The guns were firing right over our heads. What a roar they made! As the blast went off and the shells were hurled through the air the grass and weeds for a hundred yards would be flattened down as if a great freight car had passed them by.

In the few intervals of quiet the French artillerymen crowded around. They were most optimistic—told us that the Germans were heading back to Germany. They offered us wine and cognac, and constantly reiterated that soon it would be " finis la guerre. Oo la-la c'est finis maintenant."

There was an American battery a bit farther over. They had their guns tilted high in the air and must have been firing at some targets very far back. There was a balloon company and anti-aircraft guns, both artillery and machine gun, here. The observers in the balloon were busy during all the hours of daylight sending ranges and changes in the ranges to the artillery. As far as I could see the artillery seemed to be at work.

It was truly a magnificent sight, although I could not help but think of what those shells must be doing to the men and horses who were over there back of the German lines. Later I was to learn that the guns were inflicting little enough damage, for the Germans were quartered, horses and all, in tremendous cave-like galleries under the hills. There were many of these in France. They had been used originally to quarry or mine the soft stone of which most of the houses were made. The stone had been taken out with galleries which extended far back into the hills, similar to our Pennsylvania coal mines. Many of these stone mines were being used in years past for the growing of mushrooms. Most of them would easily quarter a regiment or even a division of Germans. They were frequently sheltered in them.

The hundreds of guns in action along that front reminded one of a terrific lightning storm, such as occasionally occurs in the summer. The tongues or jets of flame would leap out from the woods at irregular intervals, shooting far out into the darkness. They winked and flashed, making a spectacle that was truly wonderful to behold. Scores of us just stood there and watched this great display as we would watch the fireworks on the Fourth of July at home. It was a never-to-be-forgotten sight.

The Vesle River— Fismes and Fismette

We remained there near the guns all that night and the next day. The Germans were no longer retreating, but were making a serious stand at previously-prepared positions at the Vesle River and Fismes, we were told. I looked at the map and saw that we weren't many kilos from that town. Since they refused to retreat any farther, evidently it was our work to drive them out. That night, with little more than the flickering light of this same artillery, we swung packs and started toward the front lines. We knew it wouldn't take us long to catch up with the actual fighting, for it was standing still and we were approaching it with each step we took.

A few hundred yards farther on shells began to fall. They seemed to reach us just as we went over the top of a small hill and there far below us we could see the flares far back of the German lines on the hills beyond a town that turned out to be Fismes. Gas seemed to be everywhere, but not in sufficient quantities to require the wearing of a mask. We seldom put on our masks until we received the order to do so. Wearing masks at night made the hiking difficult and it was almost impossible for us to keep together. We approached a crossroads and shells were falling rather rapidly. For a time we took shelter in a sort of trench beside the road. It had been a ditch, but had been changed into a trench during the fighting that had taken place at this point. Dead Germans were still lying about, just beginning to take on that faint aroma always indicative of the dead. The shells that were landing were not high explosive, but just plopped down about us. Suddenly gas was so strong that we all held our breaths, hastening to put on our masks without being ordered. There was a continual plopping of the shells as they landed. There was a piercing scream from the man right next to me. A big gas shell had come right over my back and horribly mangled his legs. Amputation was later necessary. I was the nearest. To me fell the task of getting him out of there—to call for stretcher bearers and to send him to the rear. He needed immediate aid, however; our Red Cross bandages were applied, and as the blood was pumping out in great dark jets, we made a tourniquet of his puttees to stop the flow of the blood. Soon he was on his way back to better treatment than we were able to give him.

There were only occasional high explosive shells, but one did land near and create terrible havoc. I could hear the shell approaching. It seemed to be coming our way, but it landed among a group of men about fifty yards away. It killed a number of them. What a lot of screeching and moaning, wailing and shouting for first aid that shell produced! I won't live long enough to forget the mark a single shell left on my memory— men alive and well one minute, shattered, dead bodies or maimed human beings the next instant.

We lay in that vicinity all night, being intermittently shelled and never knowing which shell might land right on top of us. As dawn came, other companies of our battalion moved into the long ditch or trench we occupied. It gave us an opportunity to see just where we were. The flares and star shells of the night before had made us believe that we were just a few hundred yards from the Germans. But it was farther than that.

There was a little village right near us with the usual shattered church steeple. Church steeples invariably served as a target for the artillery and they and the houses closest to them were always the most devastated part of the town. Studying my map seemed to indicate that this little town was Mont Saint Martin. And down there along the river, what seemed to be one big city or town, must be Fismes and Fismette.

The position we occupied was part way down the hill toward the river, for looking back I could see row after row of hills. There was a gentle slope in front of us, a road lined with fields and an occasional house. From this gentle slope the ground then fell away rather sharply toward the river well below in the valley. We lay in the trench all that day. It seemed that we had gallery seats to some gigantic theatrical performance. The town far down in the valley looked deserted at this time; we could not see a sign of movement there.

But there were watching eyes, for a small group of tin helmeted men had hardly started to go past us in single file when shells fell surprisingly close. Evidently there was nothing to do but keep under cover the entire day. Far in the distance we could hear the faint popping of machine guns which we expected must be in Fismes. Trench mortars fell at times there too. First we would see a cloud of dust, falling walls, and then long afterwards—it seemed long, for it was three or four seconds —would come the sound of the explosion.

It was evident that some parts of this hill were under constant observation by the German lines, for the passing of a working party, men carrying food, supplies or wounded past a certain part of the road, always brought German shells. When the wounded would pass us we asked them what was going on over in the town, but they knew little enough about it. Most of them had a knowledge only of their own little sector. Many of the injured men passing were what was known as " walking wounded." Shot in the shoulder, upper body, or only slightly in the leg, they were able to make their own way toward the rear. Quite a few men were carried on stretchers. It was a trying job for the stretcher bearers—two to a stretcher, for some of the men were quite heavy.

The ambulance made trips with fair regularity down over the hill, but not enough trips to take care of all the wounded. Hence the necessity for the carrying and walking back of some of them. There was one particularly bad place in the road where the ambulances had difficulty getting through. The Germans could apparently see this part of the road, and were ready to drop shells on it when any vehicle attempted to cross. Later from the town of Fismes I was to see the ambulances dashing past this same spot. It took a while for the shells to come over so the Germans soon learned to drop the shells on the road in front of the ambulance, hoping that they would either strike the ambulance as it ran into them or would fall into the hole left by the shell. The German seventy-sevens were not as fast as the French seventy-fives in their firing. There was always a space of at least fifteen seconds between shells when one gun was firing. Several times I saw an ambulance driver wait for a shell to fall, then dash across the open space full speed ahead, before the next shell could get there. This took considerable nerve, but these men, whom many believed to have a soft job, braved the shell fire, gas, and other dangers to do their work.

I haven't said a great deal about meals. But there was usually something to eat three times a day—seldom hot meals, though. It never seemed to me that we fared as well in the meals served as did other companies of our regiment. Frequently we went without while they had an almost warm meal which had been prepared by their cooks and sent forward with the men. There were many occasions when it was not possible for the kitchens to keep up with us, and other times when it was not possible to send the food forward which our organization needed. Entirely too often our meals consisted only of what we could obtain from cans which we opened with our bayonets. Meat and bread, corned beef, monkey meat and bread—filling, but not much variety, and not nearly enough to supply all the needs of one's body.

Additional supplies of ammunition and rockets were issued that night. I went around to inspect the equipment of the company. Where possible, additions to the equipment were made. Such an inspection as I had been ordered to make of our men usually meant that we were to go up front. We thought that we might move early in the evening. But hour after hour passed and still no order to move. So most of us fell asleep. It seemed that I had hardly fallen asleep when I was awakened and asked to report at company headquarters. We were told that we were to go down into the town and relieve the organization which was holding the line there. Time now to awaken the men and prepare to move. I went along waking men and with the help of the platoon sergeants soon had the men up on their feet and out in the white road. In a few minutes we were moving down the hill toward the Vesle River and Fismes.

We didn't have far to go, for in a short hike we reached a point where we could see our own machine gunners firing across the small river, the Vesle, to the Germans in the town of Fismette or in the fields beyond it. I can say here that few rivers in France were rivers as we know them. This Vesle River, which figured so much in dispatches and the news of August and early September, 1918, was just a fair-sized creek across which we could easily toss a stone.

We came down from the hills and went along a railroad track. There was considerable shelling here and some machine gunning. But we were safe for the time from either. The smell of gas was in the air, particularly mustard gas. It was a chilly night, and as the cold air hit the warm ground, a great deal of fog was in the air. One of the German shells had landed in an ammunition dump made up chiefly of machine gun ammunition. The resulting fire was burning brightly and shells were popping like a bunch of firecrackers on the Fourth of July. A bit farther along, we crossed a trestle bridge over a little stream which ran down into the Vesle River. Where it passed under the bridge at Fismes, our men were working in the stygian darkness to repair the bridge. It had been hit with German shells so that nothing but a footpath was left of it. It made a difficult and dangerous crossing, was always under fire from snipers and machine guns, and about every three minutes a shell fell nearby too. Many men were to lose their lives crossing that bridge. It was far safer to take a chance and wade and swim the Vesle.

We must have been seen as we passed the burning ammunition dump, for the shell fire which had been desultory in its effect during our first hour on the railroad track now doubled and redoubled in its fury. An increasing smell of gas was in the air, and I, like the remainder of my comrades, put on my gas mask. By this time I had two pieces of German equipment. One was a German shovel (which I carried through the war and brought home with me) which I found quite serviceable after my own shovel had been demolished on Hill 204, and the other was a German gas mask, which I preferred. Our masks were made with a cylinder filled with chemical, a mouthpiece and a clip to place over the nose. Long wear of them made a man sick and many a man took them off too soon and shortened his life from the effects of gas rather than wear the sickening mask. The glasses on these masks steamed up very easily so that it was almost impossible to see. Rubber with the Germans was as scarce as the proverbial hen's teeth. At this time everything they had was made of leather—their haversacks, gas mask holders, their gas masks, even the wheels of their autos were protected with leather tires. The German mask had no mouthpiece or nose clip, just a close-fitting leather covering, and the glass composition had been so treated that it did not steam up. I found it much more comfortable and serviceable.

The word was passed along here that we were to go over in the town and relieve the 112th Infantry of our division. Day was breaking about this time, and it seemed that we could not relieve them that day, but must remain along the railroad embankment until the protection of darkness again came our way.

A runner had come over from the 112th Infantry to lead us to the positions where we were to relieve them. It was decided that we had better not cross the river in the daylight, for our losses were sure to be heavy. Fismes lay down in a valley like any river town must do. Already we could look back and see our own observation balloons, and not far over the way the balloons which were serving a similar purpose for the Germans.

The runner told us something of the situation in the town. The larger town just before us was Fismes. We held that pretty well although there was considerable sniping and machine gun firing from the Germans across the small river. Most of the 112th were in Fismette, chiefly in the cellars of the houses. There was considerable fighting from house to house; constant counter attacks took place during the day. There was scarcely a time when some shells were not falling into Fismes. The Germans had held the town for long and they knew just where to shell—at the source of water supplies, the pumps and springs, as we were to find to our sorrow. Aside from the 112th, a battalion of machine guns, the 109th, from our division were holding a position back of Fismette.

The men of the 112th had been rather hard pressed, and it was imperative that we relieve them soon. There were many wounded and killed and all of one company had been captured as they kept under cover in one of the cellars. They had failed to leave guards and the Germans had come on them and forced the entire remnants of the company to surrender.

The artillery was very active at this time. An average of a shell every fifteen seconds was falling near the bridge over the Vesle. We hugged the safe side of the embankment, and even then there was a constant whirring of pieces of shell over our heads and we were forever being showered with debris.

A Counter Attack in Fismes

AFTER noon (it was lunch time for some people but only twelve o'clock to us, as rations were already becoming quite scarce) a runner came dashing madly across the bridge. Several runners had already been killed as they attempted to cross, and their bodies were still lying along the bridge. Aside from the shells falling regularly there were the snipers and the German machine gunners who could so easily see the bridge. Afterwards we were to find the garrets and points up in the field from which the Germans had been firing, and from their emplacements the bridge could be seen as plainly as the thumb on one's hand.

The runner gasped out the information that a heavy counter attack was taking place and the officer in charge must have reinforcements or they could not hold their positions. A quick council of war brought the decision that we would cross the bridge in daylight. The men got ready to move and we prepared to rush across the bridge three or four at a time. After each shell had landed a few of us would make a dash across the bridge. We went up the street into Fismes in the face of machine gun fire, but it did little damage; we later learned that it was coming from the high land back of the town nearly a mile away and accuracy of fire was hardly possible. Our entire battalion crossed the bridge and we were in the town with a minimum of losses. The ranks of every company had been decimated and probably our outfit consisted only of four or five hundred men instead of the full-strength one thousand men there should have been.

We avoided the open streets as much as possible and made our way through the buildings, and back yards. All around us was the pandemonium of the German barrage for they could see any activity in the town so easily and they were gunning for us as fast as they could fire. Fismes had apparently been a large and prosperous town before the war;

it had been the center of activity and fighting over a period of four years, being occupied in turn by French, German, French and German. In the days of constant fighting with snipers and resisting the German counter attacks I was to find souvenirs of the first German occupation of the town nearly four years before.

Our progress was slow; if we did not avoid the ceaseless barrage there would not be enough of us left to be of any service when we relieved the 112th. We were held up for long periods at certain stages of our infiltration into the town. I remember at one point, shortly after we got in the town, a shell falling right in the enclosure which a group of us occupied, killing seven or eight, among whom were the two Spencer boys— just kids, fifteen and sixteen years of age, respectively.

At one point I had been in the club rooms of some sort of a big society. It had been occupied by the Germans. Sofas and stuffed chairs were all around and tapestries and pictures still flapped around on the walls. A bit later I was in a particularly dangerous place—the City Hall. Its location was well known by the Germans and shells fell constantly. I climbed up into the bell tower to take a look and had a good view of Fismes for the first time. The City Hall seemed to be in the center of a square. From it extended at right angles the street through which we had come into town. I could see back to the river, see the sloping hills on the other side of the river, with the rows of poplars flanking the road as far as I could see. Down the road an American ambulance was coming to the town. Shells were falling around it and it was making a mad dash for the shelter of the town. It finally got in the town and shelter from the shells. I could see another car down the street a bit. From its color I could see that it was an American car. Badly shattered, it had stopped right in the middle of the street, and the driver was still sitting dead at the wheel.

There were dead Germans all around, but I could see one particularly well. He had been coming up the street past one of the garden walls, and had been hit with a shell. His legs were lying on this side of the wall—were lying there like they had been taken from some gigantic frog—while on the other side of the wall through the hole the shell had made I could see the rest of his body. He was a powerful-appearing man in his early twenties, with a thick shock of blond hair. His eyes were wide open. He never knew what had hit him.

Looking up the street, which ran parallel with the hills back of the town, I could see the famous Rue Cervante, which I came to know so well. For the next five days that was to be the scene of my worst battle of the war. What happened during those five days alone could easily fill a good-sized book. It was one of the most futile, most horrible experiences of the American army. German soldiers were lying the entire way up this street. There was a barricade part-way up, behind which either the French troops long before, or the Americans, had made their stand. The Germans had come down the street under cover of machine gun fire and artillery fire from the hills, as they were to do several times during our occupancy of the city, only to be stopped by our troops at the barricade.

The bell tower was a dangerous spot as the German artillery was constantly gunning for it; but the view of the town I had was most valuable to me later. It gave me a pretty good idea of the lay of the land; the part of the city occupied by us, the part of Fismette held by the Germans, and the little village and the fields up over the hill which they also occupied. I could see a church across the way, and the Hotel de Ville on another part of the square. The windows and doors of the stores gaped open. They had long been deserted and looted. We had been warned to keep off the street owing to the activity of snipers, particularly for the full length of this street, Rue Cervante.

German planes flew over the town on several occasions this day. They were so low that we could almost recognize the pilot. After each trip there was more shelling. The Germans were very adept at shelling their old homes. We were to find later in the war, as the Germans retreated, that we were wise to avoid any spring or building in which they had been quartered. They had the proper coordinates of these places and it was as much as a man's life was worth to be near them when the shells started dropping. Our company was too close to the City Hall during the slowly passing hours of that day, and shells never ceased to fall.

At times considerable machine gun fire came down the street. I could hear them going zst-zst-zst as they passed. The next morning we were to hear them crack, for the gunners were so close. About the middle of the afternoon the Germans tried another counter attack, and we helped the defenders behind the barricade and in the houses farther up the street, by sniping from the second floor of the houses we occupied. We were prepared to stop the attack if it had penetrated down the street to our positions. Firing over the heads of the men behind the barricade we were able to assist in stopping this counter attack. The Germans too had their snipers to cover the advance of their men. I remember one who was firing very carefully from a window in a house well up the street. I took careful aim, and he fell forward out of the window.

During all this fighting, the air was filled with dust and with the fumes of powder. They burnt our noses, throats and lungs to such an extent that we could not tell if gas was in the air. We didn't expect it, however, for we were too close to the attacking Germans. About dark the shelling quieted down for a time. I suppose the German gunners had to eat. We had several hours of comparative rest, and then were ordered to be on our way again. We were to relieve the 112th finally. I felt that we had been in action long enough, that we should be relieved, and wished that they were relieving us instead of us relieving them. But it was our turn to be at the front of the front. I had seen several graves of the 110th Infantry, also of our division, in the yards which we had passed. They had been in before the 112th, and now it was our turn. I admit that I was not greatly enthusiastic over the prospect of making an attack the next morning as we were expected to do. Volunteering for our first action on Hill 204, and seeing the men who did not get to go crying real tears, was some different from the inferno, the cemetery, we were in in this battle. We were becoming war weary, ready and willing to do our duty, but not anxious enough to rush forward before our turn came. It was only the eighth day of August, 1918. (I didn't have any idea of the date then, but the citation I received from General Pershing, which is framed in my home, cites me for " extreme gallantry in action and brilliant leadership during the fighting in Fismes, August 8th to 13th.") We were just going into action in Fismette, so it must have been the 8th. I have little recollection of day or night which followed. There was little difference—fighting every minute, attacking or being at- attacked. The sun rose and set, but a few of us went on indefinitely without pause for food which we didn't receive or sleep which we did not have time to snatch.

We went farther up Rue Cervante, and finally stopped for such a long halt that most of us fell asleep. About three o'clock in the morning I got the men awake again and we started on our final trip to take the places of the 112th. I was told that Captain Lynch of B Company was to be acting major, and see us safely into the lines. Our major was to remain back in his dugout, his point of command, from which he would direct remotely and report the progress of the attack. " Lucky major," we thought at the time.

The men were as quiet as possible, but noise was inevitable as they walked and crawled through the litter of debris—of stones and roof tiles, and of broken glass that lay everywhere. Jerry was awake as usual, constantly shooting flares overhead, which came right down into town as they hung suspended in air from the tiny parachutes which bore them. They were close. It was not necessary to tell the men to be still when flares were lighting the town; they instinctively "froze" as does any animal when it thinks it is observed. The snipers and machine gunners were on the job. We were to learn that they crawled into the edge of town every night, and went back to their lines on the hills each day as the dawn came. We found their vantage points and their sniping posts and sometimes we found them to their sorrow.

While those who were far on the other side of the river believed that we held the entire town, we had just part of Fismette. The Prussian guard held the other half and during much of our stay here they were right across the street, never very far up the street.

I'll try to paint a brief picture of this single street in the town of Fismette where so much action was to take place. Fismes was the older part of the town, the principal part. Evidently Fismette had been built along what had once been a country road. The houses extended out to the sidewalk, and were made of the usual stone and plaster. They were built solidly against each other up this long single street of the town. Every house had its cellar and its garret covered with red tile. Uniformity of building construction is one of the rules in France. On the opposite side of the street, possibly forty feet from front door to front door of the houses which lined each side, were houses whose back yards extended in a gentle slope down to the river—perhaps two hundred yards away. But the houses on our side were set right against a steep hill. Almost at the end of the short back yards of these houses was Hunland, for they were close enough to be shooting flares down to us with their Very pistols, and the range of such implements was short. The street was comparatively straight as it extended through Fismette, and then it took a turn to the right up the hill toward the German lines. It was from this direction that the almost constant counter attacks came. Nearly every house had a deep cellar extending into the hills back of them. These had been used for the storage of wine, but served admirably as safe dugouts. Later in the action it was difficult to keep the men out of the safety of these dugouts and on the line where they could repel attacks.

A number of these back yards had springs which ran from spigots. We thought we were to have plenty of water at least, but it happened that the Germans knew where these springs were, could see them during the day, and often at night, when the blackness was lighted by flares, many of our men were killed and wounded as they tried to get water here. At the ends of the comparatively short and steep back yards was a stone wall which extended parallel with the street clear to the end of town. Although somewhat straight, it varied in height, at some few points being as high as a man's head and at other points being little more than a marker approximately two feet high. This was to be our front line for the days of our battle of Fismette. Above this were gardens, farms, orchards, vineyards, and farther up woods. It was as much as a man's life was worth to look over the wall, but I did catch a glimpse of it at times and saw that a young pear orchard was just over the wall from my particular part of the line. I could see a haystack up in the field and it was from there that many of our men met their deaths. The Germans were hidden by the hay and were sniping and firing machine guns from that vantage point. There were occasional wagons, outbuildings, and storage houses. The Germans had their trench there. They were on higher ground and could see us so much easier than we could see them. Later when I led so many patrols through the German end of the town to put the snipers and advanced machine gun posts out of action, I gathered a better idea of what lay behind us. But even I knew little about what lay behind the stone wall when we occupied it in the black darkness of this August morning. We stumbled along through the darkness, crawling behind the stone wall.

G Company was far down to the left, B Company next to us, then our own Company A and D Company to our right. The defenders of the wall were firing through openings in the stone wall. " Where are the Germans? " I asked. " Out there somewhere," the gunner replied. " How can you tell what you are shooting at? " " We can't, but we keep firing and they know we are on the job and are less likely to attack." In the distance it was very dimly becoming light. The men of the 112th sneaked away from the line, and here we were in a rather thin line with the flower of the German army, the Prussian guard, occupying the vantage points ahead and above us.

We were scarcely settled when someone said, " Come on. We're going over." I could see the men to the left of us climbing over the wall and we climbed too. How different from our first experience at going over the top. Then we had a beautiful day, the sun was shining, the birds singing, we had laughed and talked all day with our Allies and among ourselves. We knew what we were doing and where we were going; we had the advantage of an intense preparatory barrage to pave the way. We were new to war, enthusiastic, even anxious to prove ourselves.

But here we had crawled through a pretty good example of Hell, and were going out to face the unknown in what is always the time of the twenty-four hour day when spirits are at their lowest ebb. Already bullets were flying overhead like a swarm of bees. They passed closely over our heads in endless streams, with their zst-zst-zst apparently searching for us in the dark. We were about level with the roofs of the houses below us and most of the bullets were crashing against the tile roofs. Worse yet, we were being enfiladed by machine gun fire from our left. No one could know at the time when we occupied these positions in the dark that we would be subjected to this destroying cross fire. But it was killing us. It was evident that we could not remain in this place long. There would not be any of us left. We were later to learn that the cross fire came from the garrets of many houses farther up the street. Frontal fire is bad enough, but flanking fire is suicidal. Men were getting hit all around us. They were calling for stretchers, trying to apply their own first-aid kits on every side, and some of them were gasping out their last breaths. To have come so far, at least four thousand miles, and to have their lives snuffed out so wantonly, so uselessly, behind this wall in the back yards of a remote French village that the world would never have heard of were it not for the action which took place there.

Over the Top Again

WE were going over, right into the rain of death which was coming from in front and to the left of us. We couldn't see much—just the ruined house and outbuildings, the haystack, and the wagons. But they were out there somewhere, for from this apparent void was coming a veritable hail of death. We were so close to the guns that we no longer heard the zst-zst-zst of their searching fingers—just the wicked crack they made as they went past our ears. There must have been a battalion of machine gunners in front of us. I was to face machine gunners many times in later actions, but never before or since had I heard gun fire like we faced. The noise they made was not unlike hundreds of riveting machines such as can be heard in building a skyscraper in New York or some other large city. Seldom had such a chattering and banging of machine guns and rifles ever been heard before. We were fortunate, if we only knew it, that they did not turn the Flamenwerfers (liquid fire) upon us that we were to feel later.

We advanced possibly fifty yards. There was absolutely no place to advance to. The machine guns must have been placed in concrete pill boxes closely spaced, and well camouflaged so that we could not see them. Enfiladed fire of such type would not permit a rabbit to go through. The only possible means to advance under the circumstances is with the help of artillery support. We had to fall back to our lines. There was nothing else we could do. We left some of our men lying dead and wounded in the orchards and fields. It was light enough now that the machine gunners from our own division had been able to locate the German machine guns in the garrets, and they blasted them out of there with a withering fire. Some of us carried rockets, and one—a red one—was sent high in the air to call for the support of our artillery. The barrage came in a short time but, as happened so often, the range was wrong or the shells had been made with less explosive power than they should have and the shells fell right on us, instead of on the Germans. At such times the wily, war-trained, war-hardened Germans would open up with every available gun, artillery and machine gun fire. They would know that the men would be running and would get many of them. What a shame! As if enough death was not coming from the German lines! Our men, every one of them some mother's son, were being killed by our own gun fire. We ran down off the hill in a hurry and took shelter in the cellars and wine vaults. For a period our line was completely undefended. Had the Germans attacked then they could have gone right through, have retaken the town and killed or captured every one of us. But they had been in the war too long and were super- cautious.

I stood at the foot of the hill, looking up to the wall where we had been. I saw many dead and wounded men around, but particularly Philip Beketich of our own company. He was rolling around on the ground, apparently in great pain, and soon would be picked off by some sniper. I knew that he should be brought down, but I was reluctant to return immediately into that inferno of American and German shells, direct and enfilading German machine gun fire. I had to talk to myself. " What's the matter, Bob? Are you yellow? Why don't you go up and get him? " My inner self persuaded me to make the short rush up the hill, lift up Philip's body and prepare to dash down the hill again. It was on this short trip that Philip received the two additional wounds which, added to the first, quickly resulted in his death.

But I had seen something when I went after Philip— a German soldier lying just outside the wall which we had occupied. The Germans had sent over this patrol to see if our line was undefended. I pointed my gun and bayonet at this small German and he Kameraded and surrendered as quickly as he could. It had been his purpose to surrender, and as he was dancing around there, trying to look several ways at once, so that someone would not stick a bayonet in him or shoot him, one of his own men shot him—a flesh wound in the gluteus maximus (the big muscles of the buttock which provide a seat for us when we are tired).

In the next few hours I was to get his story. He was a German Jew who had been captured once before in the war. He had been a prisoner with the French for nearly three years, and had been exchanged with a lot of French prisoners. It was agreed that none of these prisoners would be sent to the front again, but here he was. He didn't want to fight and die in the first place—especially not now after what he had seen during his years of war service. It is quite likely that the Germans knew of his intention to surrender at the first opportunity, and when they saw him giving up, the sniper fired, wounding him. This little fellow was pretty much of a man. Jews make good soldiers—courageous fighters if they feel that they have something to fight for. This man was smarter than we were. He knew that he was expected to suffer and die for a cause that he felt was none of his affair. I presume it is this independence of nature, so foreign to the regimentation of the German people of the last war and of today, that causes the Germans to thoroughly dislike the Jewish race; and although they force them to serve in some capacity in the present war, they do not trust them at the front.

By motions this German Jew asked for a rifle. I didn't know that we should trust him, but finally decided to take the chance. He knew where the snipers were hiding and with his first shot he got the man who apparently had shot him. He stayed with us all day, in spite of his wound, firing at snipers, and did us inestimable good. Later he gave helpful information through our interpreters which aided us immensely. It was evident that he was no coward. He just didn't wish to fight for the cause for which he had been drafted. He was once again a prisoner and no doubt survived the war.

Here we were on a battalion front where there should have been four full-strength companies, a thousand men, and there was the merest handful of us. Nearly all the officers were gone. Our captain, Arch Williams, had been wounded. A bullet had run around his ribs, and was imbedded in his spine, making him quite helpless. But he was cheerful and smiling and did all he could to be helpful. Captain Lynch, a big stocky man who had led us over, was lying out in the pear orchard, quite dead. It was said that he had a large sum of money upon his person, the equivalent of two thousand dollars in U. S. money. Later this amount was offered to the man who would go out and bring his body back. Many tried. Some lost their lives in the process, for the Germans made a practice of not shooting wounded men again, who were in front of the line, but to leave them there as decoys to bring other men to them who would in turn be killed by the snipers. Many of our wounded lay in front of that line suffering for days and nights before they could be brought back to the line. Captain Law had been killed. Lieutenant Glendenning of the next company had been killed. So had Lieutenant Larned. Lieutenant Miller had been killed some time before. Captain Haller of D Company was the senior officer and was in charge of what was left of the battalion. The lieutenants of our own company had been decimated and I didn't see any of them around. Evidently I was the senior non-commissioned officer and took command of this advanced line.

I was sure that we could expect an attack soon. The German reconnaissance patrol would report that we had retreated, that our lines were unoccupied and there would be no opposition to their attack. I found one sergeant and a crew from the machine gun battalion. I got them up on the line back of the wall with their machine gun and a fair supply of ammunition. I managed to dig up two Chau Chat guns still ready for action and improvised crews. I remember that one of these men was a former cook in our company by the name of Riley, a man who had drunk, gambled and went A W O L to an extent that he had lost his position and was now a buck private. One of the men on the gun was an Austrian miner by the name of Otte. I understand that he was later to receive a D S C for crossing the river under fire with important messages. He had been considered an enemy alien and it was doubtful for a time if he would come overseas with his company. There was a squat, bow-legged, heavily-mustached Turk, who also had been a coal miner, and was considered to be an enemy alien. With the machine gun crew and two small nondescript crews for the Chau Chat rifles we were as nearly ready as we could be—six men on a thousand man front.

We weren't ready much too soon, for shortly we saw the Germans coming, with full packs and ready to march along—perhaps to Paris, no doubt they thought, for they had seen us retreat and felt sure they would at least regain the city and the ground across the river.

They didn't even come forward cautiously—no points or flankers, no line of combat groups, just marching along at ease and carelessly as you could please. They thought they were going right through. We waited until they were quite close. Then I gave the signal for the other two guns to open up, manned one of the Chau Chats myself with Paddy Riley to feed me ammunition. Such expressions of astonishment on their faces! Such scrambling and running for cover, crawling back to their former positions! We had a good share of revenge for what they had done to us that morning.

I missed my equipment about this time. I had thrown off my pack at the beginning of the battle because it interfered with my firing as we advanced through the pear orchard. That pack was constantly pushing the helmet down over my eyes, interfering with sighting my rifle, so I had discarded it. It contained my iron rations, several small cans of corned beef and hardtack. Many of the fellows had eaten theirs, but I had saved mine for just such an emergency as this. Now it was gone, lying out in front where it might as well have been a million miles away. I crawled around to a number of dead men who were lying near, but their iron rations were gone. Nothing to eat—and nothing for the full five days I was in that town. Between the cats and the rats, and the hungry soldiers, everything eatable was gone, for we weren't cannibals enough to eat the dead Germans as the cats and rats were doing.

In the next two hours, I got every available man I could upon the line. We had to defend it and hold it. I found able-bodied men in the headquarters dug out, in the cellars of the houses, in the wine vaults. Some insisted that they were sick. Everybody was sick. I got them out just the same. I used strong arm methods if necessary, even kicked them in the pants. One of these fellows, a corporal in the adjoining company, had been treasurer of a big company at home. My elder brother had worked with him. But I yanked him out just the same. We needed every available man. After the war, when we had returned home, I went to see a football game at Forbes Field. Here was this man selling tickets. I thought this was his chance for a minor revenge—at least to give me a ticket back of one of the huge pillars which supported the upper stands. He gave me the best ticket in the place. There were many men whom I handled a bit roughly during the war to get them on the front line. But none of them permanently resented it. They seemed to admire me for having stronger nerves or more physical strength and courage than they. I believe it was the reporting by these men of my deeds that caused me to receive the decorations which were later awarded to me, for I didn't tell anyone about it when I returned and certainly there were no officers around who were close enough to see how I spent my five days in Fismette, and recommend me for any sort of decoration for any deed which warranted some reward of distinction. There must have been a hundred men on the battalion front by this time and once again we were ready for what came.

Back Across the Vesle

AFTER we had repelled the German attack, and had the line at least partially reinforced, I knew that we must quickly plan to coordinate our forces and prepare to endure greater bombardments and even more severe counter attacks. As yet the higher officers of our regiment—the major of our battalion across the river in Fismes, or Colonel Shannon—did not know just what had happened in this early morning attack, or perhaps even that the Germans had counter attacked.

I was able to leave the line in charge of those who had performed such splendid work in stopping the attack; to consult with higher officers of our regiment and lay plans for the future defense of Fismette.

While I had been searching out every able-bodied man to place them in defense of our line behind the stone wall in the back yards of Fismette, I had found Captain Haller, who by this time was actually in charge of the remnants of our battalion. Major Kelly was across the river in Fismes, so I went first to see Captain Haller and apprised him of the situation—told him what we needed to hold the line.

The advanced post occupied by Captain Haller was a big wine cellar. It was right at the end of a little street and extended far back into what had been a cave in the solid rock. A blanket covered the opening to the cave and when it was pulled aside there could be dimly seen the group of scouts, runners, liaison men, orderlies, wounded, and an officer or two. It was difficult to keep men from " gold bricking " in these dugouts, for everyone who had the slightest excuse—and some without excuses, just slackers—was always crowded into these places of safety.

It was decided that I should endeavor to find the major of our battalion. It was quite a trip to his post of command but it was necessary that he, and the colonel behind him and the general behind him, know the exact situation in Fismette. I had to find my way through the town, and to avoid in some manner the corners where machine gun bullets and snipers' bullets created a dangerous condition. There was a great deal of shell fire too, for the Germans had occupied Fismes and Fismette so long that they were as familiar with these towns as they were with their own villages at home. They knew every building, every street, path and the crossings at the streams. It took good judgment and considerable luck to cross the river without being killed or wounded. In the days to come we were to never cease a stealthy man hunt for snipers and machine gunners throughout the entire town, but on this first day of the battle we had done nothing to wipe them out and they were so close that many runners and men who had to go from place to place lost their lives. The town was being shelled constantly from the heights back of the town of Fismette. We could easily see the German observation balloons. As usual the Germans had command of the air and their planes frequently came over, flying low to see what they could see. After such a visit we could expect additional shelling.

The Germans were especially efficient in all phases of war, particularly in their air reconnaissance. It was their habit to constantly take photos of our lines all along the front. Officers well back in the seclusion of some distant and safe dugout Would study these photos carefully, and if they found the slightest change—digging, even the moving of supplies, wheelbarrow or broom—shelling could be expected in the very near future. We were always careful to leave things as near the way we found them as possible.

I left the advanced post of Captain Haller on the run. I was partially familiar with the town and had a fair idea as to the path I should take. Fritz was quite methodical in his shelling. It was usually safe to cross a street, a corner, or bridge immediately after a shell had fallen. He might be shelling that point every fifteen seconds, or every minute, and usually we could get across in safety between shells.

The really dangerous time was when a barrage or more active bombardment was taking place. Then one didn't know when or where to expect shells. There were few times when at least an occasional shell was not falling somewhere in Fismes. Each falling shell was followed by the tinkle of breaking glass, the crashing or sliding of the tiles from the roof or the stones from the walls of the homes.

At this time of day it was rather quiet after the great activity of the night and the morning, but I heard the occasional crack of a rifle. This told me that a sniper somewhere was on the job, and the body of a runner with his red band was lying dead in the street right in front of me. I slipped along as warily as I could, hugging the walls carefully, and travelling through the back yards close to the houses as much as possible. Not a soul was to be seen anywhere. All the Americans were under cover. The village was as deserted as is the usual cemetery at midnight. But men were everywhere, particularly the enemy. And it only takes one shot to end one's life, no matter how quiet things may seem to be.

No doubt if I were over in France, strolling over this same path, in peace time, the distance I had to traverse would seem short, but the devious and dangerous path I followed made it seem much longer. During my observations of the day before I had noticed that right behind the houses on the opposite side of the street were the usual outbuildings and a path at the end of the garden which ran down to what seemed to be some sort of a foundry or steel mill. Just beyond that I had seen piles of coal and then a bit farther the Vesle River. The river was in flood, sparkling in the sunlight, unusual enough at the middle of August, but there had been a great deal of unseasonable rain. It seemed that nature was conspiring against us to make travelling and fighting more difficult—conspiring against me in this particular case, for I had to cross the river. The bridge in broad daylight was too dangerous. I didn't wish to have my young life ended on the little smashed bridge which extends across the Vesle River between Fismes and Fismette, so I already had decided to try swimming the river. The brown flood of the raging torrent of what should have been a small stream at this season, the middle of August, would make the crossing very, very difficult.

I had hoped in the beginning to cross the bridge, but the unusual number of shells falling there made that impossible. A machine gun was firing from somewhere up on the hills back of town and while accuracy at such a great distance was hardly possible, there were enough bullets flying near the bridge that some of them could strike.

The river was filled to overflowing and extended well up into the fields. From where I stood in the shelter of the old iron foundry, I could see the river less than two hundred yards away through the fields. A city street led down to the masonry bridge over which it was customary for heavy traffic to cross. But about two city blocks below this were the remnants of a wooden suspension bridge, a footbridge, similar to those which we see on country streams in parts of our own country. The bridge had been damaged and most of it was level with the rapidly moving river. Some of it was submerged. By this time it seemed that a real barrage was falling at the big bridge. Some of the shells were hitting the already badly-damaged bridge, but most of them were falling into the water, throwing up showers of water and mud. Dead fish too! The explosion of a shell would kill all the fish within a considerable distance. Under quieter circumstances some of us could have had fried fish to supplement our usual meager rations. It was evident that anyone attempting to cross the masonry bridge at this time would never succeed, and if I didn't get across and get reinforcements and additional ammunition the brave men of our organization would lose their lives in an endeavor to hold Fismette.

It seemed that I might be able to cross near the footbridge. Shells weren't being directed at it, although an occasional one fell too close for comfort. A path extended down the slight slope from my present vantage point, the old iron foundry, to the ruined wooden footbridge. No doubt in times past, in normal, peaceful times, it had been the means by which the field workers and those of the foundry had crossed the Vesle to and from their homes in Fismes. The path followed a gully which had been chiselled from the hillside by countless rain storms of the past. I intended to attempt the crossing by crawling down this gulley, and then swimming or pulling myself across the Vesle below the bridge.

The houses of Fismes appeared far away, as they gleamed in the bright French sunshine. It didn't seem right, at times, that the sun should shine so beautifully when men were killing and being killed beneath it. At first thought one would expect the fighting to take place in rainy, cloudy or stormy weather. But just the opposite was the case. Moonlight nights were the most prevalent source of air raids, and beautiful weather meant more shelling, more attacking and more frequent death.

The machine gun bullets were hissing down over the entire area of fields approaching the river. It was customary to use machine guns with a sweeping action, swinging the gun back and forth in the hope of putting out of action any runner or group of men who endeavored to cross the space swept by the guns. Although I only had two hundred yards to traverse to reach the river if I could have travelled in a direct line, it was easily double this distance following the tiny ravine, which was little more than a drainage ditch, to the river. At places it barely kept me beneath the level of the fields, as I could hear the " zst-zst-zst " of the flying machine gun bullets as they just cleared my back, seeming to search for me.

I crawled so long through this ditch, through the mud and water, that I felt little different from some turtle, and the crawling method which I was using seemed like the most natural thing in the world. The smell of gas became strong as I neared the river. There had been considerable shelling, with mustard gas in particular, all along the river on this sector. Gas would remain, particularly in a damp place, for at least two weeks. I could smell it strongly, and soon I could feel it smarting upon my hands. It was a hot day, with considerable humidity in the air. I was perspiring profusely and I wondered if I would get enough of it that it would put me out of action. I hoped not, for I wanted to get back to my comrades behind the wall of the back yards in Fismette.

A miracle happened as I crawled down this ditch. A shell landed not fifteen feet from me—a big shell, at least six inches in diameter; had it been a high explosive shell my chances of surviving the explosion would not have been great; had it been a gas shell, particularly mustard gas, I would have been so sprayed with its deadly contents that my chances of living would have been slight. But by a miracle it was a dud; it did not explode. As I crawled past it, I could not help but think that perhaps some careless worker in a German munition factory had done me a favor of tremendous proportions.

Yard by yard, almost foot by foot, the smell of gas became stronger, and soon I thought it best to put on my gas mask. It was dangerous to be without a mask, and nearly as dangerous to wear one. Here I was crawling from the direction of Germany, as well as of our own outposts, wearing a German gas mask, my clothes so wet and muddy that they could have been American or German. My helmet was one distinguishing feature, but some American sentry, too hasty on the trigger, could have disregarded that. Many men fire before they get a good look. Men are killed in hunting every fall because someone fires at the movement of a bush without seeing what caused the movement. In several instances our own men had been killed by our own fire. Just that very day Charlie Wright of B Company had stepped out from the shelter of a house wall for some unknown reason and had been promptly shot by his comrades who expected only Germans to appear from that location.

A human in a gas mask is not a pretty sight, particularly one covered with mud, slime and filth. The human race has not advanced far since that day, perhaps hundreds of millions of years ago, when the first reptilian monster crept up out of the warm seas to the land, through slimy ditches such as the one I was traversing. Human ingenuity was being directed into ways to destroy one another.

I was gradually approaching the edge of the flooded river; there was no bank as usual—the water was merely lapping against the sides of the fields. As I neared the stream I had to detour for a moment to circumnavigate a very dead German who smelled to high heaven, having been lying in that ditch for a week or two. Apparently the river had been defended by the Germans very desperately, until their troops had withdrawn to the vantage points they now occupied above the town. Just a bit up to the right, I could see a group of dead Germans, who apparently had been killed as they tried to hold the lines and prevent the crossing of our troops. Some of them seemed to have been bayoneted.

Barbed wire was everywhere, much of it submerged beneath the surface of the muddy water of the ditch and of the stream, and it made forward progress constantly more difficult and more painful. Finally I was sliding down the bank and getting into cold water up to my neck. It seemed particularly cold after the near tropical heat I had experienced crawling through the drainage ditch. I held onto the submerged portion of the bridge and pulled myself along hand over hand, just as I had so often done in the Pittsburgh natatorium at home while learning to swim. There came a gap in the supporting cable where that portion of the bridge had been shot away and I had to swim a few strokes to grasp the cable on the other side. I was glad that I had grown up along the rivers of Pennsylvania, that I was a good swimmer, or I easily could have been swept downstream to become a target for our own or the enemy's guns.

It took considerable time to work my way up the Fismes side of the bank, for our own machine guns were firing from there at targets farther up upon the hillside and I particularly did not want to become a target for our own guns after coming this far through dangerous and difficult ground and water. But I was up over the bank in time, up through the back yards on the Fismes side of the Vesle, and finally came into a house which was only across the street from the major's dugout, as I was told by the first group of Americans when I asked, " Where will I find Major Kelly?"

In a moment or two I was in the major's dugout apprising him of the situation. He said that he had just called the colonel, and told him that things were going well, that we were advancing and taking prisoners. The only prisoner I knew of was the little German Jew who was then with our troops on the line. I told the major that the captain of B Company was dead; Captain Williams of our company seriously wounded; Captain Haller serving as officer of the advanced line from his place in the dugout; nearly all the officers dead or wounded; only a handful of men to hold the lines; scores of fresh wounded and the wounded from the 112th still in the town; very few dry bandages and no other means to care for the wounds of these sorely injured men; very little rifle and pistol ammunition; no bombs; our own artillery falling short, and killing us; the snipers and machine gunners of the enemy surprisingly close, where they could enfilade our lines and make it very difficult for us to hold our positions; no food. All in all, our experience in the Great War was at its very lowest ebb.

The major very quickly saw that his battalion over in Fismette was facing a very grave situation. Immediately he sent a true picture of the conditions back to Colonel

Shannon. I knew that within a reasonable time we could expect reinforcements and the needed material. As it turned out we were to desperately hold the advance line for four days before the third battalion of our regiment, under Colonel Dunlap, would come over to sell their lives rather futilely in making an attack upon the German positions above the town. It was to be an equal number of days before I ate a mouthful of food. Had I known that, I would have eaten some of the salmon and " monkey meat" which lay around the major's dugout in abundance.

I understand that this major was relieved of his command approximately eight weeks later because he disregarded an order to go forward at any cost—an order similar to the one which was obeyed in this town when we were instructed to hold the line at any cost. We had spent weeks of intensive, terrible fighting in the Argonne forest from September 25th to October 14th. We were endeavoring to drive from Chene Tondu to Chatelle Chaherry when we encountered one of those previously prepared lines to which the Germans would fall back successively as they slowly retreated. Concrete pill boxes, enfiladed fire—this was a line which the Germans had had four years to prepare. I was leading the advance guard and quickly recognized the fact that it was impossible to advance farther. Men can't go through the cross fire of machine guns when the guns are properly placed. Even a rabbit or a bird could not expect to go through the hail of crossed bullets such guns can fire. As I crawled up through a tiny gully, somewhat similar to the one I had traversed to reach our battalion commander, I could detect the fact that the guns were close, so close that they were shooting the pack off my back. I could easily hear the crack of the gun.

I sent a runner back to tell the major of the condition and ask what we should do. He ordered us to go ahead. We crawled ahead perhaps fifty yards through this little gully. I knew that the entire army could not crawl through this point—that they would be cut down instantly when they tried to follow us—so sent back another runner. This runner came back again with the order to keep going forward. Another fifty yards and the guns were all around us. I could see that it was impossible to go any farther. We would all lose our lives and accomplish nothing toward winning the war. I sent back another message to tell the major of the condition, and this time he said that we would not go forward without artillery support. It saved our lives and lost him his command. We were relieved there by an organization which had never been in the lines, and they lost hundreds of lives in a foolhardy attempt to go through this fortified position.

But back to the battle of Fismes and Fismette. An artillery lieutenant had come into the major's dugout who was supplied with more authentic information concerning our exact positions. There was difficulty with shorts ever after that.

And now I had another job on my hands, as bad as the one I had just completed—going back over the river again. I must admit that it took courage to repeat the same performance I had just gone through. I could see the river from the street in front of the major's dugout. The bank of the stream was still a target for many shells; they were landing all around the masonry bridge, falling into the stream, the fields and the town. Before I started back our own barrage came over with a roar and fell in front of our lines on the hillside. There was a constant booming, roaring, whistling and howling as the shells passed overhead—I could almost see them—then clouds and geysers of mud and dirt from the hillside above Fismette.

I knew that our own barrage would keep the Germans busy for a time and give me a chance to cross the river. The engineers took advantage of the lull in the German firing and were desperately trying to repair the bridge with planks. I crossed the bridge on the first plank they laid, and dashed down the stream toward the small gully which I intended to follow up into the foundry. Soon I was crawling up the ditch and found a hole where the dead German had been. A direct hit had landed upon him, blowing him to pieces. One thing sure, his relatives back in Germany would never know what had become of him. I made rapid progress up the ditch and soon approached Fismette.

And here I was again in the back yards of Fismette, still all in one piece and alive. I had been in a frying pan, but now I was in the fire. The men were still on the job back of the stone wall, but were suffering from machine gun and sniper fire from well over to the left.

We were lying pretty close to the wall, and the snipers continued to fire. Right in front of me was a little hole in the wall through which I had aimed my Ghau Chat rifle when the Germans were coming over. But now I couldn't get near that opening. If I had held my finger in the open space between the stones it would have been shot off. The sniper was on the job and mighty close. To test him, several times I put a stone in the opening and almost instantly, almost before my hand was removed, the bullet hit the stone and it was down. Probably a score of times I placed that stone in the opening to have the sharpshooter knock it down. It was while engaged in this form of play that I saw my friend Michaels coming along well bent over. It was tiresome to crawl on one's hands and knees from one part of the line to the other, but it was the safest way. I warned Mike to get down, telling him that a sniper was shooting through the hole in the wall; but he either did not completely comprehend what I had said or did not get down soon enough, for it was here that the sniper shot him through the heart, killing him almost instantly.

From where I lay I was partially sheltered to the left. The snipers could not reach me at that particular spot, but when I moved a bullet would instantly come perilously close. Immediately after one shot I took a quick dash down over the hill where I was sheltered by the back wall of the houses. We needed water, but the spigot was in plain sight of the German sniper, so we had to do without. No food and water! Our supporting troops could not get across the river with food or ammunition or to remove the wounded. Things were in a ghastly state. Ammunition was running low. There was not a single bomb left among us; no rifle grenades. Everybody had long since thrown away their trombones, which were used to fire these grenades. No trench mortar men or one pounders were near; when we called for our own artillery to support us it would fall upon us. There was a rumor at the time that the guns behind us were being directed by a German officer—that later he had been shot by his own sergeant when it was learned that he had been killing the Americans. We were always hearing rumors. Few of them had any basis of fact. I don't know what truth there might have been to this one, but I do know that our own artillery hit us every time they fired.

Later we were to repel an intense German attack, before which we had been deluged with trench mortars and artillery shells. The Germans came over with everything which could be used in modern war—hand grenades, rifle grenades, machine guns, and Flamenwerfers. We had nothing but a very moderate amount of rifle and revolver ammunition.

There were a host of dead Americans in the town. It was impossible to bury them, so they had been piled like logs of wood in the lower rooms of the houses. It was August, you must remember, and flies swarmed by the millions in this place where the dead had held sway so long. The rats and cats had their inning. In fact the rats were nearly as big as the cats, and the cats kept well away from them. The cats were only around for their share of the plentiful repast when the rats had gone.

Wounded were everywhere—not only our wounded, but the men from the regiment we had relieved. There was nothing left by this time except dry bandages, and few enough of them. The doctors and their helpers continued for long hours at their task, doing all they could until they were completely exhausted. One doctor had worked so long and hard, back in the wine cellars where the Red Cross dressing station had been located, that he forgot himself and stepped to the front door for a breath of air for a minute. A sniper from well up the Rue Cervante shot him right at the intersection of the red cross he wore over his heart.

The wounded with each passing day were in a worse state. They knew that things were going badly for us and each time the door opened they thought a German would enter and blast them out of there with potato- masher grenades. I tried to reassure them—would lie like the proverbial trooper; tell them that we had chased the Germans well up over the hill, at least a kilometer back; that the town was no longer in danger; that we would soon be relieved and that they would be evacuated. I reassured them for the moment, cheered them up a bit, but their spirits would fall again as soon as I left. And I had work to do and could not be with them long. Captain Williams was there in the dugout being eaten by a myriad of flies, but cheerful and brave through it all. I saw him just once after the war—at a hockey game in Pittsburgh.

It was evident that our only hope was to do something about the Germans in the upper end of town— particularly the snipers. If we didn't drive them out of town they would continually pick us off until there weren't any left. Food could not come to us, nor the sorely needed medical supplies; nor could ambulances cross the river. So a battle against the snipers was determined upon.

The smaller photo shows Lieutenant Hoffman in March, 1919 with the ravages of war still showing plainly on his face. The photo, in which he is wearing the Belgian Order of Leopold, the D. S. C. and the French Croix de Guerre, pictures the author at the age of 20—in July, 1919.

Battle With the Snipers

I TOLD my friends what I intended to do and enlisted a group of them to help. Leaving another sergeant in charge of the lines we went down to the houses below. We could find our way through the walls of the first several houses, as they had been shelled. We would slip forward with the stealth of Indians on the warpath. The deserted houses were quiet enough that I believe a good-sized cockroach walking across the ceiling would have sounded a lot like a walking German. We would hear a sound upstairs in one of the houses. Thinking that at last we were in a house with snipers I crept softly up the stairs. Hugging the wall, keeping my weight at the edge of the floor boards so as to reduce the possibility of creaking boards, I spent an endless time going from the first floor—through the various rooms of this floor. Finally as I worked up to the second floor I heard slight noises again. Perhaps the Germans heard me too and were waiting for me at the top of the stairs. I crept from room to room, and the slight noise that I heard seemed finally to center itself in a big closet in one of the bedrooms. So he was hiding in there, was he? I crept closer, finally throwing the door open with my bayonet held in readiness. And there sat only a big black and white cat, one of the villains, no doubt, who made daily forays, dining upon the Germans in the street.

I continued up to the garret. There, lying face down, was a big, powerful-looking German sprawled with his legs apart. The bullet which ended his life had hit him right in the head and his face had turned almost as greyish green as his uniform. The floor was stained with blood of a dark elderberry color. The man seemed to have been a working man. He had callouses and warts upon his hand, and a stubble of whiskers upon his face. He had been firing through an opening just at the eaves of the roof. As I looked through his former porthole I was surprised at how easily I could see the men on our line. It's a wonder that he hadn't picked us all off one at a time. But he had paid a price with his life for coming down so far into the part of the town that we held. I wondered who had seen him and had shot him—probably some sharpshooter from the 112th, for he seemed to have been dead for some time.

There was little in the way of furnishings in these old houses. The bedclothes were gone, the mattresses had been removed and utilized by the Germans in the many dugouts throughout the town. A lot of rubbish lay everywhere. There was a small printing press and some type in this attic. Evidently the owner had used it to print some sort of small magazine or hand bills. In a short time I regained the cellar with my companions and we were ready to continue with our hunt.

This house had no openings so that we could continue through. We couldn't go out on the main street, for snipers were watching that carefully. I had seen several men try to cross the street and get hit before they could get to the other side. I noticed here, as I had several times before, that the men of Anglo-Saxon extraction would take their wound without a sound—perhaps a look of startled surprise—but the Latins would permit a terrific scream to burst from their lips, screams that 1 remembered for long afterwards. Only those escaped in crossing the street who were particularly agile. I had occasion to cross this street numerous times during our stay in Fismette, and always managed to make it safely enough. I would start well back in the hallway of the house I occupied, get a good start and go across just about in a hop, step and a jump. Invariably the bullet would crash against the door jamb as I had gone within. It was far from safe to go through the back yards of the houses, for they too could be easily seen by any snipers who were still at work. It seemed that the best plan was to tear a hole through the cellar walls so that we could go through. I sent one of the men back through the houses toward the battalion dugout to see what sort of an implement he could find which would help us batter our way through. A telephone line had been extended to this advanced post. The officer in charge was able to call the commanding officer of the engineers who were endeavoring to throw a temporary bridge over the Vesle. In about an hour they came up with a good old American crowbar, a pick and two shovels. We set to work in earnest. At this stage of the battle I was quite strong and could swing the crowbar at the stone wall for a considerable time without a rest. Days later, one or two swings was all that I could muster, so weakened did I become without food or sleep for such a long period, for I was to divide my time between keeping the town free of snipers and protecting the line. Were it not for the action which we now took, I don't believe that we would have been able to hold the town. It was customary for the Germans to slip down the street at dusk, and to go back at the break of dawn, keeping close to the buildings where we could not see them. Some of them would bring food with them and remain for a longer period. These were the men who worked the day shift and the men we wanted in particular.

As we battered our way through the houses, a group of us would go through every room in the house as well as the garret. With the great noise that we were making in the cellars quietness was no longer needed. If there were snipers in the upper stories they would endeavor to slip out—slip out they must have; at least we didn't catch any, although in several of the houses we found where they had been. There would be quite a pile of empty clips and empty cartridges, perhaps the remnants of a tin of food, and a bit of that evil-smelling black bread the Germans were using. Just about a block up from our lines we came to a cellar which apparently had been occupied by a large body of troops. We came to the conclusion that this had been the place occupied when the remnants of one company of the 112th Infantry were taken prisoner. Many months later I was at St. Agnain when the Americans who had been German prisoners came through. I talked to men of the 112th and they described the manner in which they had been captured. They had gone into a cellar on the main street in Fismette, each one believing that the door was guarded by one of their companions. But they were too careless. The guard had decided to rest and sleep, too, and all the patrol of Germans had to do was to open the door. Threatening the Americans with machine gun fire and bombing, they forced them to surrender.

Our progress had been slow this day, for night was falling and we had gone perhaps a hundred yards, the equivalent of a full city block, however—had gone through the cellars of perhaps fifteen homes. I told our men that they could stop for the day and to go back to our lines. I decided to stay at this end of the street for a little longer and see what I could see. Not a single soul was in sight, in spite of the fact that I knew some thousands of men were within a stone's throw. They were all out of sight. You have no idea how dismal a deserted, shattered town such as this can be. If you could think of your own town, completely deserted, shattered, partly burned and entirely unlighted, you will get some idea of the state these deserted towns were in. As I stood on the second floor watching out the window, I saw a bent figure come running from the direction of the German lines toward the very house in which I was—into the house and then moving around downstairs. I supposed that this was the first of a group of returning snipers who were here to prepare for their night's work. With my big .45 in one hand I started to slip downstairs. Just as I did, another figure ran across the street. This time I could see that it was a woman, or, at least, dressed to appear as a woman. She too came in the house.

I took long minutes in going down the stairs, only to confront my twilight visitors at pistol point. I could see that they were truly an aged couple, apparently returning to their former home for a short visit. Then too they could have been pro-Germans, searching for what information they could obtain. They had come from the direction of the German lines. Evidently the Germans knew them and had not harmed them.

I tried to tell them that they had better leave the town. I said, " Beaucoup boom boom," trying to tell them that there was to be a big bombardment and an attack and they would be caught in it. The old man said not a word, but the woman made up for his silence with her loquacity. She chattered along and all I could make of her talk was that she said, " Petite pickaninny " —that this had been her home since she was a small baby. She refused to go. I remonstrated with her for a time, trying to urge her to leave. She did start out the door, but I grasped her just as she went out. I thought, " Perhaps she'll go back up the street and tell the Germans, and they can be prepared to escape our barrage—fall back and be ready to meet our men when we try to advance into the end of the town." I thought I had better take her back to our headquarters. She refused to go. Finally I picked her up, and she kicked and scratched, tearing at my face with her nails, and calling me all sorts of names. I herded the old man before me through the openings in the cellars, carried the old lady back to battalion headquarters, and left her there. I heard afterwards that they were sent to the rear, and that there was a strong belief that they had been serving as German spies.

What a mob there had been in the headquarters dugout when I went back—just proof that it takes ten men in reserve or support (the engineers, hospital or service of supply) for every man at the front. Here we were at the front—all of us apparently first-line troops—and there were nearly as many men in the active major's dugout as there were on our entire battalion sector at the front line.

In the dugout were a lot of officers, some non-commissioned officers, and battalion scouts. (They seemed to do little scouting; we never had their help for a single minute and had to do all the scouting and patrolling ourselves. I wondered then if their work was to scout out the deepest and safest dugouts.) There were a great number of runners from all the outfits which had any sort of connection with us. There were a lot of wounded in the dugout, but most of the men were just gold brickers who had taken refuge in the dugout to get away from the battle. Officers from our third battalion, which had just entered Fismette, were there getting the lay of the land—machine gun officers; a large enough mob to fight the German army, it seemed to me.

First Night in Fismette

I WENT back to my place on the line prepared to spend another busy night. It had been a terrific day. Almost the events of a lifetime had been crowded into this one day. In the moments of quiet before we were to undertake our next job I reviewed the events of the day—crawling up through Fismette to relieve the 112th, the shelling, the constant flares, the firing from behind the stone wall in the direction of Germany, the attack. I wondered who ordered the attack; if they knew what they were doing. We weren't told about going over; there was no plan, no instruction as to objectives, no preparation—just "We're going over," and the men were climbing over the line. In a few minutes nearly all the officers were dead or wounded. I could never learn exactly who had ordered the attack, but the captain of B Company was the senior company commander; the major was back in his dugout, so the command to go over must have come from the captain. Nothing could have been more useless, more futile—the wiping out of nearly all the leaders of a well-trained regiment, uselessly, in just a few minutes.

We weren't prepared to go over; the Germans were more than prepared for us. Many times during the war I advanced in the face of machine gun fire, but never before or afterwards did I hear as many guns or almost feel as many bullets going through the air.

The retreat to our line, our own artillery falling upon us, the dangerous trip across the river to see the major of our battalion, the patrols, searching for snipers—it had been a long day filled with excitement. There are few hours of darkness in the summer in France—hardly more than six hours of absolute darkness. If men slept at all, it was for only an hour or two, for they should be on duty twenty hours a day—no forty or thirty-six hour weeks in the army. The time before dawn is the most dangerous—that is the time when attacks are most likely to take place—so every man had to be up and around an hour or two before dawn to be ready for any eventuality.

I thought of my friends who had died that day. I had been saved by some strange fate while Vaugn and I had been firing over the wall. How easy it would have been for the sniper to pick me instead of Vaugn! I would be dead as he still was lying almost beside me in a kneeling position with the top of his head gone. Although I was to have many miraculous escapes, this one escape remains in my mind stronger at present than any other. I was to be the only man back from many patrols, many dangerous missions. But this case was different: two heads above a stone wall belonging to men who were firing at any available target. A German sniper, hidden somewhere out in front, sees these two heads. For some reason he chooses one as his target. " Why," I wondered, " did he choose Vaugn?" In action a soldier shoots first at a man who is bigger, dressed differently, apparently giving commands, a leader. But here we were, just two helmets, two faces, the ends of two guns over the wall. Vaugn was on my right; this would place him on the sniper's left. If I were doing the firing, I would select the man to the right of me. Was the sniper left handed? Or by what strange fate had he selected the other target instead of me? I was to wonder about this hundreds of times during and after the war.

Many things were hard to understand, especially why one man would die, hundreds, thousands, even millions (nine million, counting all the men on both sides who were killed) and some were to live. I couldn't help wondering why. Only ten feet from me Lester Michaels was lying dead. What a fine fellow he had been—the salt of the earth; the kind of man who makes the world a better place to live in; yet a bullet, going through a small hole in the wall, found his heart, and he was dead. He hadn't been touched. There he was lying just as if he were still alive and about to go on this patrol with me. I thought of the times we had been together;

of our experiences while guarding bridges in the United States. He had been with me on the bridge outside of Wampum. We had accidents then too. One man had been hit by a train, and parts of him spread over about a half mile of track.

We had searched for his gun in the creek below the bridge for weeks before we found it over a hundred yards downstream where it had been thrown from the force of the train's impact. Another chap had accidentally shot himself through the hand. The wound would not heal. He did not get to France and he is still alive, no doubt. I knew Michaels and had been with him so many times. We had been seat mates on the long journey by train to Augusta, Georgia, and there, in the beginning, we had been tent mates. Later I was promoted to a sergeancy and moved to the sergeant's tent. But Lester and I had palled around a lot together. He had become a corporal and lived in the next tent. We were both members of our regimental football team. He was a half-back, I played full-back. I remembered a day down at Camp Hancock in Georgia, when we had won a game by a six point score. Lester had been a flashy, speedy runner; he had been responsible for most of our march down the field. When the ball was near the opponent's goal line, I was given the ball and crashed through for a score. But that wasn't all I crashed through. Our playing field not long before had been sparsely-covered with scrub oak and southern pine. The trees had been removed, but not too well, for my nose came in direct contact with a short stump which extended a few inches above the ground. My nose was never quite the same again— always turned toward the left.

I thought of another day—a time down in Augusta when Lester and I had gone to church together. We had been invited to the home of some new-found friends and spent a quiet but enjoyable evening playing and singing. Lester was the pianist j we all sang the old songs, and forgot the camp and the war and the impending trip to the battlefields for a time.

And there was poor " Mike," as we called him, lying dead. I had spoken to him last. " What's the matter, Mike? " " They've got me," he answered. He was shot directly through the heart, but even this had not stopped his fine, strong heart instantly for he had still time to say, " They've got me."

Two others of my particular pals were out there somewhere in front—Buck Krause and Fred Wilner. I had lived with these men for just sixteen months by this time. I knew them as well as my own family. I had been a good soldier, was so often held up as a shining example of what a soldier should do (the white pants and white leggings nearly ended my life), but I had had my moments of trouble. When we first landed in Georgia we were rather hungry—had left our posts guarding bridges and tunnels two weeks before; had camped at Schenley Oval in Pittsburgh for some days. We were expected to be there for only a few days and the proper rations were not served there. Then the trip to the south, with two sandwiches per man at each meal. And at the new camp the kitchens had not been set up as yet. We were really hungry. So I suggested to two of my sergeant pals, Krause and Wilner, that we could go down to one of the homes nearby and see if we could purchase some southern corn bread. I still had thirty-five cents. We went far over the hill to a little cabin and there the woman had promised to bake us some southern corn bread. We went back the next day and found to our disappointment that she had hurt her hand and could not make the corn bread. Walking back to camp we passed a corn field and Fred said, " I'm so hungry I could eat raw corn." I said, " I'll get you an ear." Buck said he could eat some too. So I pulled off an ear and gave it to him. When he pulled the husk off I saw it was not a very nice ear, so I said, " Wait. I'll get you another one." And this was a big one. Just then two men in civilian clothes confronted us with drawn revolvers. I didn't think it was anything serious and kept walking along. But Buck and Fred after a time called for me to come back. I saw them both handcuffed and they put handcuffs on me too. Fred was in the center. He had huge, powerful wrists and the handcuffs were most painful. We were taken down to the old Civil War jail in Augusta, and there spent six days before we were brought to trial. Many fellows had been raiding fields to obtain all they could. They had dug up sweet potatoes and peanuts; had eaten melons and fruit, even persimmons. It was unfortunate for the poor southern farmers, but it was unfortunate for us, too, who had enlisted to fight for our country, not to obtain sufficient food in our own land of plenty. But during war time most everything is punishable with death or imprisonment, and as it turned out we were to be the goats. We were to get years in Leavenworth for stealing corn when we were hungry. Six days we spent in that southern prison designed only to keep colored men over night. They didn't serve meals. But one of the kind-hearted police officers went to a restaurant across the street and got us some coffee, some soup meat sandwiches. This was the only other time in my life that I drank coffee with the least bit of relish aside from the time in the first-aid station on Hill 204. But I had had nothing warm in my stomach for some days and it felt comforting when it was down in spite of the fact that I didn't like the taste. But something was wrong with the meat. Buck and Fred contracted ptomaine poisoning from it. They suffered during their stay in jail. It was not a nice jail—three of us in a cell six feet square. I couldn't stand up straight, or lie down straight with my height of six feet three inches. There were four bunks in the cell, two on each side, which prevented even satisfactory sitting. There was a light on one side of the cell room, and the bugs started to bite pretty badly under the light. But the other fellows were sick so I had them lie on the dark side. I was nearly eaten to pieces with a great variety of hungry southern insects. And the rats—I don't believe that

I'll be accused either of exaggeration or prevarication when I tell you that they had to " duck " to run under the bunks.

Finally the fellows in our company got paid, and they came down to visit us. Each one of them, I believe, every man in the company came to see us, and they brought food—fruit, bananas, apples, lemons and oranges, cake, candy and all sorts of delicacies. Yes, the men who were lying out in front dead and wounded had been to see us in the jail at Georgia. I was a friend to all of these men and had my particular pals too. But the other fellows were too horribly sick to eat. Not me! I had a cast-iron stomach and ate thirty-six bananas with plenty of other food in one day. The ladies in Augusta found we were there and they brought fried and roast chickens and other delicacies. The business men of Augusta tried to get us out. My father went down to Washington, and soon the papers were filled with our plight. I was especially uncomfortable, for, with the bugs, I had a horrible case of poison oak. I was particularly susceptible to poison ivy and poison oak. There had been a storm at camp and we had run out in our bare feet to tighten the tent ropes so that the pegs would not pull out and the tent collapse. Roots of poison oak were everywhere and what a case I had! I could wring drops of water out of my socks.

We were moved from that cell to the women's quarters after a time; but not for long, for soon a disorderly house had been " pulled" and the tobacco-chewing women were brought in, and back we went to our own cell.

Finally, on the sixth day, we were taken back to camp and court-martialled. I pled " not guilty." I didn't have any corn in my possession. I had " swiped " plenty of melons, peanuts and fruit the day before but I didn't get caught with it. I was liberated. The other fellows didn't get off so easy. There was so much about it in the papers, about putting men in jail who had enlisted to fight for their country, because they were so hungry that they had stolen and eaten raw corn. But the officers felt that discipline must be maintained at any price. Buck and Fred were reduced to the rank of private, given thirty days in the " brig," and fined two-thirds of three months' pay. Expensive corn! They were never quite the same again after that experience. And now they were lying out in front, unable to get back— dead, perhaps, or severely wounded. In an hour or two we would find out.

It is too dangerous to go out in front of the lines early in the evening. Even soldiers don't sleep until near midnight at the front—that is, those who are not on duty. And then there is the alertness just before dawn, so we weren't to have so many hours. All was quiet at this time. Both sides had had a pretty hard day, and were willing to let well enough alone. I looked at my luminous wrist watch. Only ten o'clock—at least an hour before we could go. I should have slept, but I couldn't. There was too much on my mind. I hadn't felt the war so much in previous experiences. There was the novelty of it on Hill 204. But here it was different. The men who were killed near me on Hill 204 weren't my special pals. I knew them, spoke to them, liked them well enough, but only Sergeant Amole had been a tent mate. And he was twenty years older, and such a stickler for discipline that none of us had liked him very well. He had ridden us almost to death when we were 1 rookies," and even when I had gained equal rank (except that I was somewhat his junior), when I too had come to know and quote the various books of instruction so well that I could occasionally outscore him in a tactical argument, I didn't like him too well. Nor did others in the company. He was a very good soldier, but I am sorry to say that I have always strongly suspected that he received what was often called a " blue bean"—a shot from his own men. There were men in action that day who had occasion to actually hate him. He had been a martinet, unfeeling in his allotment of punishment to those who erred in the slightest. He had far too much to drink before this battle, and the last time I saw him he was waving his pistol around his head telling our men that he would shoot them if they didn't go forward to the attack. That was not necessary and I have strongly suspected that a certain one of our own men fired the shot which ended his career.

Bill Felix I knew and liked, of course, but he was at least alive, there beside me. The Texans I did not know too well. I had been with them three months but there weren't the many close ties of friendship I had had with these other fellows. Vochona, I just knew. But here my special pals were in difficulty and it hurt a great deal more.

I had been told that Sergeant George Endy was out front there too. He had been a tent mate, occupied the cot next to me. He is dead now, but I thought a lot of him then. I don't believe that two men more unlike could have been brought together by the bonds of friendship. We certainly were direct contrasts. I washed and scrubbed, shined and polished. Endy never washed. He was one of the old national guards, the town " ne'er- do-wells " who had been members of the guard in peace time. He had been on the Mexican border and owing to his long period of service had become a sergeant in spite of some careless phases of his personality. But he was a diamond in the rough. I believe he lived only for pay day, for a bottle of whiskey or two, and women (any shape, size, type or color, it didn't seem to matter). I would be back in camp early enough after my trip to the movies, a half-dozen fried oysters and a glass of limeade, which was the extent of my dissipation, hours before Sergeant Endy would come back, and fall all over me, laughing uproariously. I would angrily toss him off on the floor, but you couldn't get really mad at the big bear or tame ape as he was sometimes called. He labored along under the name " Bouzoulle " Endy. Where he got the name I don't know, but any unusual name would have been appropriate.

A short time prior to our stay in camp at Augusta I had been reduced to the rank of private—not for a commission, but an omission, one day when I was sergeant in charge of quarters. There were two officers who were heartily disliked in our organization. One was a lieutenant in Company C and one was the colonel who was in command of our old regiment before our fine new Colonel Shannon took over. It was raining one day in Pittsburgh and I was lying on my cot playing solitaire. Others were playing " Black Jack " or " penny ante." Someone tired of the game and started what was often a familiar pastime: " Three cheers for Colonel Keel " (the colonel was relieved of his command later under unpleasant conditions and accusations concerning behavior with his fourteen-year-old niece, so I was informed, and there is no need to mention the real name), one man shouted and then the chorus, " Oh, S-," and again and again until finally they got down to the officer of the day, the lieutenant from C Company. He went around to find the colonel, and both of them nearly exploded, for by this time practically the entire regiment had joined in the chorus, and the men who were suffering from inactivity had offered their respects to any officer in the regiment for whom they felt any sort of a grievance. I wasn't shouting, but they were echoing my sentiments. So when the furious colonel and the officer of the day came into my tent, I kept on playing cards. I didn't even get up off my seat, for I saw that I was in for it, and why try to cover up? I was responsible at least for the men in my tent who had started the explosion. The colonel lined up the entire regiment and said, among other things that made my ears burn, " Here's a man that I sent to Fort Niagara to be an officer, a man whom I selected from among thousands as the material of which officers and gentlemen are made, and after all of that, his special training, he doesn't have respect enough, knowledge enough, or decency enough, to salute his own colonel or to prevent others from being disrespectful," etc., etc. " I give orders that this man be reduced to the rank of private and never be made a non-commissioned officer again." I was a private as long as he was our colonel; but I was a sergeant the day we got our new colonel. Were it not for the fact that I was under age I could have gained a commission several times early in the war, for Sergeant Wausnok, of the group in our tent, received his second lieutenancy and later his silver bar, and commanded our company in the Argonne battle.

When I was a private I became number one man in the front rank. Sergeant Endy was the right guide. That meant that we marched side by side in the parade in Augusta. I was tall and straight, deep in the chest even then (although I weighed but 170 pounds), spotless and looked like a soldier, if I must say so. Endy was short, broad as a barn door, held one shoulder much lower than the other, was bow-legged and pigeon toed, marched with his gun wrapped around his neck, and rarely washed his clothes until they were in such bad shape that he got new ones. I was in snowy white— he in a very suspicious-looking, unwashed, nearly new suit of khaki. And all along the way I could see the people pointing, saying, " Look at those two." " Look at those two." We were a direct contrast physically, morally and mentally. I was studious by nature; he never looked inside of a book. Years of experience brought him enough knowledge to hold his sergeant's stripes. I didn't smoke, drink, chew or swear. Endy did them all. I thought he was a roughneck. He considered me a sissy. But we were real pals. I was strangely drawn to that man—enough so that he is the only man I have actually hunted up since the war, hoping to see him again. But when I arrived at the George Amole American Legion post in Pottstown, named after Amole of course, I learned that Sergeant Endy had died. Too bad; he was a great fellow.

One time down in Georgia we were bringing in wood for our tent. Four of us were struggling along over the uneven ground carrying the trunk of a pine tree with considerable difficulty. " Get away. Let me carry it," Endy roared. We didn't take him seriously. It was all the four of us could do to carry it. But carry it he did, more tha i a quarter mile up to our tent, and we had more than our share of wood for a few days.

The man had absolutely no feeling. Pain was foreign to him. He could practice every form of dissipation and go on without rest or sleep endlessly. I was told that he was suffering from some physical trouble while on the Mexican border; that he was confined in the hospital with a plaster cast upon one side. He learned that our team was losing the football game. He was no athlete, but he was a powerhouse, strong as an elephant; he could go through a line with half of the other team suspended from various parts of his anatomy. He got right out of bed, broke off the cast, and reported to the football field to play the second half. They told him he could not play. But he insisted and did play, and his side won the game. He must have been a throwback to cave man days—the sort of man we would expect the Neanderthals to be. When we finally did get him back wounded, he was blown up again when a shell struck the ambulance in which he was riding. Again when he was back in the tents of the field hospital I was told that another bomb, an aerial bomb this time, fell near and blew him far into the air and nearly fifty feet away —wounded and rewounded, but not killed. He seemed too tough to kill. I learned in Pottstown that it was a recurrence of his old habits—constant drinking, absolute neglect of his physical self—that finally brought on the illness which ended his life.

I hope I am not boring you who read this book with reminiscences of my comrades. They were the men who fought the war—the men who made me desire to rush back to the front when I was back at the hospital. There were all kinds of men in our company, but the same common purpose, the same aim, had welded us together, each striving to do his part to win the war and to bring honor to our organization. We were proud of the i nth. And now Sergeant Endy, Buck Krause and Fred Wilner, among many others, were out front. Sergeant Haas should have been out there too. I thought of a fight or near fight he and Endy had had in Georgia. They had never quite forgiven each other. Endy was outside the tent. Haas was inside shaving, and threw the water through the tent door right in Endy's face as he attempted to enter. It was an accident, but Endy roared out that he was going to kill the fellow who did that. He dared him to come out and fight. Haas became angered and rushed out with both fists clenched. Two blows were struck. Endy hit Haas in the eye, Haas hit the ground and the fight was over. For hours afterwards Haas sat on his cot, with his hand over his eye, endlessly saying, " And he hit me right in the eye," " And he hit me right in the eye."

He had rushed out of the lighted tent into the Stygian darkness of the cloudy night, and before his eyes could become accustomed to the darkness, he had a huge fist, with plenty of power back of it, right in his eye. It was tragedy for Haas—mighty funny for us. I never saw them speak after that. I wondered if they were lying together on the outside of the wall and if they would speak under the present circumstances.

In Front of the Front

I LOOKED at my watch. One minute to eleven—time to go over. The men all along our line had been notified that a patrol was going out for the wounded at eleven o'clock and to hold their fire. I took off the wrist watch. Its luminous face could too easily be seen by the enemy. We blackened our hands and our faces—used soot obtained from the chimneys of the houses below us. It was dark enough that there was little likelihood of us being seen while it was dark, but the wakeful and perhaps nervous Germans were always shooting flares into the air to make sure that they were not being attacked.

Eleven men including myself were going out this time. I had spent some time crawling along the wall. I would find a man in the darkness. I would say, " What's your name?" Upon his answer I would quickly make a decision as to whether he should go or not. If he was a good man, I wanted him; if he was careless or clumsy, we didn't want him to bring destruction to the rest of us. That's why the best men get killed off in a war. No one wants to take the poor excuses of soldiers on an advance guard or advance patrol, but the good men are worked to death.

Promptly at eleven I sent a whisper along the line: " Come on, fellows; over we go." We had left our guns behind—even my forty-five revolver. We needed our hands free to bring back our comrades, and we wanted to avoid any possibility of making metallic noises when our equipment would come in contact with some hard object such as a stone. We had only our shirts—not even our cartridge belts. Each carried a trench knife, for we could not go toward the German lines entirely devoid of weapons. These trench knives were wicked- looking implements—short in the blade, hardly more than six inches long. The blade extended from a razorlike point to a good half-inch in thickness near the handle. They were triangular in shape and designed to make a wound that would not heal. A round hole will heal; the cut left from a flat bayonet or sword will quickly close; but these triangular wounds might never entirely heal even if the man who received such a wound did live. I had heard that Civil War veterans, who had been stabbed through the arm, leg or shoulder with the three-cornered bayonets used in that war, were troubled by the resulting wound as long as they lived.

The blade of the knife was bad enough, but to protect the hand and also as a means of inflicting additional damage upon the enemy, there was a guard made of roughened metal, designed to tear or rend if the blade missed and the handle came into contact with the enemy. This could extend in front of the knuckles of the hand, so that it made the most terrible set of brass or iron knucklers anyone could use to strike a blow at another. This trench knife belonged in the same category with the German saw-tooth bayonet. Both would inflict an almost-impossible-to-recover-from wound. We had been told that every German did not carry a saw-tooth bayonet—that only one man in each squad (in each eight) had one; that they were used to cut pegs for the shelter tents when they were behind the front, or to cut wood for their fires under similar circumstances. Whether this is true or not, I do know that I found a great many of them on the field. I brought seven such bayonets home with me. It seemed to me that there must have been more of them than one to eight men.

All of our men had one of these terrible trench knives. We had been told that it was as much as a man's life was worth to be captured with one of these on his person—that the Germans would more than likely stab the captured American with it if he was found carrying one. I not only carried my trench knife through the entire war, but brought it home with me as a souvenir. During the hostilities, I determined to throw it away promptly if I was ever so situated that capture seemed inevitable.

Each of us carried the naked blade thrust into the belt of his trousers. We slipped over the wall, sliding along on our stomachs, using the elbows as the sole means of propelling ourselves forward. We were as quiet as we could be, but every tiny sound seemed to be amplified by the absolute silence that surrounded us.

No one who was not at the front will ever realize how quiet things can be. The sound of a wagon miles away can be heard. The thump of a pick, the scrape of a shovel a quarter mile away, become actual noises at the front. The moan of the wounded and the shouts and cries for help when a shell falls far behind the line can be heard almost for miles. The click of the bolt of a rifle as some alert sentry prepares to fire—even the sound of pulling the cord of a German potato-masher grenade—can be heard. And darkness! I had read books in my youth which often mentioned darkness so great that you could not see the hand in front of your face. I had never experienced such a condition in America. I could always at least dimly see my hand. Perhaps there were nights that dark, but I didn't happen to be out in them. But this night, when there were no flares in the air, it was impossible to see a hand four inches away.

Whispering was dangerous, so in a short time it was every man for himself. What a dangerous place to be! What an eerie feeling one gets! Can't see a thing—creep along and find a pair of shoes with feet in them; a pair of trousers with legs in them. To whom do they belong? Is it one of our patrol, a wounded man, a dead man or a German? One never knows what minute the man who has been touched may turn around and thrust a knife into you. When I found my first pair of legs, I whispered, " Who are you? " No answer. Again I whispered. Meanwhile I was feeling the feet and legs. It was an American all right—no high leather German boots here. But closer examination determined that rigor mortis had already set in. He was dead. And we had more serious work to perform than to try to bring back the dead at this stage of the battle.

I could hear slithering, creeping sounds over to my right. I hoped it was one of our men. It could easily be Germans, too, for their men were also lying out here in this fresh graveyard. We had lost our great number of men in the morning; they had counter attacked a bit later and lost a great many men before they could return. It might have been nice if a truce had been declared as is done so often in fiction, so that both sides could fraternize for a moment as they brought back their own dead and wounded. The French and Germans probably would have made such an agreement. They had been in the war long enough that they preferred not to molest each other when they were on the quiet or rest sectors. There were sections where the Germans and the French had their days to go down to the river to bathe and to wash their clothes—just as the Germans are now holding up signs where they can be seen by the French, " Don't fire and we won't fire." At places the Germans had their latrines out in front of their lines. It was much more sanitary and far nicer than to obey the call of nature in a trench. A man never likes to be outside of his trench performing that act when there is firing, for, of all parts of his anatomy, that is the place he expects to get hit first. In the Argonne, later, we were to relieve the French on a quiet sector where they had lived and " fought" together with reasonable intimacy over a period of four years. Our men waited until the German latrine was filled with five or six Germans obeying the call of nature in the morning, as all healthy people should do, and then they opened fire. Those poor Germans dashed back to their trenches without even pulling up their pants. It was a big laugh for our young soldiers, but we paid for it later. The French could dig their trenches right out in No Man's Land with long shovels in reasonable ease and comfort. We had to lie on our faces and dig little by little until we were reasonably safe under the ground. Perhaps if we had been in the war longer, we would have learned to take it easy when we could. But all we knew at this stage of our war careers was the fact that there was a war on and we were going to try to win it as quickly as possible.

I heard a click over back of the German lines. It was the shooting of a flare. Every man automatically froze in the position he was in. If men are stooping when the flare is in the air, they remain stooping; if lying, they remain lying. In this case it was so easy for us to be mistaken for the bodies of the dead and wounded. I found myself lying beside a small pear tree. An American was lying to my right. I could raise my head just a little in the deep grass, and with the small trunk of the tree to protect me I was able to see that he was one of our men. I saw the dead man I had just passed lying face downward, but I couldn't see anything of the big man I knew Captain Lynch of B Company to be.

On my several trips into No Man's Land I could never find the captain, but I understand that a little fellow who later opened a garage in Pennsylvania, Christie Champ by name, found the captain, managed to bring his body back and claim his reward.

It seemed to take a lifetime for the flare to burn itself out. Not a shot was fired. Evidently the Germans did not detect us, or they too were being quiet because they had a patrol out. I didn't like this shooting of the flare. It could mean too many things: certainly wakefulness and alertness on the part of the Germans, perhaps worry and fear, which loosens a man's trigger finger and makes him a bit careless where and when he shoots; next that they might suspect we were out there and had fired the flare so that their own patrol could see us; and still more and worse, that perhaps they were planning a night or midnight attack on our lines. It was near midnight and we would be in poor condition to be caught between our lines. There was nothing to do but continue on as carefully and quietly as possible, hope for the best, and " cross our bridges when we came to them "; in other words, meet any form of attack or danger when it presented itself and not worry until we were confronted with it.

I thought I had seen an American lying well off to the left. I made my way in that direction. After slow minutes of crawling, inching forward a bit at a time, stopping to listen, then another six inches, finally I came to him. But he too was dead. I could not identify him in any manner. I turned to my right again, which meant farther toward the German lines. The next man I felt was a German, dead too. I went on—perhaps fifty feet farther—before I came to the edge of a shell hole. I lay still for what seemed to be minutes; but it may have only been seconds. I heard a slight moan. Now a moan from a German or a moan from an American should not be unlike in their sounds. I believe a moan is a moan the world over, no matter what color, type or race of man it comes from. But there seemed to be something about that sighing moan which was a bit American. I lay still for a time. If he was wounded badly enough I had nothing to fear whether American or German. But wounds create unusual fear and if he was armed, he might feel that I was there to destroy him instead of to help, and would kill me before I had the opportunity to tell my mission. The moans continued at almost regular intervals, and finally I kept low back of the loose earth the explosion had thrown up and whispered, " Who's there? What's your name, fellow? " " Who are you? " came the reply. " Bob Hoffman." " Boy, it's good to hear your voice. I'm Philip Miller." "Hurt bad?" I asked. "Pretty bad, I believe. Can't move my right leg, and my left arm seems to be broken. Couldn't even attempt to crawl back. Do you think you can get me back tonight? " " I think so. There are ten more of us around here somewhere and they ought to be able to get you back." " Do you have any water? I'm just about dying from thirst, and almost freezing to death." " Sorry, didn't wear our belts as we wanted to avoid noise; but we'll get you back. Any more wounded near here? " " I kept under cover all day, but at dusk I could see a man moving over toward that farm building. He looked like an American, and he may still be alive. And there's a German over there about fifteen feet from me. Maybe he's dead now, but he's been giving me the creeps almost all day. I'm hurt bad enough, but at least I haven't made noises like he has. He keeps wheezing and gurgling, gurgling and wheezing; he must be hit in the chest or in the throat from the sound. For hours I wished he would die, so that it would cease to bother me, and for the last few hours I've been afraid he would die and leave me alone out here in the dark. If I ever get back out of this place-, they'll never see me around the front again if I have to shoot myself."

One of our men had heard our whispered voices and joined us. It was Jim Oliver. " Try to help this fellow back, Jim," I said. " There is nothing you can do under the circumstances except pull him little by little along the ground. It's not so far, and you may encounter one of our men who can help you. I'm going forward to see what else I can find."

But first I crawled over toward the wounded German. All was quiet—not a sound or a gurgle. I finally reached him, identified him through the peculiarities of his uniform. He was not stiff, but there seemed to be no sign of life. I felt where his heart should be and it was still. Evidently he had just died—another young man who would never see his father in his Fatherland again.

I didn't come across any more Americans. It was difficult to tell how far I had gone, but I must have been out in front of the lines for two hours, and even with the slowest of progress one can come pretty far in that length of time. Perhaps none of our men had managed to get this far. Then I heard a whisper. " Herman."

" Yaah, Adolph." Then one of the few bits of German I knew, " Geben sie mir wassa." (You students of German, kindly pardon my German—I only know how it sounded—" Give me water.") A flare went up and in its blinding light I saw two young Germans in a shell hole. One was about to give the other a drink; he turned and saw me, and dashed terror-stricken in the direction of the German lines.

In a short time the bullets started to fly in my direction. Two or three machine guns were firing, sweeping along the ground. I could hear the bullets striking here and there—no fire from our lines. They knew we were out there and no doubt thought that we were discovered, but there was nothing we could do about it except wait and hope. I knew if I remained where I was it would be just a question of time until one of those bullets got me, to leave me lying and suffering in No Man's Land, or be with the dead. I had no choice. I slid forward as rapidly as possible and into the shell hole with the German. By the light of the dying flare I saw the terror in his eyes.

I didn't know whether he knew English, but I said, " Never mind, Fritzie. I won't hurt you. I don't feel in a particularly murderous mood tonight." He was still for a moment. Then he said, " Are you an American? I " Yes, sir," I replied. He thought we were English, he said. They had only encountered the French in their actions prior to the last few weeks, but had noticed that the men who were now in front of them wore different uniforms than the French. So I was from far-off America. How he would like to be there! Not a word about his wounds. He talked fairly good English—quite meticulous in his pronunciation. He told me that he had gone to school in England for several years and had learned the language there. " What are you doing in this shell hole? " was my next question. " Why don't you go back to your lines?" "Can't," he said; "shot through both legs and can't move. That was one of my friends here when you came. They were going to try to get me back." " That's what we're trying to do—get our wounded back, too," I said.

I asked him if he was in much pain. He said that he couldn't feel his injuries—that they were still numb. Evidently the reaction had not yet set in. When it did he would suffer enough to make up for the respite that terribly injured and deadened nerves had given him. I chatted with this young German for some time—the usual talk about his home in Germany, his people, their reluctance to fight, but their domination by the ruling classes. This was his first summer at the front and he was just seventeen years of age. He had been in the attacks at Fere en Tardenois, down through the drive to Chateau Thierry, and had retreated back up to this point as the counter drive of the Americans had its effect. His organization was worn to death, he told me, but they could not get relief.

They had been told that they were winning the war—that this was just a small setback on this front, but that they were advancing and winning the war in other sectors. They too had been told that they need not fear the Americans. First they were informed that they could not get to France, and then, when the Americans were driving them northward, that there were just a handful of us in France and they were all on this sector.

Twice since the memorable days in that town of Fismette I have met men who were around me that night, ready to kill me if possible. Coming back from the Olympic games which were held in Germany in 1936, I went down to the dining room for my first meal on board the liner Roosevelt. The table at which our particular group was being served seemed to be entirely filled, so a waiter directed me to a small table set for two nearby. In a short time a fine-looking, well-dressed man came along and said, " Do you mind if I sit with you? " I assured him that I didn't. After the usual pleasantries about the weather, the calm sea, the ship and the passengers, he asked me if this was my first trip to Europe. " Not my first," I said. " My first to Germany; but I had been in France during the Great War." He asked me if I had been in the fighting. Upon my reply that I had been, he asked me where I had fought. I replied, " Hill 204, drive up from Chateau Thierry, Fismes and Fismette." He stopped me there and said, " When were you in Fismes? " " August 8th to 13th," was my reply. " I was there at that time, too," he said. " Were you in the 28th Division? " I asked. " No, I was in the German army." I was surprised. He was a fine-looking fellow—looked too young to have been in the war; was perfectly groomed and handsome in appearance. He told me that he was now with the United States Lines, who operated the Roosevelt, Manhattan, and other steamers from New York to Hamburg. He had been with them since the end of the last war. Owing to the fact that he spoke English as well as German he had secured advancement and now held a responsible position with the steamship line. What a coincidence that we should be thfere eating, having a friendly chat, when a few years before we would have been trying to kill each other. He might have been the same fellow I met in the shell hole, but as it turned out he wasn't.

And a year afterwards in Cincinnati, serving as an official at a weight-lifting contest, I found a German who also had been in this battle of Fismes. It was nice to fraternize with them after the war. We never dreamed of another war. When the German team of weight lifters were here last year, two of them spoke English rather well, one fairly well. When they found that I had been in service during the Great War one of them said, " Oh, an enemy, eh? " But he told me afterwards that he was just kidding. But I wonder! Germans are Germans and it has been drilled into them for all the years of their lives that they are a nation with a destiny. In spite of all we hear about Germany—about the depredations and restrictions forced upon them by the Nazis, the prevalence of ersatz material (imitation), the absence of fats, sugar, eggs and butter—the captain of the team said to me, " You have no idea what a wonderful place Germany is to live in." They either know no better or they have just come to be accustomed to the conditions of their manner of living and are satisfied.

But here I was in the shell hole uncomfortably close to the German lines. Dawn might be coming before I knew it. I thought I had better be getting back. I told the young German that I was sorry there was nothing I could do for him. I wished him luck, hoped that he would recover from his wounds and that we would meet again sometime under more favorable conditions. He grasped my hand and wished me luck, too.

For a moment I was not sure of the way I should go, but after a time I oriented myself, and with a brief good-bye started back toward the town of Fismette and our lines. I made better time going back, for with each foot I crawled, I was farther from the German lines, closer to the comparative safety of our own lines. I could go in a direct line, and did not need to be quite so cautious as I got nearer to our stone wall.

I don't believe that I had gone more than two hundred feet in a direct line toward Germany, less than a city block. But during the day just passed, the German sniper who had killed Lester Michaels and had been firing through the small opening in my wall was much closer than that. He was lying out front somewhere in a carefully hidden, previously prepared position which he must have crawled up into during the day and back away from at night. At least we never encountered him again after his firing of the first few hours of the 8th of August. Perhaps, as I expected, the little German Jew had permanently put him out of action.

I was over in the pear orchard now and in a short time back of the wall where we had found the German the previous morning. There was an ever so slight streak of light off to my left as I faced our lines. Dawn would be with us soon, and another busy day of killing and being killed. I lay outside the wall for a moment. " Hey, fellows," I said, " it's I, Bob Hoffman." " Come in; you're the last one to come back."

" Did they all get back? " " No, not all. Two are missing. But they brought back three wounded men." That was a gain, lose two to get three. Sometimes we lost six or ten to get one.

A Wounded German

I KNEW that the regiments which had held Fismette before us had lost many prisoners. We determined to be ready for any eventuality. Long after the war I read a communication from Major General Bullard, which was as follows:

*Headquarters 3rd Army Corps, American Expeditionary Forces, France. A. P. O., 754, August 28th, 1918.
General J. W. McAndrew, G. H. Q., A. E. F.
My dear General:
I am informed that today's German communique (which I have not seen) states that the Germans captured at Fismette yesterday two hundred and fifty Americans. A part of my command until yesterday occupied Fismette. I had there some one hundred and ninety officers and men, altogether—infantry. If you will look upon the map you will see the position of Fismes, a large village on the south bank of the Vesle. Just opposite Fismes, on the north bank, is the small village of Fismette; opposite Fismes, the village of Fismette and no more was occupied by us. Ten days ago, after a German attack upon Fismette, which almost succeeded [referring no doubt to the action during the time that our organization was in Fismette], I saw that Fismette could not be held by us against any real attempt by the Germans to take it, and that to attempt to continue to hold it would, on account of the lay of the surrounding terrain, involve the sure sacrifice of its garrison, to which help could not be sent except by driblets at night. I therefore decided to withdraw that garrison of Fismette some three hundred metres back across the Vesle River into Fismes. Before this was finished, the French general commanding the 6th army, to which I belong, arrived at my headquarters, and learning of my orders for withdrawal from Fismette he himself, in person, directed me to continue to hold Fismette and how to*

hold it. My orders were changed in his presence and his orders were obeyed. Yesterday morning the Germans made a strong attack upon Fismette from two directions, taking the village and killing or capturing almost all of our men who were in it.
I request that the commander-in-chief be acquainted with the facts in this case.
R. L. BULLARD, Major General, N. A., Commanding 3rd Army Corps.

Later General Bullard wrote as follows: "A few days later I saw General Pershing himself. He told me that he had seen the letter; that he understood. He was much irritated and asked with vehemence:

"[4] Why did you not disobey the order? [5]

" I did not answer. It was not necessary to answer. The general had spoken in the vehemence of his irritation.

" While I recall this incident with some bitterness, I must give the French general credit for being ever ready to help me and my corps. He was a fighting man. He never ceased to press the enemy."

As dawn approached it was evident that something unusual was going on over in the German lines. Many more flares were fired, and the trench mortars were firing rapidly. It must be an attack, I thought. Our guns were so enfiladed that we were well protected in the front and felt sure from the former experience the Germans had had that they would not attempt to come over our wall, but would attack from the flank.

Sure enough, firing and explosion of grenades started up the Rue Cervante. I quickly gathered a group of my men and we dashed down into the cellar below us, then worked our way as fast as we could through the holes in the stones of the cellars. I distributed these men throughout each house and I myself went on to the last house in the block which we had tunnelled. I was hardly in place when I saw the Germans coming down the street. Clumpety-clump, they were going, with their high boots and huge coal bucket helmets. I can see them coming yet—bent over, rifle in one hand, potato-masher grenade in the other; husky, red-faced young fellows, their eyes almost popping out of their heads as they dashed down the street, necks red and perspiring. Far down the street was the barrier usually occupied by Americans. They were centering their attack on that part of the town and never dreamed that we were in the houses so far up the street. It would have been impossible for us to be there if it were not for the work we had done the day before.

I was standing back in the small hall of this house on the corner when in popped a powerful young German. He did not see me. It was not quite light and his eyes could not penetrate the semi-darkness of the interior of the house. He leaned well out of the doorway, planning to run to another doorway. This was their usual system in making an attack.

What was I to do? What would you have done— shoot at close quarters, yell at him to turn around and then fight a bayonet duel with him; or just stick the bayonet in him? I chose the latter system as being the safest and easiest. He was so surprised, and died there on the end of my bayonet.

The attack had passed. There were only fifty or so of them, but none came back. We had them between the defenders of the barricade and ourselves, and picked them off as they continued down the street and tried to return.

The work of the day before in making these holes through the cellars had paid us good dividends. We intended to continue working with the same system later in the day. I believe that only this tunnelling of the cellars made it possible for us to hold the town. I still do not understand what happened to the organization who lost the town two weeks later. Perhaps they were troops of inexperience. I understand that a New York City national army division received their baptism of fire in that district after we had left. They were inexperienced troops and very likely they each depended upon the other fellow, as so many of our men had done, and had no means to protect themselves when the German attack came. If they had used our system of tunnels surely they could have held the town. We drove the Germans well back, and it should have been as possible to hold Fismette against an attack as to hold Fismes.

There were a lot more dead Germans on the street now—probably a hundred of them in all lined the street for these two short blocks. Once again we got our crowbars and started to work up the street.

Going through two more of the houses we found a cache of German ammunition and grenades. They had enough there to make several counter attacks. No doubt this equipment had been carried down here during the day and left there for those who wished to use it. We later carried all of this material back with us and made use of a few of the German grenades later in the battle.

I had been told that a trench mortar had landed among a group of our men the day before near the end of the line which we were paralleling—that one of our men, a chap by the name of Henshu, had had his leg blown off. Comrades had made a tourniquet and were forced to leave him. As we got well up to this end of the street I seemed to hear someone yelling in a weak voice, "Ho, Bob! Ho, Bob Hoffman!" I thought it must be Henshu. The calling came from the other side of the street and was weak and indistinct, but it could have been a trap too. Our foes lost few opportunities to take advantage of any ruse that might defeat us, their enemies. The calling continued and I decided to run across the street. I took the usual fast start and made it without a shot being fired. Perhaps we had already driven the snipers out who had been making things so difficult for us. We were pretty well up the street by this time, and had reached a point about a block and a half from our starting-point, not so far from the end of the street. In fact the place where the sounds seemed to be coming from was not a house like the rest, but some sort of stable or outbuilding, although in line with the remainder of the houses. I waited until more of our men had crossed the road. They too did not bring a single shot.

We went toward the sounds of the shouting as carefully as we could, and then popped into the room with pistols and newly-found potato-masher grenades. There we saw that our fears were misplaced, for there was only a young German fellow lying there wounded. I then was able to distinguish the cries that he had been making as " Kamerad," in a weak, drawn-out voice, instead of Bob Hoffman as it seemed to be. One of the fellows in our party, Sergeant Gunther (I understand that he received a Distinguished Service Cross for this very exploit), interpreted what the young man had to say, which was as follows: First that he was too young to die; that he didn't want to die; that he hadn't wanted to fight; that he had been going to school and was drafted; that his father was rich and would give us 100,000 marks ($40,000 at the present rate of exchange) if we would save his life. I had the sergeant tell him that we didn't want the money, but didn't know, anyway, whether or not we could save him.

" Carry me down to your first-aid station," he said.

" Can't do that," was my reply. " They shoot every time we show as much as our nose on the street."

" Why, our men wouldn't shoot anyone carrying the wounded," the lad said.

"Yes, they would; they've done it too often before. Why, they have been shooting at every man who tries to bring in wounded or dead from between the lines."

" But they are the Prussians. They hold the center of the line. We Bavarians hold the end. The Prussians hate their enemies and give no quarter. But our men are different. They are home-loving men, who didn't want to fight. They were forced to come here. They know I am here. They like me and they would not harm anyone who tries to save me. In fact, they would help if they could. See over there! During the days I have been lying here they have brought me food."

I noticed that the dishes beside him were partially filled with bread, meat, and milk. Little of it had been eaten because he was sick from his wounds. His wounds were ghastly enough. The very evident wound was a bullet through the neck. He couldn't stand; he must have been hurt in his legs too. When a bullet enters the body it makes just a small hole the size of the bullet, but when it leaves it tears and leaves a big hole. This bullet had left quite an enlargement where it had passed through the neck, and the entire wound was literally filled—crawling—with a seething mass of maggots. It was the first time I knew that maggots could get in the bodies of living men. I had seen enough of them in the dead. I had seen them crawling in and out, leaving nothing but a rotting shell when they were done—finally just the bones of the skeleton after they had completed their work.

I knew that something had to be done for this boy or he would not be in this world long. I dug out the maggots, great handfuls of them, with my fingers. I pulled them out, where they had burrowed into the hole, by the tail. There were enough to have filled a good-sized sugar bowl. Had the young German lain there much longer, they would have enlarged the hole in his neck to the point where the jugular vein would have been severed and he would have bled to death; or they would have cut through the windpipe so that he would have drowned in his own blood. I have seen this happen so many times—many men were hit in the neck. After I completed my simple operation, I turned to the group of soldiers with me and said, " What shall we do, fellows? Will we take his word for it that his men won't fire if we carry him to the first-aid station? " The men hesitated a while. Finally one of them said, " I'll take a chance—can't let him die here even if he is a German. He wants to live as badly as we do." We tore a wooden shutter from the side of the house, placed the German upon it and prepared to carry him down the street. Not a shot was fired. We were the center of all eyes as we were the first to march down that street in many a day. The doctor who attended this young German found him to be the straw that broke the camel's back. He became deathly sick himself with what he had seen from the long hours on duty, and had to give up his work. I was told later that the young German died. It was some time before they could evacuate him. There were so many of our own wounded that no place in a regular ambulance could be found for him, so he went along with a man driving a light truck who volunteered to take him back. This man hit all the bumps in the road; drove everywhere to show men that he had a Jerry in the truck, and finally the poor boy died just as he reached a place where he could have received proper medical attention. I for one felt sorry for him. He wanted to live, to go back to his little town in Bavaria, and live out his life in a normal, happy manner. How pitiful it all is! No one in the world wants war—that is, not the common people who fight the wars. They want peace—to live their lives in happiness and content. It is far better to experience reasonable privations than to suffer and die in the war. Mothers don't want their sons to die; the sons don't want to die either. But there is fighting over much of the world, and dying also—all to satisfy the ambitions of a few of the countries' leaders. Humans will never learn.

A Night Attack

THE hours of the day had passed rapidly, and the sun was setting in the west. I had not slept for even a moment since I had been in this town, for the excitement had been holding me up; nor had I had anything to eat. Hunger after a time is not troublesome. A man can live a long time without food if he is inactive, but not long if he is working as hard as we were—fighting and burning up energy.

It has been said that the best defense is a good offense. We intended that night to turn the tables on the Germans. While we were penetrating their lines they could not be making an attack on ours. Attacking is always by far the most dangerous, but wars are not won by sitting and waiting. We would carry the battle to our enemies. Things were quiet enough at the edge of town, where we had made the first attack. There our lines were constantly on the alert, ready to repel any attack that was made. From time to time there was shelling but the men were standing it pretty well. There was considerable grumbling owing to lack of food; they had to be careful of their ammunition for one never knew when we would get any more. The hand grenades and German ammunition we had found were brought up to the lines. It would fit our guns. The French guns had ammunition different from many others. The rifle ammunition was of larger calibre than the .30-06 we and the Germans used. The automatic rifle ammunition was large and angular in shape. Therefore it was necessary in the French army to have several kinds of ammunition—one for the rifles, one for the Chau Chat guns, and another for the Hotchkiss machine guns. The same ammunition which fitted the German rifles also was used in their machine guns—a great advantage. Fortunately we could use their ammunition, and the potato-masher grenades were of considerable use to us.

When we had gone into action we had been issued a few of the French Citron grenades. They are oval in shape, and have a covering which fits over the detonating mechanism. This is removed, the plunger is hit upon the hat, and five or six seconds later the bomb explodes. We had to be especially careful, in using these, to hold them long enough for there were many cases of the enemy being able to pick them up and throw them back into our lines to explode, thus completely turning the tables upon us. It was dangerous business to pick them up and throw them, for one never knew when they would go off. I heard a tale about this time of a group of wounded who were sheltered deep in a dugout. A German opened the door and threw a potato-masher grenade down the stairs. One of the wounded threw himself upon it, knowing that he would be killed, but that it would save all his comrades from death. Few men would have the courage or presence of mind to perform such a feat, but this is an apparently authentic case.

There were two ways in which the Germans seemed to enjoy having their photos taken. One way was looking as fierce as they possibly could, with their bayoneted rifles, knives, and bombs strung in their belt so that they would look like dangerous customers. I always felt that it was quite dangerous to roll around and crawl around with potato-masher grenades in one's belt. They are started by pulling a string, creating friction, heat, then a spark which causes the bomb to go off. Too many accidents could happen when carrying them around. Yet in these pictures a dozen bombs around the belt was quite the ordinary thing. Another way was looking as happy as possible, sitting at little rustic tables, made of branches of birch trees, at their card games, with bottles of beer or seltzer, smiling and happy— showing that it was a pretty nice war after all. Humans are wonderful at times. They fight, suffer and fear, yet most of them can still muster a laugh or a smile. I often saw Germans going through the wood or through a town laughing and talking as they went—as if they were getting a lot of fun out of the trouble they were causing us. Sometimes I hated to spoil their fun by shooting, but, as the French said, " C'est la guerre" (" It is war ").

Under the surface a lot of the Germans—I should say most of the Germans—were regular fellows. We came to know a good many of them. There are what I call the " stiff-necked Prussians," the arrogant devils, who cause the endless war and strife. These feel that they are a superior people, and constantly want to prove it by winning athletic contests at any cost, by weight-lifting contests, or by force of arms. Usually their coal bucket helmets and the huge, rough and heavy boots, with their ill-fitting clothes, made them look particularly brutal, but we found many of them to be very nice fellows. Nevertheless it was our work to fight them and to give them as good or better than they sent us. When one nation declares war on another, one must fight every person connected with or allied with the other side.

Too bad that a vote cannot be taken so that those fire-eating generals who want to fight should be given the opportunity to fight. I think it would help prevent war if an international law could be made that the leaders must do the fighting—say, for instance, Stalin and Hitler, as well as Chamberlain and Daladier, or the big fat generals of either side, stripped to the waist, wearing only a pair of B V D's. I would suggest that each one sit on a pole which extends out over an evil- smelling pig pen. There they would swing at each other with stuffed clubs. The one who lands in the mire loses. How many wars would be fought if they were to be decided in such an undignified manner? It is the uniforms, the medals, the gold braid, the cheering people, the bands and the strutting soldiers that make war interesting—the adoration of the fair sex. The way to end war is to take the profit and glory out of war.

Make it impossible to win a war, and then nations of the world will learn that war is folly, war is silly, war is useless.

But back in those days in 1918, when we were living with the rats, the cats, the flies, the cooties, the filth, the wounded and the dead, we still had a war to win. It was my intention to lead a small group of men, a mobile group, up into the German outposts and give them a taste of what they had inflicted upon us—work our way to the edge of town, station some men in the garrets so that they could shoot anything that moved, fire some of the German flares at the German lines, throw German bombs back at them and use some of their ammunition against them.

The plan was for half of us to crawl up through the edge of town, the other half to do what damage they could by sniping at the Germans up over the hill.

There were about thirty of us in this party—all set to get a bit of revenge for the difficulty we had experienced for some time. Although the Germans in the picture carried the potato-masher grenades in their belts, we preferred to carry ours in the boxes in which they came. Heaven help us if something happened to hit the grenades and cause them to explode. It would have been the end of the carriers, and the rest of us, too, no doubt.

We carried our equipment as far up through the town as the holes in the walls permitted. There we left the bulk of the grenades, each of us taking two in our hands—sixty bombs—with which we hoped to do some damage. We crawled along the street hugging the buildings, stopping to listen every little while to make sure we were unobserved. This form of attack was much easier than that we were to experience in the Argonne forest. There we were to crawl through dry leaves, finding the Germans in concrete pillboxes, unable to detect them until they fired first at us. But here we had solid walls at the beginning of our trip, and then the solid ground of the back yards of the town and the gardens.

The hillside back of the houses was occupied by the Germans. There were little draws or gullies leading up to the heights above. There was an occasional road leading to the farms, vineyards, and orchards up on the hill. This night there wasn't a living thing in sight, but we knew they were up there somewhere. We kept to the gullies as best we could so that we could remain unobserved. Far down the road there was a big building, a tannery, so we had been informed from a preliminary reconnaissance that had been made. We knew that this was occupied by the enemy but did not know whether we could penetrate to that point or not.

We had left word with our troops that we would be out in front and told them not to fire at any movement or unusual sound they heard. We had little confidence of escaping unscathed from the fire of our own men if we caused any difficulty out in front, for there were many from organizations other than our own who might not have received the word that we were making a small attack. One of our objects was to get a prisoner, if possible, bring him back to headquarters and try to learn from him what were the Germans' intentions. We kept crawling up the road until we had passed the advanced sections of the enemy. Only two of us had gone on at this point; the others were remaining in the ditch at the side of the road. Finally we saw a group of men lying upon the ground near the big outbuilding that we had seen from our lines. They were lying there laughing and talking. I knew only a few words of German, but could not detect a single word of what they had to say. It was evident that they formed an advance guard of some sort. We could dimly see their machine guns in well-built emplacements. Inch by inch we crawled along until we were almost as close to the Germans as we were to their guns. I prepared to draw the string of one of my grenades and hurl it at the group that lay talking at the side of the road.

I pulled the string, waited three seconds and then let fly. My aim was good and it went off right in the midst of the dozen or so men. Some were killed, others wounded. They milled around like a lot of sheep and didn't know what to do. My companion and I rushed forward, throwing other bombs, and soon our entire group was at this advanced post. One of the men who was familiar with the operation of a German machine gun turned this gun around, and opened fire in the direction of the German lines.

How puzzled they must have been! It is so easy to distinguish the sound of a German machine gun's " ta-ta-ta-ta-ta-tat " as compared to the slower " chung-chung-chung" of the French guns. They must have thought that their men were making an attack and that the bullets coming toward them were from the American lines. A great many Germans rose up from somewhere in the back and rushed forward to help. Their own guns were turned upon them and our men were firing from all along the lines.

The German casualties were heavy and we escaped, with a young prisoner, almost unscathed. It was a great surprise to them and I believe some of them are puzzled yet as to what had happened. The prisoner we had was just a boy. He didn't seem to be over sixteen years of age, was small and immature. If he was older he did not look it. Upon interrogation at headquarters he told us that they expected relief that night—that they were to be replaced by shock troops whose intention it was to make an attack on Fismette and Fismes and take the town from us. This was interesting news indeed. When was it to come? How were we to repel the attack, and what with? We didn't have enough men to stop a real drive, nor enough ammunition.

We didn't expect the attack on the morrow. The troops who were expecting relief surely had had enough with the attack we had just made, and would be only too glad to remain inactive until they got out of there. Attacks were usually made in the early morning, so we need not expect an attack until the fourth day of our stay in Fismette.

The Daylight Patrol

WHILE the men were hard at work drilling through the cellars one afternoon I decided to take two companions and cross the street and see what we could find on the other side. It was almost as important to work up through the houses on the river side of Fismette as on the hillside. A sniper could do just as much damage over there. Three of us, one at a time, were able to cross the street in safety, although the last man just managed to beat the bullet to the doorway. A fraction of a second before or after was the difference between life or death. From here I had a different view of the town. I could look across and see the houses with[1] which we had become so familiar; through some of the shattered walls I could see the men lying tight against the wall back on the hillside. I could see a bit farther up the hill here. The German sausage balloon was hanging so close to us that I almost felt I could see the color of the observers' eyes. It must have been a half mile away, but the air was so clear and the sunshine so bright that it seemed to be much closer.

In this part of town—what must have been the suburbs—were many really handsome houses. From my vantage point they stood side by side, row on row, as far as I could see up or down the street. It reminded me of the ghost towns I had seen in the mining districts of the west. The doors and windows hung ajar in both Fismette and the mining towns, but there was a great deal more refuse or junk in Fismette. It was in this first house which I entered that I found a souvenir I managed to bring back home to America—a leather German helmet of the vintage of 1914. It was years since this type of helmet had been worn. It was evident that some French soldier years before had sent or brought this " Boche " souvenir home to his native village of Fismette. Here it had lain as a souvenir of the distant war—to once again become embroiled in the center of the fighting. I was a souvenir collector. At home I had enjoyed collecting relics of previous wars, and I constantly collected them during the Great War. I collected them, but few of them could I keep. I was always out there somewhere in front of the front. We had been told that crucifixion was the least a captured American could expect from the Germans if he was found with some of their belongings upon him. Nevertheless I had collected a great lot of photographs, some hundreds of them, which I had found in the pockets or haversacks of dead German soldiers. Many of these were more than risque and really came under the head of the " French type " of pictures. I could never understand why men who were at the front, away from the opposite sex for months at a time, would wish to carry such pictures. But carry them they did and I obtained quite a collection, partly from the belongings of Germans we buried, but chiefly from houses and dugouts which had been occupied by the Germans.

In the fine big home I now found myself in, the Germans had apparently really made merry and maybe " made Mary " too, for once again we found considerable of women's clothes. The towns of Fismes and Fismette contained wine and cognac in great abundance. The Germans must have drunk all of it they Could, but there was still more than plenty left. The wine cellars were literally filled with it. In this house, the beds apparently had been used by the Germans, perhaps the German officers. And the remnants of the last meal they had enjoyed here were still on the plates on the dining room table. It was too old to be of any use to even hungry men like ourselves. A few crusts of heavy black bread remained, most of which had been eaten by the town's population of rats. There were lettuce leaves with dried mayonnaise on some of the plates. It seemed that the meal had consisted of pork and sauer krout, as well as wine and salad. There was always sauer krout when we came in on the Germans soon enough to find it. At times we found the pots of sauer krout still boiling. But the plates here bore the unmistakable marks of rats' feet over the still greasy surfaces.

In this house there was a little organ which had been operated by foot power and played until it was completely worn out. What a collection of junk there was in this house, all worthless, left there by the men and civilians who had been there before us—the early German souvenirs, some French equipment, cartridge cases, belts, a battered helmet, straps, empty cartridges, a German Very pistol. I carried that behind the lines and sent it home too. It was used to shoot flares at night. There were worn-out articles of German clothing. Some German had changed his shoes and socks there. The shoes were without toes—perhaps he had received a new pair; but more than likely he had taken a pair from one of the German dead. Torn papers and magazines were all around, some of them German, and of rather recent date. I remember one copy of the magazine, " Die Woche," was a July issue.

All the houses in Fismes and Fismette were pretty much like this one—made of white stone and plaster, with red tile roofs, and shuttered windows. Some were a bit more ornate than others, as will be noted in any town. The majority of these houses were quite similar to so many of the older houses in our own city here in Pennsylvania. This part of Pennsylvania had been Dutch, and no doubt the European forms of architecture found their way here when our section was settled over two centuries ago. Some of the homes had fine big stairways to the second floor, but most of them had closed-in stairways which were almost as steep as ladders. Many of these closed stairways were stealthily explored by us in the days we spent in Fismes and Fismette.

There was a whisper from one of our patrol: " Boh, look over there in the next house. Isn't that a German sitting there at the window? " " Looks like it," I said. " Wait a minute. I'll see if I can get him," one of my men said. He took very careful aim and fired. The man didn't even move. He tried again, and only then did we find that he was shooting at a man who was already dead. We spent some time in the attic of this house, looking all around the town. Occasionally we could see one of our men on the other side of the street come to the window or the door of the house he occupied. I looked down the street and saw an American try to cross. He was not quick enough and we heard him scream as the bullet from the sniper at the edge of town got him just as he was about to go in the doorway of a house on our side of the street.

We determined to never relent for a minute until we had cleared the town of the snipers. The next building seemed to have been some sort of a Catholic institution. There was a dormitory and the German soldiers had slept here too in the little iron beds. They had lived well, making use of everything the French people had left in their haste to evacuate the town. And they in their turn had left in tremendous haste. Some of them had even run out without their haversacks. There must have been a score of them in this house. I opened many, but there wasn't anything I would want or could use. During the war I opened hundreds of German haversacks, and invariably found nothing but a pair of socks, a suit of underwear, a blanket, and some eating utensils. Evidently more personal belongings were carried somewhere else on the bodies of the Germans.

Everywhere we looked was more junk—cast-off German clothing and bedding in particular. But the French had been here, too, as we saw their refuse as well as a great deal of garbage and excrement. Flies crawled over everything—more flies than I ever saw before in my life. Flies and rats are at home wherever there is filth or dead things. They made the wounded's lives almost unbearable and would have nauseated us to the point of making it impossible to eat if we had had anything to eat. The roof had been blown from this house and we could see the fine blue sky above us. Hard to realize that there was a war on! But soon I heard the roar of an airplane, as one of the Boche planes flew low. Nearly everyone took a shot at him, disregarding the fact that he might return with his machine guns and make it pretty hot for everyone. He went on through the town without apparent damage and circled toward the hills and the German lines. As he circled up past our lines on the hillside, the machine guns of the 109th let go at him with the steady riveting of their guns. " Tac-tac-tac-tac " they seemed to say at this point.

The German planes had control of the air. I didn't see a single one of our planes during the first few months of the war—always planes with the black cross. Back over the river I could see a German plane attacking our artillery balloon. The crew tried to pull it down as they saw the approach of the German plane, but they were not quick enough. The aviator fired burst after burst of shells into it, with tracers and inflammable bullets at regular intervals. Soon there was a great cloud of fire and smoke, the shrivelling up of the huge gas bag, and then its rapid descent to earth. In the meantime the observers had jumped and were gliding to earth with their parachutes. Usually the aviators let the observers descend unharmed, but at other times they returned to fire at them and destroy them. On this particular afternoon the German aviator must have been in a somewhat benevolent mood and let the observers come safely to earth.

Almost numberless times I saw hundreds of men fire at a low-flying German plane but never saw one brought to earth. Occasionally we saw the charred remains of a plane, often with the burned and shrivelled corpse still strapped in the plane, but these could have been brought down in a multitude of ways. I saw a number of air battles later in the war, but it was not until well along in the Argonne battle that our aviators were able to sweep the sky reasonably clear of enemy planes. And here we were without the eyes of our observation balloon to note where shells were falling, whether on our own or the German lines, while the German balloon was still there to report the slightest movement in the town or across the river.

'We had to be especially careful as we went through these houses. It was a favorite move of Fritz's to hide until the Americans had passed—hide in a cellar, a garret, dugout, under a hay pile, in a barn, in outhouses or along ditches, waiting until we had gone by—then he would shoot us in the back, and do untold damage until he saw fit to escape. Mopping up is one of the important features of modern warfare. We had not been in a position to do it thoroughly here, and were endeavoring to do so with patrols such as the one I was now leading.

The Germans were thoroughly game and they would die at their guns if they were told to do so, firing until we managed to advance to the point where we could put the gun out of action. There has been a lot written in magazine stories which apparently endeavored to prove that the Germans could be beaten as were the Indians and the Mexicans in American battles of the past. They were entirely worthy foes. I disliked them, but I was forced to admire them, too, for the way they fought. All through the war I saw examples of how they fought and died. They had been taught to believe that they were in the right. Propaganda is a terrible weapon. They had no means of hearing the other side of the story and could believe only what they were permitted to hear. Often machine gunners and snipers were left behind as suicide groups. Usually our men paid so dearly before they could take their guns that they refused to take them as prisoners when they did endeavor to " Kamerad " toward the very end.

I had lagged behind a bit, while my companions went ahead. I heard the sound of a coming trench mortar shell but I didn't pay much attention. I thought it would go over our heads as so many had done. But this one landed near—so near that I was showered with dust, and my throat burned with the acrid odor of burned powder. I went ahead to see where it had landed and there was one of my companions, just as dead as he could be. A huge piece of shell had battered in the side of his head just as if it had been a soft pumpkin. He had been a fine young fellow, one of the original members of our company. What a shame that he should die here in a miserable French garret in Fismette! He should have lived to go home and to become the father of fine children, to do his part to make the world a better place in which to live. But he was gone. Oh, the pity of it!

Out in the back yard I could see a number of rows of little crosses—two rows of little mounds, probably a score in all, with an occasional helmet hung on the cross. For the Germans were dying too. They had much the worst of it at this stage of the war and until its ending on November nth. Their desperate rear guard actions, suicide groups, who were left to hold up our advance at any price, inflicted a great many casualties upon us. But we had the weight of artillery, particularly when they were moving to the rear. At times no shells came our way, while they fell on the Germans by the thousands. Some of the most terrible experiences of the war took place for the Germans in the retreat they had made from Chateau Thierry to Fismes. The roads were choked with troops hardly able to go forward, for at this time the heavy rains had made the mud in the fields seem to be sixteen feet deep. The German troops had to wait their turn upon the road, and think of the suffering, the death that took place when the shells from a single seventy-five French gun, firing ten or more shots a minute, landed on the target of this congested road.

Many of the men who were making this desperate stand outside of Fismette had been in that terrible retreat. But here they were, still good soldiers, trying desperately to do their work, and to do what they thought was right for their Fatherland.

I looked over to the left at one time as there was an unusual amount of shelling in the direction of Fismes. There was an ambulance trying to come down the hill into the town. I could see the ribbon of the road for miles and it had absolutely no chance to get into the town safely. I wondered who had ordered it to come down into that town—probably some bigwig of an officer who didn't know just where the front was. Shells fell all around the ambulance. The driver was going desperately. I thought he would make it, but soon a shell landed so close that the ambulance was wrecked. I thought the driver was dead, but no, there he was streaking along as fast as he could go for the higher ground and comparative safety at the edge of the road.

I thought of a time before this when we were stationed in the woods not far from the front. An orderly came up the road leading two horses. " Hey," I shouted, " where do you think you are going? " " Up the hill," he said, " with these horses." " You can't go up there," was my reply; "that's back of the German lines." " But I must go there. The colonel told me to take these horses to the top of that hill and wait for him." And he would have gone up, too, if we had not forcefully detained him. He had more fear of what the colonel would say if he didn't get up that hill as ordered than he had of what the Germans could do to him if he went a bit closer.

At the British schools we had been instructed to take no prisoners. This was the wrong advice for it only caused the Germans to fight to the very last and to inflict upon us a great many additional and unnecessary casualties. The idea of war is to put the enemy out of action, and capturing him puts him out of action too. This stupid policy was changed a bit later, when special orders were issued that quarter be given at any time when the enemy wanted to surrender. This was a wise change and made it much easier to capture Germans in the later fighting, and thus end the war that much sooner. Most of our men did not have the hatred for the Germans which had been born in them as it was in the men of the other allied armies. It was hard to treat human beings with absolute savagery. We were human beings ourselves and, except when necessity insisted, we would rather have taken the Germans prisoners. We had passed many places where dead Germans still lay, and it did not look like any quarter had been given there. It takes all kinds of people to make a world or an army. We had quite a variety of people in our army; most of them were fine fellows, but we had many men who permitted the savage to come out in them at a time of stress such as during the war. The Germans were divided into two more distinct groups than were we: the Prussians, usually the shock troops, who preferred to give no quarter or ask for it; the Bavarians or Landwehr divisions, who only fought because they had to. In the quieter sectors one usually encountered the Bavarians—simple, home-loving country or small town people. But in a battle such as this we were up against the storm or shock troops, the flower of the Kaiser's army, men who were rushed in to stop an attack or to make a counter attack where needed.

 I looked down to the river and thought what I would be doing at home if I weren't in the war. The time of the year's biggest regatta was on. There would be boat and canoe races. But here we were in this lonesome land filled with death, wounds, filth and endless trouble. I had a feeling of homesickness here. I thought of my father and mother. I knew that they were very proud of me, for in my pocket was a clipping, columns and columns, from a Pittsburgh newspaper telling of my exploits on Hill 204. My mother had written that she was oh, so proud of me; that even the little boys and girls stared at her and spoke to her with respect along the street. I wondered if she would ever see me again. I had intended to die bravely, hoping and expecting that word would get back to my parents of the courageous way in which I had met my end. We couldn't foresee the future—who would live and who would die. Little did we know that the war would be over in exactly three months, nor did we know who of us would survive the war. I thought of Pagamemos, of Captain Williams, Beketich, the Spencer boys, Lester Michaels, Felix and Early, Sergeant Amole, Corporal Graves, Candidate Vaugn—nearly all dead; the others crippled for life. What would the remainder of the war hold for me? The battle of Fismette had only started. Hundreds more of our men were to die. I thought of the comrade I had just left in the back room. I had been experiencing morbid feelings—too morbid for such a beautiful summer day.

I decided to go ahead, to get out of that place of the dead, filled with the belongings and effects of men who were gone. The next building had been a store, a butcher shop. I saw the kettles, the brick stove, the hooks on which the animals had been hung. A dried-out and worn-out rope hung there. Animals had to die too. But they didn't know that they were to die, because they could not think. Were it not for the fact that they would be used for food they wouldn't be born and have the short months or years of normal life until they met their end. More than once we came to envy the animals during the war.

I was still alone. I called for my companion repeatedly, but no answer. I started back in an endeavor to find him. I detected movement under a pile of debris—of plaster and wall paper. I saw an arm extend out. He was still alive, I was glad to see. I helped him out into the open; asked him if he was hit. He wasn't sure, but he felt helpless below the waist. I asked him if he felt any pain. " Not at all," he said. But he did feel like " obeying the call of nature "—like he must empty his bowels. And not much wonder either for a piece of the shell had torn right through his buttocks into his bowels. He might have lived had conditions been nearer normal. But he was to die before we could get him out of this advanced point. He gave me a note; we all carried them into battle. He asked me to see that Grace received that when I got back to Pittsburgh. I tried to tell him that he was not hurt, but he knew I was lying. He could see it in my face and in the tear in my eye. I told him that I would return with stretcher bearers in a little while.

Our Last Battle of Fismette

THE night passed uneventfully. We weren't called out to repel a counter attack that morning. In fact all through the day everything was serene and peaceful. It was a beautiful day, about the 12th of August. It was such a day as usually brings joy to living. But we knew that it was only the quiet before the storm—a great storm. Runners had carried messages across the river concerning the impending attack of the shock troops. They got through easily enough this time, which was quite unusual, for ordinarily there was a great deal of shelling, and dead runners were all along this path down to and across the river. We could not rely on our artillery after the unpleasant experiences we had had, so did not call upon them for a barrage. The German artillery were quiet. They did not fire, thus avoiding any retaliatory fire on the part of our batteries. We had no trench mortars, as I mentioned before, so could do nothing but lie there and wait.

All that afternoon the town was so quiet and peaceful that one would expect a group of children to come happily home from school at any minute; to see a motor car chug up the street; or a farmer with one of those high two-wheeled carts, followed by powerful peasant women with their rakes and hoes. Somehow there was a breathlessness, an expectancy in that afternoon's unnatural calm that gave us forebodings of the days to come.

That night the engineers were to try to rebuild the bridge. It would have made possible the bringing over of additional supplies. At times the telephone line could not be used and the runners dashed back and forth. When the wire was open the line was kept hot. Our fine old colonel—Colonel Shannon—was notified of the stern situation at his point of command across the river. He asked for support and planned to send over some of the companies of our third battalion. I saw Captain Thompson of M Company, and Captain Keel of

L. They had fine-looking organizations which had not been as badly decimated by the war as was our first battalion.

Early that evening, just after darkness, these supporting companies started across the bridge in single file. We had the snipers and machine guns pretty well cleaned out of our end of town and there was little firing. One gun from a great distance was covering a street corner near the City Hall and there was difficulty getting the troops over. But they finally arrived and pulled in to where Captain Haller, our acting major, was in charge.

Some of the new men were sent up to relieve the worn-out sentries on the line so that they could get a bit of sleep that night in preparation for the stern events we expected on the morrow. The German artillery became more and more active. They started to shell the bridge every minute or so. Before an attack there was always great artillery preparation. The barrage would lift only slightly, and remain just behind the troops—partly to prevent them from retreating and partly to prevent other troops coming forward to reinforce them.

It was fortunate that our reinforcements were across the bridge, or there would have been many casualties with the rapid shelling. Our own barrage was called upon, so that under the cover of our own fire there could be an attempt to evacuate some of our wounded. They were in bad shape. Some of our own men had lain there three days and the men from the 112th were much worse off. Some of them were getting maggots in their wounds. There was great danger of tetanus, or lockjaw, and gangrene. They had been treated with nothing but dry bandages—no hypodermics, no pain tablets, such as we had in abundance in our first attack. I paid them a last visit, and gave them some more good news. They had heard of our little attack on the German lines and I enthusiastically told them more about it—how easy it had been, how far back over the hill we had chased them; that there was no danger in a bombardment—just a little careful figuring and spacing of the trips across the river between the regular falling of the shells. I believe that some of them almost believed me.

Captain Arch Williams was still there. He was one of the first to move, and although he must have been in great pain, he was still patient and cheerful. He was one of the finest men I ever knew. We were fortunate to have such a man as our captain. My friends, Buck Krouse and Fred Wilner, were here. I was pleased to see that they were alive and had a good chance to recover from their wounds. I never saw them after that, so I don't know what happened. As the men from I Company carried out our wounded I said good-bye. It was fine to see them go. If we failed in repelling the attack we expected the next morning, it might have gone hard with these poor fellows. Often enemy troops, particularly in the heat of battle, generate tremendous hatred which they will vent upon anything they come in contact with, whether the men are wounded or not.

Some men were trying to dig a tunnel across the street to remove these wounded, and, as fate would have it, a direct hit from a trench mortar landed right where they were working, killing nearly all of them. We wondered how there could be a God when He let such things go on. There were so many other places where that shell could have fallen. Most of the men were killed or wounded. Others were badly damaged. There was one man who did not bear a noticeable wound who had been blown clear out of the room and was horribly shell shocked. Some people believe that shell shock is a sign of weakness or cowardice. It is something real, something that no man who has not experienced it or seen it will really appreciate. The men were buried right in the hole they had dug. It was necessary to carry the wounded right over the top of the ground and the bridge. Nothing could be more pitiful than seeing and hearing some of these poor wretches being hit again after they were already so sorely wounded.

I learned at this time that the orders had been changed somewhat. The first two battalions were to hold their lines at any cost, while the third battalion, under Major Dunlap, was to attack. I knew enough of the circumstances surrounding the town to know that this was murder—actual murder. The men had no chance—no more than we had had when we made the attack our first morning in Fismette. We wondered if the powers that be, safe in their deep dugouts, did not know that they were throwing meat to the lions in the nature of three companies of our battalion against an overwhelming, well-equipped number of the finest German shock troops. They knew but, as we afterwards learned, they had been ordered to attack and to hold the line at any cost. The orders for all this fighting and holding of Fismette had come from the French army commander through our own major general as you have read in the published portion of General Bullard's Memoirs. It seemed that the bridge head at Fismes and Fismette was worth anything that it cost in human lives to the Americans and French. At times it was necessary to hold a point at absolutely any price, as was done here, even letting the Germans advance somewhere else so that we could start a flanking attack as had been done toward Fere en Tardenois at the beginning of the American French counter drive July 18th.

Early in the morning every available man was prepared for action. Squads had been going everywhere to rout them out. Just a few men held the front line, so that they could notify the remainder of the battalion when the barrage had passed and the German troops were coming.

About this time the 3rd Battalion attacked up the hill far to our left, where we had made a patrol and captured a prisoner the night before. Real Hell broke loose now and a barrage was laid down on our lines that beat anything we had ever experienced up to this time. We were too busy for a time to feel sorry for the men of our 3rd Battalion. Captain Thompson, one of the finest men in our regiment, was killed in this absolutely futile attack. Survivors said that he was killed by shell fire while he was endeavoring to rally his men and go forward for the third time. When this action was over, Captain Haller, acting major of our battalion, and former captain of D Company, was the only available captain in the entire regiment. The other men were all killed or wounded. When you consider that the captain is far less exposed than the buck privates and noncommissioned officers, you can imagine what was happening to the men on the line when nearly all the officers were casualties.

Machine guns, trench mortars and artillery were massed almost hub to hub on the hill above us. For once our artillery did their work and laid down a barrage that almost tore up the entire hill for an hour or two. It silenced the German machine guns, trench mortars and artillery for a time. Certainly it prevented an attack that fourth day of our stay in Fismette. At this time the remnants of the 3rd Battalion came back and they were just remnants. Only a handful of men were left of some of the companies. The 28th Division lost more men than any other of the former National Guard Divisions; the 111th Infantry lost more men than any former National Guard Regiment. This defensive battle and two attacks on Fismes were one paramount reason for the heavy losses.

The attack had shown the Germans how small was our force. There were very few effectives able to be on the line. Ammunition was still scarcer than ever. While some of the men had been in reserve and had eaten, there were others like myself who had been four days without food. We were very, very weak. Later that day, when we tried to continue with our passages through the cellars, I found that I could hardly lift the crowbar that had been so easy to handle some days before. We didn't get far—just two more houses up the street. We soon gave this up as a bad job and did what we could to help the wounded. In spite of the fact that some had been evacuated, there were far more of them now than ever.

They lay two deep in every available dugout. The men who had died early in the attack stunk to high heaven, aided, of course, by the dead Germans, and the troops from the 112th who had given up their lives there a week or two before. It seemed that all the flies in France must have learned of what was going on in Fismette and rallied there. They almost carried the wounded away.

Some gas had fallen which added to the pain and bleeding of the wounded, and proved to us that no hell in the hereafter could be greater than this man-made hell that we were enduring. Men began to go out of their heads—shell shocked if we could call it that, or just crazy from weakness, strain, suffering and hunger, with death all around them.

It was near the breaking point for all of us who survived. We would ask ourselves, " How can there be any more? " But there was more, and worse. The night wore on and the morning of the fifth day was about to break. The German artillery speeded up again. We knew that an attack was impending. Everywhere I looked were dead men. There seemed to be no live men around to man the guns.

" Here they come," was shouted along the line, and many of the nearly dead men rose up to man their guns behind the wall that had become almost a part of us. Wave after wave of Germans were coming through the pear orchard—rifles, hand grenades, and machine guns; but worst of all the Flamenwerfers. I could see the men plainly. They had tanks on their backs, and from the ends of their hoses came great masses of liquid fire, shooting toward us a distance of at least fifty yards. The smoke went far beyond us. We felt that the heat would burn us up. Every man able to fire concentrated upon the men who were operating the flame throwers. Almost immediately they were out of action, their tanks perforated, and each man's body a mass of flame. The flames leaped and shot into the air. Thus was the attack stopped by the Germans' own diabolical weapon. They suffered far more than we. Never after that in the war did we encounter that type of flame throwers I again. They were the real suicide squad. The men who operated those tanks were sure to suffer a terrible and quick death.

It was a narrow escape. There were just a handful I of us left. When we were relieved that night and stag- 1 gered across the river, there were just thirty-two of us left. This included the runners, headquarters men, and the skulkers who kept hidden so well somewhere that we could not find them. Our companies on the line were almost completely wiped out. But we had held the line! I believe this battle of Fismette to equal any battle of the war—not in size, but in horror and death per quota of men involved in the action. I believe it was the worst experience of the entire American army—that no war of the present with their slightly improved technique at killing each other could be worse. Any man who lived through that inferno did so only by a series of miracles. It was an example of stick-to-it-iveness and courage on the part of the line soldiers; of efficiency of the artillery and supporting troops; of a willingness on the part of our Allies to hold the line to the last American. It was only what we can expect, except on a larger scale, in a new war should the expert propagandists succeed in getting us into another war. The war will be bigger; it will last longer. Instead of one hundred and twenty-five thousand dead Americans there will be a million or more. Let's save our young American lives for the defense of our own country.

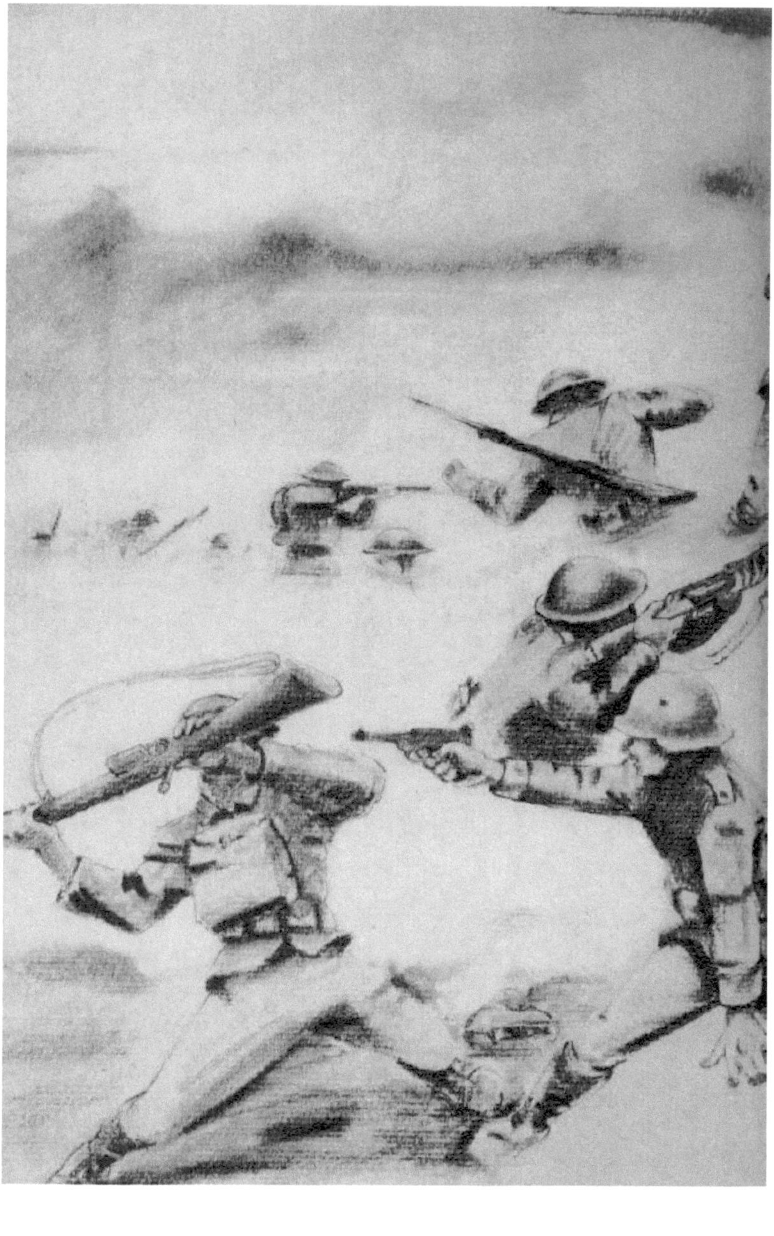

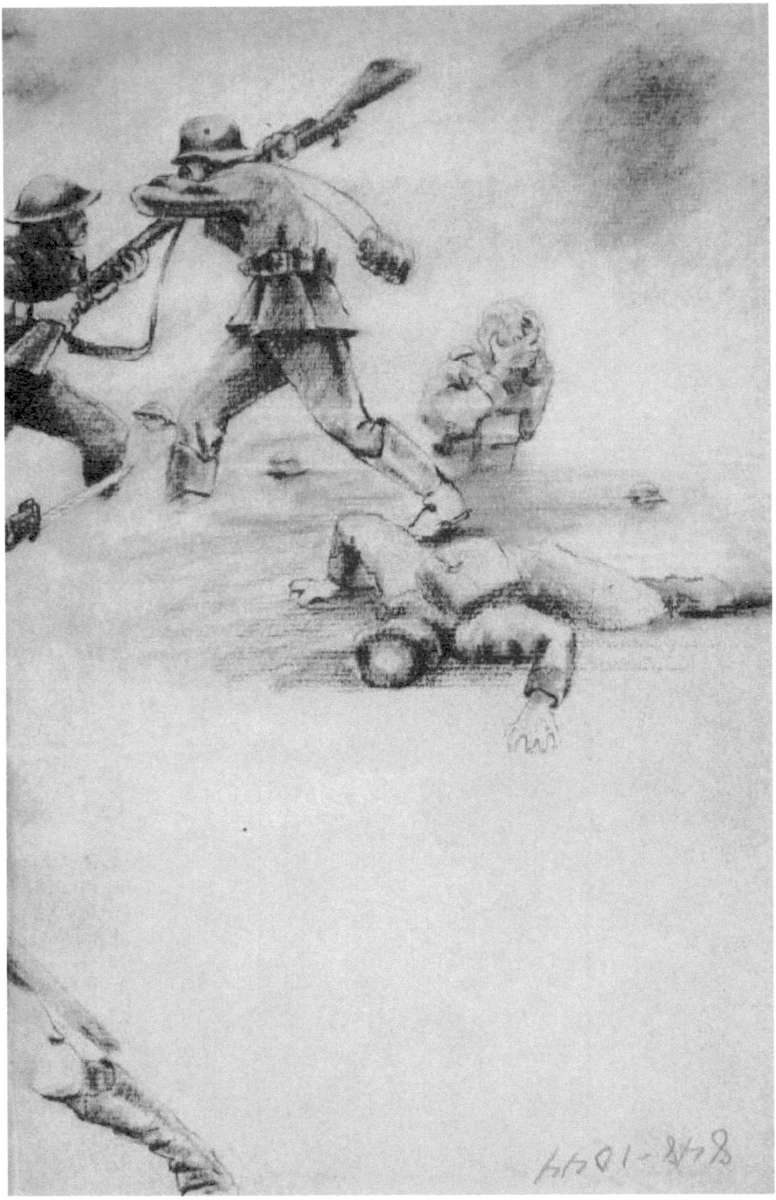

Made in United States
Troutdale, OR
06/27/2023

10841736R00146